T0315034

The Cultural Logic
of Computation

The Cultural Logic of Computation

DAVID GOLUMBIA

HARVARD UNIVERSITY PRESS

Cambridge, Massachusetts

London, England

2009

Library of Congress Cataloging-in-Publication Data

Golumbia, David.
The cultural logic of computation / David Golumbia.
p.   cm.
Includes bibliographical references.
ISBN 978-0-674-03292-7 (alk. paper)
1. Computers—Social aspects.   I. Title.
QA76.9.C66G68 2009
303.48'34—dc22   2008039331

For My Parents

Contents

The Cultural Logic
of Computation

The Cultural Functions
of Computation

THIS book is not about computers. It is instead about a set of wide-spread contemporary beliefs about computers—beliefs that can be hard to see as such because of their ubiquity and because of the power of computers themselves. More specifically, it is about the methods computers use to operate, methods referred to generally as *computation*. Computation—as metaphor, method, and organizing frame—occupies a privileged and under-analyzed role in our culture. Influential new concepts often emerge alongside technological shifts—they emerged alongside the shifts to steam power, electricity, and television, for example (see, e.g., Marvin 1988). Like enthusiasts during these other shifts, computer enthusiasts suggest that their bedrock principle is *the* one people need to use to resolve our most pressing social problems. To a greater degree than do some of those earlier concepts, computing overlaps with one of the most influential lines in the history of modern thought, namely the rationalist theory of mind. This may account in part for the strength of computing's influence in contemporary culture. I argue that the current vogue for computation takes this old belief system—that something like *rational calculation* might account for every part of the material world, and especially the social and mental worlds—and repurposes it in such a way so as to give every appearance of its being something very new.

This book foregrounds the roles played by the rhetoric of computation in our culture. I mean thereby to question not the development of computers themselves but the emphasis on computers and computation that is widespread throughout almost every part of the social fabric. In this way, despite its critical orientation, I do not suggest that computers are useless, that we should discard them altogether, or (in the spirit of some recent popular commentators) that computers are destroying the fabric of expert reason and judgment on which our society supposedly rests. To the contrary: my concern is that belief in the power of computation—a set of beliefs I call here *computationalism*—underwrites and reinforces a surprisingly traditionalist conception of human being, society, and politics. In other registers, we might imagine these views to have long been abandoned, in large part because their faults as part of a total account of human being have been long ago demonstrated conclusively.

Like all the other things human beings build and discover, computers can only be understood productively when they are seen as part of the cultural and historical contexts out of which they emerge—when, to put it in a colloquial and potentially misleading manner, they are read like texts. The primary goal of such an investigation is not to understand computers, though it may have the effect of providing new analyses of them in context. The primary goal is to understand our own culture, in which computers play a significant but not decisive role. As such, the guiding argument of this book is not and cannot be that our society and human beings are in the process of being *fundamentally* transformed by computers, if by fundamentally we mean that we are becoming something categorically unlike ourselves as-we-are and as-we-have-ever-been—in Katherine Hayles's (1999) term, "posthuman." Of course, our society and human beings are changing, but they are also always changing. Change that is so fundamental as to redefine altogether what it is to be human and what it is to participate in a society therefore must be either that same kind of change to which we are always subject, or a kind of transcendence of the human lifeworld that arguably we cannot comprehend, because it is by definition beyond our human understanding.

Too often the rhetoric of computation, especially that associated with so-called new media, suggests that we are in the process of experiencing a radical historical break of just this millennial sort.[1] My bedrock conviction in this study is that whatever the range of historical and cultural difference may mean, it does not entitle us to posit such radical breaks lightly. Until and unless evidence to the contrary presents itself, and with reference to other significant and in their way world-changing technologies, we must assume that technological shifts are best seen as changes in degree and not in kind; that human beings remain what they are (however we decide to define such a vague concept), and that human societies, too, remain largely bound by much the same fundamental forces by which they have always been characterized. In a time of the most extreme rhetoric of cultural change—which does not, at the same time, accompany a concomitant recognition of the possibilities for radical cultural difference—the need for resistance to the rhetoric of novelty seems especially pressing, not least when such claims are so often based on willful avoidance of the existence of analogous phenomena in the recent historical past. Networks, distributed communication, personal involvement in politics, and the geographically widespread sharing of information about the self and communities have been characteristic of human societies in every time and every place: a burden of this book is to resist the suggestion that they have emerged only with the rise of computers. In a familiar phrase whose import we sometimes seem on the verge of forgetting: the more things change, the more things stay the same.

The Circulation of Computational Discourse

This book focuses primarily on the ways in which the rhetoric of computation, and the belief-system associated with it, benefits and fits into established structures of institutional power. I investigate these benefits in two ways: first, by looking at those aspects of institutional power aided through belief in the superior utility of computerization as a form of social and political organization; second, by examining how the rhetoric of computerization circulates throughout our society, both inside of powerful institutions and outside of them, and then how that rhetoric entails beliefs about human subjectivity that endorse institutional power in a reciprocal manner. Because of its focus, this book is meant as a complement, rather than a direct contribution, to what is generally understood as the field of digital media studies. Computers and beliefs about them pervade our society through forms other than the ones usually designated by the term *media*; they are ubiquitous, playing vital roles in nearly every institution and nearly every product. "Digital media" names only a subset of the modes in which computers influence social formations; it must be the task of cultural criticism (as practiced by writers like Jameson 1981, 1991) to address all of these social forms and not confine itself to those that can legitimately be referred to as media.

I focus on the institutional effects of computing not merely to ensure that cultural criticism fully addresses our moment; rather, I am convinced both intellectually and experientially that computers have different effects and meanings when seen from the nodes of institutional power than from the ones they have when seen from other perspectives. If an unassailable slogan of the computing age is that "computers empower users," the question I want to raise is not what happens when individuals are empowered in this fashion (a question that has been widely treated in literature of many different sorts), but instead what happens when powerful institutions—corporations, governments, schools—embrace computationalism as a working philosophy. I am convinced that from the perspective of the individual, and maybe even from the perspective of informal social groups, the empowering effects of computerization appear (and may even be) largely salutary. But from the perspective of institutions, computerization has effects that we as citizens and individuals may find far more troubling. Here, computationalism often serves the ends of entrenched power despite being framed in terms of distributed power and democratic participation.

Too often, computers aid institutions in centralizing, demarcating, and concentrating power. It is not that individuals lack power to affect aspects of the computer system, or that new media art, hackers, and open source software are wholly ineffective; much the contrary is true. But it is a mistake to see these often beneficial effects as ameliorating the institutional effects of computerization, and it is also a mistake to give too much credence to the ways that the structures of capital and authority retreat in the face of relatively more democratic, resistant, and responsive public/individual uses of computers. A part of my argument is that this public existed well before the Internet did, and seeing public resistance too much in the context of computerization aligns too closely with the technological progressivism that conditions so much computational discourse.

Inside our existing institutions of power, computerization tends to be aligned with relatively authority-seeking, hierarchical, and often politically conservative forces—the forces that justify existing forms of power. This is true in academic disciplines (where it is especially visible in analytic philosophy, the subject of Chapter 3, and in linguistics, the subject of Chapter 4); it is true in corporations and the corporate monitoring and control of everyday life, including the worldwide spread of capital and accompanying surveillance known as globalization (Chapter 6); and it is true even in politics, despite the obvious utility of computers for communicating and political organizing (Chapters 8 and 9). It is those in power, and those who align themselves with existing structures of power, who are most often (but not exclusively) served by the advancement of computerization, and who make the fullest use of computers; it is they who endorse most fully the computational rhetoric and the computational beliefs that have become so widespread in our society. Following a line of criticism that extends at least as far back as Kant (at least on one interpretation of Kant's views), and that has recent avatars in figures as diverse as established scholars like Lewis Mumford (1934, 1964), Harold Innis (1950, 1951), Jacques Ellul (1964, 1980, 1990), Joseph Weizenbaum, Martin Heidegger, Norbert Wiener (1954,

1964), Terry Winograd, and Theodore Roszak (1986), and more recent writers like Langdon Winner (1977, 1988), Mark Poster (1990, 2000, 2006), Michael Adas, Philip Agre (1997), Christopher May (2002), Kevin Robins and Frank Webster (1999), Alison Adam, McKenzie Wark, Scott Lash (2002), Vincent Mosco, Dan Schiller, Lisa Nakamura, and others discussed below, I argue that computationalism meshes all too easily with the project of instrumental reason. Because of this commitment and its strength in our society, it seems problematic to put too much emphasis on computers in projects of social resistance, especially that kind of resistance that tries to raise questions about the nature of neoliberalism and what is (too often, disingenuously) referred to as free-market capitalism.

This book examines the ties between institutional power and the rhetoric of computationalism, in the hopes of helping to develop an even stronger political resistance to the power-effects of institutional computerization. In addition, therefore, to championing practices such as hacking (Wark 2004), network "exploits" (Galloway and Thacker 2007), transgressive computer art (Galloway 2004), resistance to overarching schemes of copyright (Benkler 2006; Lessig 2002, 2005; Litman 2001; Vaidhyanathan 2003), open source and free software (Stallman 2002), etc., I argue that we must also keep in mind the possibility of de-emphasizing computerization, resisting the intrusion of computational paradigms into every part of the social structure, and resisting too strong a focus on computationalism as the solution to our social problems. This study is written in the belief that computationalism aids some of the pernicious effects of institutional power; and that the best solutions to our pressing social problems lie in the social fabric itself and in social action, and less than we may imagine via computational transformation.

At the same time, I distance myself from certain lines of popular criticism of computers themselves, most especially that line of criticism that suggests that computers produce unsupervised interference with expert discourses and/or a crisis of legitimate authority with regard to the presentation of factual information. To begin with, I am less than persuaded that the democratizing effects of computers outweigh their tendency to centralize and concentrate power, as I discuss throughout this book; at another level, I endorse the demotion of expert opinion via tools like Wikipedia whose proliferation worries critics like Keen (2007). To a large degree, my concern is much the opposite: that the recent left-liberal adoption of computational evangelism (historically best documented and analyzed in Turner 2006) fails to offset the profoundly authoritarian bent of computationalism, so that radical democratization only appears likely if one avoids looking at the computational boon to centralized power. Thus both Keen and the wave of upbeat "democratization of information" writers (e.g., Shirky

2008; Surowiecki 2005; and Weinberger 2003, 2007) seem to look almost exclusively at what one might think of as the "good side" of the web, and in so doing nearly ignore the countervailing tendencies that undermine the movements they champion. These writers also endorse a radical populism that around the world only sometimes aligns itself with democratic social justice.

A second form of popular critique, this one having more exponents in academic circles, meshes more closely with my argument. This critique is often dismissed due to its first and best-known presentation in Birkerts (1994), where computerization is associated with a tendency to privilege the visual (a real worry, on my account), a decline in the ability to read (a real but more complex worry), and a decline in cultural standards that resembles the Keen (2007) attack on "amateurization" and lack of "expert oversight" of cultural production—phenomena that I would in fact find salutary if they were as widespread or as powerful as their advocates and their critics claim. Put simply, such critiques are elitist. But Birkerts also points to a line of critique that must be taken more seriously, which goes something like this: how do we guarantee that computers and other cultural products are not so pleasurable that they discourage us from engaging in absolutely necessary forms of social interaction? I see the current emphasis on the "social web" as not so much an account of a real phenomenon as it is a reaction to what we all know inside—that computers are pulling us away from face-to-face social interactions and in so doing removing something critical from our lived experience. While I am more skeptical about the implicit value of reading *per se* than Birkerts, the question of what that activity is being replaced with, raised more pointedly in Bauerlein (2008), must give anyone pause. In the Epilogue below I also discuss in some detail the pointed version of an allied critique offered by developmental psychologists, who examine the impact on personality formation of decreasing direct social interaction and unstructured play, as articulated by Adele Diamond (2006) and others (see Spiegel 2008a, 2008b).

This book is philosophical in form, but interpretive in method. Its form proceeds from one familiar throughout a number of philosophical traditions, in that it builds from discussions of the way people are constructed— via discussions of mind and then language—outward toward discussions of the consequences these particular notions have for culture and politics. Unlike some works in these traditions, my goal is not to articulate a philosophical system. Rather, and perhaps more in line with some recent works of this form, such those by Rorty (1979) and Putnam (1981a, 1992), it emerges from the conviction that there is no strong way to separate these kinds of issues, even if specialization might suggest otherwise. We are always talking about cultural politics, even when we appear not to be doing so. More overtly than those works, however, I adopt Louis Althusser's post-structuralist conception of the project of philosophy: not a "demonstrative discourse" or "discourse of legitimation," but a "position on the philosophical battlefield: for or against such-and-such an existing position" (Althusser 2006, 256–7). My goal is not to articulate an alternative to computationalist presumptions about language, mind, and culture. It is to show the functions of that discourse in our society, to think about how and why it is able to rule out viable alternative views, and to argue that it is legitimate and even necessary to operate as if it is possible that computationalism will eventually fail to bear the philosophical-conceptual burden that we today put on it.

Computationalism

Computationalism is a word that has emerged only recently in the literature of analytic philosophy (see, e.g., Copeland 1996, 2002; Davenport 2000; Hardcastle 1995; Scheutz 2002; Wilson 1994, 1995). In that discipline, computationalism is used as a successor term to *functionalism*, notably deployed after the heyday of the doctrine, as discussed in detail in Chapter 3 below. Today, philosophers write about computationalism not as a view to be embraced directly, for the most part, but instead as a problematic doctrine which raises as many questions about philosophical practice as it does about its own putative subject matter. In its received (sometimes called its "classical") form, computationalism is the view that not just human minds are computers but that *mind itself* must be a computer—that our notion of intellect is, at bottom, identical with abstract computation, and that in discovering the principles of algorithmic computation via the Turing Machine human beings have, in fact, discovered the essence not just of human thought in practice but all thought in principle (see especially Kurzweil 1990, 1999, 2006).

Today, few philosophers can accept any of the straightforward versions of computationalism (although there are certainly exceptions to this rule), generally because, as Scheutz writes, "computation, assumed to be defined in abstract syntactic terms, necessarily neglects the real-time, embodied, real-world constraints with which cognitive systems intrinsically cope" (Scheutz 2002, ix). For Scheutz's cognitive systems we must read instead "human cognitive systems," since part of the failure of computationalism has been to show that we really cannot come to general conclusions about cognition per se—we are not even sure we know what that is. Defined this way, however, the recent reevaluations of computationalism pose a question that this volume seeks to answer: not merely why was computationalism so attractive to philosophers—and why does it remain so attractive to many of them—but also what is at stake in the deep cultural commitment to this view, both inside and outside of philosophy?

In this sense, despite the widespread availability, indeed ubiquity, of computational systems throughout world culture today, I suggest that we must all the more urgently step back and ask questions that are not, in their essence, technological at all. In the terms used by Scheutz and other recent writers, it is clear that computationalism is not so much a commitment to the idea that our brains are fundamentally the same thing as personal computers (what would it mean, in this sense, for our brains to be "running programs" the way that computers run Microsoft Word or a web browser?) as it is a commitment to a set of views that are not at all new to Western or other imperial cultures in our history: views according to which cognition is a process of abstracting away from the embeddedness of material culture, and human beings can not merely be separated hierarchically from animals but also amongst themselves in terms of their cultural deployment of abstract rationality, of so-called "reason." This is a view of human being that is familiar as what Deleuze and Guattari (1983, 1987) call "State philosophy" from as far back in history as we care to trace, although it reaches a certain apotheosis in at least one brand of European Enlightenment, especially the high rationalism associated with Leibniz—who has become, not coincidentally, a kind of patron saint for computationalism (Saul [1992] is a particularly trenchant historical analysis of rationalism in the sense I am using it here).

While philosophers use the term *computationalism* to refer to others of their kind who believe that the human mind is ultimately characterizable as a kind of computer, here I deploy the term more expansively as a commitment to the view that a great deal, perhaps all, of human and social experience can be explained via computational processes. While a great deal hangs precisely on the idea that cognition in particular is computational, in the world at large the belief that computers and human minds are converging entails a set of wider beliefs, namely that any number of real-world phenomena may not simply benefit from computerization but are ultimately "becoming" computerized (precisely due to a passive agency that is here a significant object of critique). In its benign forms, this kind of computationalism manifests in the belief not just that media like recorded music, books, television, and movies are being changed by and replicated on computers, but that they are at bottom fundamentally computational processes that will be transformed quite utterly, in a long term to which we seem to lack good access today, by accelerating computerization (for a skeptical counterpoint to such views, see in particular the writings of Paul Virilio, especially

Virilio 1983, 1989, 1997, and 2000). In more malevolent guises, computationalism manifests in messianic claims about sudden, radical, and almost always salutary changes in the fundamental fabric of politics, economics, and social formations: in claims that the world simply "is" becoming "flat" (to quote one particularly popular version of the view in circulation today; see Friedman 2005); in the belief that computers inherently create distributed democratic forms; and more abstractly, in claims that we can ignore any number of pressing social problems by dint of some kind of unnamable change, a change I see as being precisely messianic, one which computers are in the process of bringing into being. In this sense, by computationalism I mean something close—but not identical—to what Hayles (2005) rightly calls the "regime of computation"; I believe it is accurate to say that the regime of computation targets the combined effects of computational rhetoric and mass computerization; here, at least in great part, my effort is to separate these two phenomena, even if we often want to examine how they work in tandem.

In the most explicit accounts of Western intellectual history, mechanist views cluster on the side of political history to which we typically think of as the right, or conservatism, or Tory politics, or in our day, and perhaps more specifically relevant to this inquiry, neoliberalism. In some historical epochs it is clear who tends to endorse such views and who tends to emphasize other aspects of human existence in whatever the theoretical realm. It is figures like Leibniz who champion such views in European history, and skeptical figures like Voltaire and Swift who call them into question. There are strong intellectual and social associations between Hobbes's theories and those of Machiavelli and Descartes, especially when seen from the State perspective. These philosophers and their views have often been invoked by conservative and neoliberal leaders when they want to consolidate power. This contrasts with ascendant liberal power and its philosophies, whose conceptual and political tendencies follow different lines altogether: Hume, Kant, Nietzsche, Heidegger, Dewey, James, etc. These are two profoundly different views of what the State itself means, what the citizen's engagement with the State is, and where State power arises. Resistance to the view that the mind is computational is often found in philosophers we associate with liberal or radical (usually, but not always, left) views, despite a significant amount of variety in their views—for example, Locke, Hume, Nietzsche, Marx. These thinkers put both persons and social groups in the place of mechanical reason tend to emphasize social and relational duties rather than "natural right."

The general tendencies of these two intellectual and political bodies are well known, but their connection with particular understanding of the nature of human being is something we discuss much less often today than we did in the 1650s. The immense proliferation of scientific specialties leaves most people arguably without even a frame from which to conceptualize a view of human nature sensitive to the vast literature on cognition. More precisely, each side of the debate continues with its tacit understanding of what is vital to human being, while technological changes subtly influence the social field out of which broad political opinion is formed. The idea that the person is somehow in essence a digital thing, especially via the sense that the mind is a computer—with no more detail than that metaphorical equation—appears to be "loose" in contemporary culture. This idea fits well with capitalist rationalism and literalist evangelical Christianity, and in some important ways meshes well with associated beliefs of both dogmas.[2] It conflicts with the traditional views of the left, but it is intriguing enough and its contradictions are far enough *sub rosa* that many there take it up as a matter of course, where computationalism has today gained a surprisingly strong foothold.

Just in order to take advantage of what Deleuze and Guattari (1982, 1987) call the "war machine," and then subsequently as a method of social organization in general, the State uses computation and promotes computationalism. This is precisely because "the modern State defines itself in principle as 'the rational and reasonable organization of a community' . . . The State gives thought a form of interiority, and thought gives that interiority a form of universality."[3] Interiority qua universal subjectivity emerges from numerical rationality applied as an understanding of human subjectivity, and not vice versa. This is not to reject the idea of subjectivity outside of rationalist modernity: it is rather to suggest that the particular and elaborated form of interiority we associate with present-day modernity underwrites an unexpected and radical mechanism. This mechanism does not seem radical if we associate it with a word like *rationalism,* because we are not accustomed to understanding rationality as a mechanical function, though that is exactly what its definition suggests. It is rationalists themselves who take the term most literally, seeing in the creating of ratios—of weightings, largely of the more and less powerful force—the characteristic computation of modernity. While Descartes himself did not subscribe to this understanding of psychology, through Hobbes in particular we associate the modern State's conception of the "free" rational individual with absolute sovereignty and natural right. Because each citizen has the power to reason (to *calculate ratios,* or in our terms to *compute*) for himself, each citizen has access to the know-how (Foucault's *savoir*) of State sovereignty.[4] Each citizen can work out for himself the State philosophy: "Always obey. The more you obey, the more you will be master, for you will only be obeying pure reason. In other words yourself . . . Ever since philosophy assigned itself the role of ground it has been giving the established powers its blessing, and tracing its doctrine of faculties onto the organs of State power."[5]

To submit a phenomenon to computation is to striate otherwise-smooth details, analog details, to push them upwards toward the sovereign, to make only high-level control available to the user, and then only those aspects of control that are deemed appropriate by the sovereign (Delevze 1992). In this sense, computers wrap the "legacy data" of the social world in formal markup, whose purpose is to provide the sovereign with access for post-hoc analysis, and secondarily to provide filter-style control. Computation can then be used, at sovereign discretion, as part of instruction, as a way of conditioning subjects to respond well to the computational model. From this perspective, it is surprising to hear prominent academics like Nicholas Negroponte state that the "digital age" is distinguished by "four very powerful qualities that will result in its ultimate triumph: decentralizing, globalizing, harmonizing, and empowering."[6] Without any consideration of arguments to the contrary, Negroponte asserts that "the traditional centralist view of life will become a thing of the past," that "in the digital world, previously impossible solutions become viable," that

> The harmonizing effect of being digital is already apparent as previously partitioned disciplines and enterprises find themselves collaborating, not competing. A previously missing common language emerges, allowing people to understand across boundaries. Kids at school today experience the opportunity to look at the same thing from many perspectives. A computer program, for example, can be seen simultaneously as a set of computer instructions or as concrete poetry.[7]

It is no surprise that Negroponte's "optimism comes from the empowering nature of being digital. . . . As children appropriate a global information resource, and as they discover that only adults need learner's permits, we are bound to find new hope and dignity in places where very little existed before."[8] It is also no surprise that Negroponte now spearheads a worldwide effort to distribute computers to children (the One Laptop Per Child program, or OLPC) that can also be seen as realizing a desire to propagate computationalism, and in this mode emerges not from a prior base of interest in the social and economic problems of the world's most marginalized people, but instead from the intuitions of computer users and developers about what it is like to engage deeply with the machine.[9]

The closing words of Negroponte's best-selling book completely lack exemplary support, and with good reason. Their staging of an artificial, precomputerization past where things like collaboration as opposed to competition existed seems purely ideological, and the observation that computers alone teach a kind of perspectivalism instanced in the ability to read code as poetry is nothing short of bizarre. "Lessons" about perspective might be thought one of the main goals of any sort of humanities education, and easily obtainable from the whole world of cultural objects—a world which, in many worlds of education, exactly requires no particular "missing common language," especially not the monolingual majority languages of computing.

Just as importantly, it is critical not to accept *a priori* the idea that computation as such refers only to the operations of the particular physical objects we understand as computers. Arguably, the major function that computers perform routinely in our society is calculation.[10] Calculation has a long history in civilization, especially in centralized, bureaucratic administrations, and in empires. Calculation is especially important for warfare, where it is deployed in a manner that must be understood as simulation, even if the simulation is represented entirely via mathematics. Turing, von Neumann, and other early developers of physical computers relied just as much on what were then named computers as they did on the machines for which we now use that name, and warfare was their main purpose.[11] As David Alan Grier has recently shown, along lines that have become accepted throughout the small field of computer history, since at least the late-19th century many sorts of institutions routinely employed rooms of human calculators, often women, and precisely enabling the exercise of administrative power to which the workers lacked access.[12]

These human computers were in fact the first operators of electronic and mechanical computers, regardless of whether they were built for analog or digital functions. In the administrative scheme, computing acts as a slave to the powerful human master, and it is always the task of imperial administration to amplify computational power. Following historians like Adas, Crosby, Headrick, and Mattelart and no less poststructuralist thinkers like Deleuze and Guattari, Virilio, and Derrida, we can see how uneven are the benefits of computational power in more aspects of their distribution than might be ordinarily supposed. This is no mere fantasy: on even cursory examination, one can easily see how many of the 20th century's most famous and infamous institutions depended heavily on computational practices. These are the accomplishments of computing, the ones its internal advocates trumpet, today more loudly than ever, as if they were devoid of politics. For a materialist study of computing to follow its predecessors, it must look not (or not only) to what computers may someday present to us, whether in the form of a genuinely "new" medium or not; it must look to what computers are doing in our world, from the implementation of widely distributed identification and surveillance to the reduction of all the world's cultures for profit.

Computers come with powerful belief systems that serve to obscure their real functions, even when we say we are acutely aware of the consequences of our technologies. The thought surrounding issues like global climate change and genetics (and, in an earlier time, research into atomic physics) suggests that technologies have strong inherent destructive potentials, even when we don't see them. The fact that computers empower users is not in doubt; what is in question is what power it gives which users, how, and why. In a world where corporations already inhabit an ideal personhood (exported uniquely from an Anglo-American model) that obscures what we understand as human being (not least because the humans who inhabit them are rarely held accountable for a corporation's actions), and as with commercials for detrimental technologies like always-on wireless connectivity, it is all the more necessary to articulate the ideological operations of the computational tropes as they come into being, rather than afterwards. We need to find a way to generate critical praxis even of what appears as an inarguable good. What historicist and poststructuralist writers like Foucault and technological skeptics like Ellul and Innis share is the view that social transformations emerge anywhere other than political movements, even when their overriding trope is technological. The lesson from that work that this book deploys is that we have to learn how to critique even that which helps us (much as computers help us to write books like this one, among many other things). It would be better not to have computers, in that sense, than to live in a world where many more people come to believe that computers by themselves can "save us," can "solve our problems."

For at least one hundred years and probably much longer, modern societies have been built on the assumption that more rationality and more *technē* (and more capital) are precisely the solutions to the extremely serious problems that beset our world and our human societies. Yet the evidence that this is not the right solution can be found everywhere. This is not to suggest that rationality is wrong or misguided or that we should eradicate it (arguably figures like Derrida and Foucault follow the counter-Enlightenment tradition of Voltaire and Swift, none of whom altogether dismiss the value of rationality); it is to suggest that our societies function best when they are balanced between what we will call here rationalism and whatever lies outside of it. To some extent this is a perpetual tension in all societies, not just in ours or in so-called modern ones; what is distinctive about our society, historically, is its emphasis on rationalism and its terrific adeptness at ruling out any discourse that stands against rationalism. In other societies and places just the opposite might be true, in a way that our own rationalist moment makes difficult to see. There is no doubt that societies have existed and do exist where there is so much emphasis on power without the appearance of rational rule that rationalism is precisely what they need to undo long histories of despotism.

Here I argue that the opposite has become the case for us. The computer, despite its claims to fluidity, is largely a proxy for an idealized form of rationalism. This book shows how the rationalist vision could be mutated into something like a full articulation of human society, despite the obvious, repeated, *a priori* and *a posteriori* reasons that this could never and will never be the case. On this view, the main reason figures like Kant, Hegel, Plato, Hume, the late Wittgenstein, and even Derrida and Spivak look odd at all to us is precisely because of the sheer power held by the rationalist vision over so much of society. It seems conceivable that someday they will be seen (again) as offering what is at least a plausible articulation of human social formation. At that point, this moment will look to be one in which we were possessed by a kind of extreme rationalist vision that carries with it at least two repressed historical formations: the absolutist leader whose will in fact transcends all rational calculation, and disdain for the "illogical" historical and social fabric of the human world.

The Deconstruction of Computation

Despite its rigid formal characteristics, in part because of them, then, computationalism is in every sense what Foucault calls a discourse, one that we are actively creating and enabling, and among whose fundamental principles is the elaboration of centralized power. Its deployment is in no way new in our world; as even computing's advocates insist, at least since Leibniz, it has been well understood that a form of mathematical calculation could be made to represent propositions that are not themselves mathematical. There is little more to understanding computation than comprehending this simple principle: mathematical calculation can be made to stand for propositions that are themselves not mathematical, but must still conform to mathematical rules.

Yet the nature of Leibniz's personal commitment to computation as a cognitive principle only demonstrates the degree to which it is culturally situated. Even orthodox computer histories have trouble making Leibniz sound like anything other than a product of the Western intellectual history of which he is a part, possessed by a belief system to which he subscribes for reasons we would today see as political at least as much as they are properly scientific. The computer historian and logician Martin Davis calls the computer "Leibniz's Dream," and leaves us in no doubt that the dream is no simple anticipation of the machines we see today: it is a full-blown wish for the elimination of everything that is imprecise or ambiguous in human social practice. Thus in one of his fullest statements about the potential of computation, Leibniz writes to his friend Jean Galloys that he is

> convinced more and more of the utility and reality of this general science [i.e., computation], and I see that few people have understood its extent. . . . This characteristic consists of a certain script or language . . . that perfectly represents the relationships between our thoughts

The pursuit of this "perfect relationship between our thoughts," while not exclusive to computationalists or rationalists, nevertheless has persistently informed a central strand of Western thought about language and subjectivity. It emerges from a terrible anxiety about exactly the ambiguity that characterizes human experience; and it points toward a seemingly perfect world in which "it will be impossible to write . . . chimerical notions such as suggest themselves to us. An ignoramus will not be able to use it, or in striving to do so, he himself will become erudite."[13]

For hundreds of years, sentiments such as this one were considered a kind of pipe-dream, the sort of stuff of which acerbic and highly rational anti-rationalists like Jonathan Swift could make merciless fun, with some confidence that the dreams would never be realized, on grounds that are philosophical, discursive, and empirical. Yet more recently, despite the strong philosophical and conceptual tradition that raises questions not about the reality of computation as a powerful praxis—its raw power should be of no question to anyone, especially today—but precisely about the conceptual underpinnings on which rest views about the general utility of computation as a form of something close to what we can call, as shorthand, "human thinking."

Few writers have doubted the importance of rational calculation in the operation of human thinking. What is in question is the degree to which that sort of calculation explains all the facts of cognition, all the effects of culture, and all that is possible in the realm of culture and cognition. Thinkers who try to construct a rationalist line extending from Leibniz through Descartes to Boole and Frege (the 19th-century logicians most relevant to computing) must conveniently put aside the most famous dissenters from the view that computation is everything, which includes figures of note such as Hume, Hegel, and Kant; and no less the 20th-century thinkers, themselves quite close culturally and personally to the birth of modern computers, like Russell and Wittgenstein, all of whom raised the most profound conceptual questions about the extent to which logical calculation could, in fact, represent all or even much of human cognitive practice.

The most thorough and most critical of these perspectives, and the one least addressed by contemporary computationalists, is the one offered by Immanuel Kant. Kant fully understood the power of logic and calculation, but he was famously not persuaded by the work of rationalists before him that this was the correct model for what humans do with their brains. Even this argument, clear enough in the main run of Kant's arguments, has started to become lost on us; today Kant looks in departments of Anglo-American analytic philosophy as if he is at least fairly close to a full-blown rationalist on the Leibniz model. Yet as one of Kant's most careful contemporary readers, Gayatri Spivak, has shown repeatedly, Kant argued that "mere (rather than pure) reason is a programmed structure, with in-built possibilities of misfiring, and nothing but calculation as a way of setting right" (Spivak 2005, 93). "Mere" reason, for Kant, is not like the two major categories of cognition, "pure" and "practical" reason, specifically because in its quest for exactness it actually eliminates the possibility of human agency in cognitive practice. Like mathematical equations, formulae that are "merely" reasonable admit of unique, univocal solutions. No thought is necessary to compute that 2 plus 2 equals 4; one can of course come to this conclusion through general thought, or through memorization, or exemplar, or through sheer calculation. But as is characteristic of such computational facts, no human being or human thought is actually necessary to determine that 4 is the unique solution to the question "what is the sum of 2 plus 2?"

It is no accident that Spivak uses the term *programmed* to describe the kind of thought that Kant did not think encompasses all of human reason, precisely the kind of cognitive practice that would eliminate the ambiguity that so troubled Leibniz and others. Jacques Derrida, who himself suggested some of the views of Kant on which Spivak elaborates, is often thought of as a thinker who teaches us to reject handed-down distinctions, showing why and how, for example, much thinking in the Western tradition has relied on an implicit and at times explicit distinction between writing and speech that is philosophically much less tenable than it may appear on the surface. At the same time, in a way that has not been so well understood by his readers, Derrida does not want to deny, exactly, that some societies, especially modern cosmopolitan and imperial societies, are everywhere characterized by writing and printing, while other societies, including the Nambikwara discussed by Claude Lévi-Strauss in the *Tristes Tropiques* and elsewhere, have historically had less formal systems of writing and have relied less on fully articulated systems of writing and printing.

Despite the efforts of pro-computer writers like George Landow to make hypertext sound like the realization of Derridean dreams of a language without binding or hierarchical structures (Landow 1992), in fact from his earliest writing Derrida has been concerned precisely with the difference between human language and something like computer code. *Of Grammatology* (1976) announces this concern in the deliberate use of the morpheme *gram* in its title, and Derrida cannily indicates that this term, associated for his purposes primarily with a history of writing proposed by the Egyptologist I. J. Gelb in his *Study of Writing* (1952), points at a more general and contemporary problematic that has been insufficiently thematized, even as he calls into question the distinction between so-called writing and other forms of inscription:

> we say "writing" for all that gives rise to an inscription in general, whether it is literal or not and even if what it distributes in space is alien to the order of the voice: cinematography, choreography, of course, but also pictorial, musical, sculptural "writing." One might also speak of athletic writing, and with even greater certainty of military or political writing in view of the techniques that govern these domains today. All this to describe not only the system of notation secondarily connected with these activities but the essence and content of these activities themselves. It is also in this sense that the contemporary biologist speaks of writing and *pro-gram* in relation to the most elementary processes of information within the living cell. And, finally, whether it has essential limits or not, the entire field covered by the cybernetic *program* will be the field of writing. If the theory of cybernetics is by itself to oust all metaphysical concepts—including the concepts of soul, of life, of value, of choice, of memory—which until recently served to separate the machine from man, it must conserve the notion of writing, trace, *grammè*, or grapheme, until its own historico-metaphysical character is also exposed. (Derrida 1976, 9)

This is not the work of someone who wants to dispose of the distinction between computer program and language. One detects, despite Derrida's suspicion of all true messianism and distinctions that are too neat, a certain wariness that "the concepts of soul, of life, of value, of choice, of memory" may be overwhelmed by a mechanistic view of language (Harris 1987) and cognition that, heedless of Kant, substitutes "mere" reason for all the complex of human reasoning that philosopher knew must characterize our experience and most especially our moral and political actions and choices.

Derrida is no Luddite, and no one would be more suspicious than he of the view that one technology or another was leading us down a royal road to monstrous disaster—far from it. But the computer in particular is a technology that caused him great concern, for precisely the reason that it offers to substitute for the flux of experience an appearance of certainty that cannot, in fact, adequately represent our experience. Marian Hobson, a critic who knew Derrida quite well personally, writes:

> The information embodied in the digital series cannot be summarized to any useful extent. A summary which can be raised to the level of theme, of next-level program, is simply not possible. Such types of binary series suggest that the much more variegated strings of signifiers in natural language may likewise not be summarized without loss, by imposition of law-like program or summary equation one to another of different scales of detail and signification—what can be generally called "thematization." The elements in the series can only be taken at the level of singulars.
>
> For Derrida, a philosophic or fictional text is neither a code which is interpreted, nor a program which is "run." (This stance takes the form of occasionally explicit resistance to a commentator in *Jacques Derrida* [Bennington and Derrida 1993] and is one of the sources of humor there.) (Hobson 1998, 194)

Hobson is right to point us to codes and programs as precisely the things which texts are not, despite Derrida's putative disregard for analytic distinctions, and it is no surprise to hear Hobson report that the notion of a "deconstruction computer program" struck Derrida as profoundly troubling, nor to read in the introduction to Bennington's "Derridabase":[14]

> The guiding idea of the exposition comes from computers: G. B. would have liked to systematize J. D.'s thought to the point of turning it into an interactive program which, in spite of its difficulty, would in principle be accessible to any user. As what is at stake in J. D.'s work is to show how any such system remains essentially open, this undertaking was doomed to failure from the start. . . . In order to demonstrate the ineluctable necessity of that failure, our contract stipulated that J. D., having read G. B's text, would write something escaping the proposed systemization. (Bennington and Derrida 1993, 1)

Perhaps just as striking is the fact that Bennington does not even propose the creation of an actual computer program, and does not make it clear how the written text that follows—merely an ordered list of terms and concepts important in Derrida's writing—might be made into something like a program. It seems to me that this hesitation on Derrida's part show just how well he understood computer programs and how they differ from written texts.

Of course, "Derridabase" is well ordered, and for this reason it could easily be made part of a functioning computer application. But its concept of system is rudimentary. It is less elaborate than the kind of logical structure computer scientists call an *algorithm,* or at any rate forms one of the most basic types of algorithm, an ordered list (and it is not entirely wrong to think that an algorithm is the same thing as a very small computer program, and so as computation itself, the principle of letting mathematical formulae correspond to logical ones; see Berlinski 2000). This helps to show the ways in which we have identified computers with every sort of logical system. This is because a computer can simulate or represent any logical system that can be precisely defined. In fact this is the definition of computation. (The thing we refer to as a computer today is a particular kind of algorithm, commonly referred to as a Turing machine.) The power and universal applicability of computation has made it look to us as if, quite literally, *everything* might be made out of computation (von Baeyer 2005; Wolfram 1994, 2002). This is meant literally: researchers have proposed, in the course of what must in part be nothing but normal scientific practice, that everything from DNA, to the interactions between subatomic particles, to the shape of space-time, might be constructed from the algorithmic passing of information in some abstract sense.

No doubt, at least some of these scientific theories will turn out to have a grain of truth to them, and no doubt others of them will fail. But what have proven to be of especially limited consequence, as this book shows, are theories that try to apply the universal representational capability of computation to the human world. The place where this is most visible is language, exactly because computers must partake of something like human language (called by computer scientists "natural language") in order to be used by human beings at all. Programming languages, as Derrida knew, are codes: they have one and only one correct interpretation (or, at the absolute limit, a determinate number of discrete interpretations). Human language practice almost never has a single correct interpretation. Languages are not codes; programming "languages" like Basic and FORTRAN and scripting "languages" like HTML and JavaScript do not serve the functions that human languages do. The use of the term *language* to describe them is a deliberate metaphor, one that is meant to help us interact with machines, but we must not let ourselves lose sight of its metaphorical status, and yet this forgetting has been at stake from the first application of the name (see Chapters 2 and 4).

Of course, from the beginning of computation as a practice and in fact as part of it, writers have proposed that language itself might be subsumed by formal systems, eradicating the ambiguity that so troubles human society. As physical computers themselves came into being, scarcely a year has gone by when several corporate or governmental entities have failed to generate multiple press stories about computers that are about to speak—and only recently, in no small part because of the heated attention they receive, have we seen fewer claims that computers are about to start thinking. But it is a core commitment of this book that neither of these events is about to happen, soon if ever. The reason is not because we and our thought and language are magical entities, beyond the science of computers; it is instead because we are material beings embedded in the physical and historical contexts of our experience, and it turns out that what we refer to as "thought" and "language" and "self" emerge from those physical materialities. Yes, we can easily build codes that are independent of our bodies; but we don't even know how to conceive of what we call speaking and what we call thinking as independent of our bodies and selves. We can't conceive that the destruction of identity that accompanies the "uploading self" fantasies of so much computer fiction has already and can always happen, because there is no self there to realize it or to feel it. Our selves can only stay where they are, in a singularity that has already happened—and is no nearer than it has ever been.

Discussions of the digital world and technology in general often are forced to hinge on conceptions of the human, and it would be easy enough to suppose that a poststructuralist perspective would have to rule out access to the concept of the human altogether. Nevertheless, like all writing including poststructuralism, cultural criticism of all sorts must inherently be concerned with something we can perhaps only vaguely call "the human world." Arguably, we would not even know what our objects of study were without recourse to such a concept. We need, then, to distinguish between the concept *human* prior to poststructuralism and after it—to keep in mind the object of criticism Derrida and Foucault meant to target, while not jettisoning a robust enough conception of human life to sustain political and cultural reflection. The most narrow, and not entirely accurate, heuristic for making this distinction is to think about the term *human nature*: do we imagine that there are many substantive features of human nature, so that much of what it is to be human is invariant over time; or do we imagine that much of human nature is flexible and open to definition, so that what it means to be human can change depending on context? The former, substantive concept of human nature can be understood as that which the poststructuralists had most in mind, while the latter, flexible conception is the one with which poststructuralism is far more comfortable.

It would be inaccurate to say that we have passed beyond the notion of a substantive human nature in our own society; such a concept functions powerfully in popular discourse around gender, race, and sexuality, among other places. Contemporary geneticists and biologists, despite the power of DNA-based analysis, recognize that human beings are far more characterized by variability than they are by substantive qualities. Persons bearing XX chromosomes and typically classified "female" usually have less upper-body strength than does a typical male of similar height, weight, and age; but this statistical observation provides almost no information for predicting whether any specific human being will be more or less strong than another. We have learned not to define women as "the weaker sex," and not to disparage women with significant upper-body strength as failing to meet the substantive definition of their kind, just as many of us have learned to assign few characteristics to any individual based on his or her membership in any given group. In this sense contemporary views of human nature dovetail with poststructuralist views in rejecting the idea that "the human" is defined by the capability for rationality, or "man" is defined by bravery, sexual prowess, sportsmanship, and so on. Whatever our particular characteristics, we are all human, and we accept the fact that this term has little substantive content. As the philosopher of biology David Hull has put it, writing against the more substantive view of human nature adopted by sociobiologists, "if by 'human nature' all one means is a trait which happens to be prevalent and important for the moment, then surely human nature exists. Each species exhibits adaptations, and these adaptations are important for its continued existence. . . . But this adaptation may not have characterized us throughout our existence and may not continue to characterize us in the future" (Hull 1986, 9).

There is no essence to human nature, no particular set of traits or forms of life that make us human or make us inhuman. Human nature is highly malleable; the ability to affect what humans are and how they interact with their environment is one of my main concerns here, specifically along the lines that computerization of the world encourages computerization of human beings. There are nevertheless a set of capacities and concerns that characterize what we mean by human being: human beings typically have the capacity to think; they have the capacity to use one or more (human) languages; they define themselves in social relationship to each other; and they engage in political behavior.[15] These concerns correspond roughly to the chapters that follow. In each case, a rough approximation of my thesis might be that most of the phenomena in each sphere, even if in part characterizable in computational terms, are nevertheless *analog* in nature. They are gradable and fuzzy; they are rarely if ever exact, even if they can achieve exactness. The brain is analog; languages are analog; society and politics are analog. Such reasoning applies not merely to what we call the "human species" but to much of what we take to be life itself, and it is notable that many animals (and even some plants) evidence behavior that falls under one or more of these headings. It is not even clear what the boundaries of "the human" might be in these regards; it is not at all intuitively clear what characteristics aliens would have to display for us to consider them roughly the same as humans, or even to be human. Presumably, the capacities to engage in thinking, language, social relations, and politics would go a long way in helping us draw this conclusion, but the problem is thornier than some would like to admit; recent suggestions that animals might deserve something like "human rights" only goes to show the dense problematic sedimented into the term.

While human beings can surely engage in activities that resemble or are even equivalent to digital ones, it is their capacity to engage in analog activities—their propensity so far in history to engage most of the time in such activities—that are of signal concern in this study. Famously, Deleuze and Guattari write at length in the two volumes of *Capitalism and Schizophrenia* (1983, 1987) that much of human life and human society can be characterized in terms of machines; they go so far as to include much of everything we recognize as part of a "machinic phylum." There is much to recommend this view, and it is not my purpose to put it under scrutiny here. But what is notable for our purposes is that these machines are generally analog: like most of our world, they are machines built for one or more specific functions, sometimes able to be repurposed for other uses, inexact, rough, fuzzy. They don't choose between 1 and 0 to build up symbolic operations; rather, the machine of the animal elbow moves at any number of stretchable angles, which no part of the body needs to decompose into numeric approximations. While enough frames-per-second can make digital animations appear as smooth as analog ones, there is still a translation occurring inside the computer that the animal body does not need to make. There is no mystery here; analog machines are at least as old as digital ones and pose no conceptual obstacles (that they might is arguably a symptom of exactly the computational mania with which this book is concerned). Lawn mowers, toasters, drills, typewriters, elbow joints, pianos, and jaws may be mechanical, but there is no reason to suspect them of being digital (Derrida [1993] offers an excellent account of the machinic qualities of the organic world that nevertheless remain different from digital representation). That digital media can approximate their function should raise this suspicion no more than the existence of baseball or golf simulations makes us suspect that these games are digital.

Few theorists addressed the interconnection of politics, culture, and technology more closely than Deleuze and Guattari. In *A Thousand Plateaus*, Deleuze and Guattari develop a concept, *striation*, that arguably emerges in part from the growing emphasis on computerization that was evident even in the 1970s, but that has sometimes been overlooked by media theorists in favor of what is clearly a misreading of Deleuze and Guattari's discussion of *virtuality* (see especially Lévy 2001). The term *virtual reality* emerged in wide use (popularized in particular by the computer evangelist Jaron Lanier) after Deleuze and Guattari's pathbreaking work, and it is clear that Deleuze and Guattari intended the virtual to refer to a generic use of the term rather than to a computer-based phenomena (see De Landa 2002; Massumi 2002; Shields 2003; and Wark 2004 for more accurate discussions of what Deleuze and Guattari mean by the virtual and how it relates to the computer). The idea that computers represent a better instantiation of "virtuality" than do the human brain or human society is a curious and curiously computer-centric notion, one that bespeaks the tremendous cultural power of computation itself.

Nevertheless, the emphasis on the virtual as Deleuze and Guattari's chief contribution to the cultural study of computers has helped to obscure their much more sustained and meaningful ideas that center on the term *striation*, and that clearly have computation as an historical abstraction, and not just material computers, as their object of analysis. Striation is discussed throughout *Capitalism and Schizophrenia* (1983, 1987), principally in its second book, *A Thousand Plateaus*, but it receives thorough treatment in Chapter 14, "1440: The Smooth and the Striated." It is important to remember that this is essentially the final substantive chapter of *Capitalism and Schizophrenia* and that the distinction implemented here builds on others Deleuze and Guattari work out throughout the two volumes. "Smooth space and striated space—nomad space and sedentary space—the space in which the war machine develops and the space instituted by the State apparatus—are not of the same nature" (474), Deleuze and Guattari write, despite the fact that in reality "the two spaces only exist in mixture." Still, we can find examples that help us to distinguish the two principles. Smooth space, where "points are subordinated to the trajectory" (478), may be represented by the lifestyles of nomads, hunter-gatherers, navigation by "bearings" rather than maps, intuition, what Deleuze and Guattari call deterritorialization, rhizomatic organization, relatively anarchic and local forms government, and relatively mobile forms of life. Striated space, where "lines or trajectories tend to be subordinated to points" (478), is the space of the State, of firm bureaucratic and governmental orders, of the grid, of maps, coordinate orientations, of territorialization, tree-like (hierarchical) organization, settlement and agriculture (see Lunenfeld 2000, xvi-xviii, for a more laudatory but, for its closeness to contemporary computing practice, all-the-more telling account of the importance of grids; Crosby 1997, Scott 1999, and Wright 2005 touch on the importance of certain views of quantification to the State-based conception of progress that are closely tied to striation).

Schematized in this way, it is clear that most of the thought and practice surrounding computers promotes striated over smooth space. It is remarkable, then, how much of the cultural-political discussion of computers uses the rhetoric of smooth space while simply not addressing issues of striation—of territorialization rather than deterritorialization. As in the case of language, computers are found on the side of culture in which people move to metropoles and then stay in them, commit to hierarchical organization, grow increasingly reliant on technologies and politics of organization and settlement, and see the world as an already-comprehended object that is available for exploitation; at the same time what is left behind is a space of relative smoothness and (although it may be heavily constrained by the pressures of global capital) mobility. While the rhetoric of computation looks for those places in which the network allows for smooth practices, arguably this is not because the computational infrastructure is itself hospitable to such practices. Rather, it is because we simply do not want to admit how overwhelming are the forces of striation within computers and computation, and we grasp at precisely those thin (but of course real) marks of smoothness that remain as computers grow ever more global in power. Of course computers contribute in some ways to what is arguably a vitally necessary resistance to global striation; but if our goal is truly to participate in such resistance, we need to see with clear eyes just how deeply computers are implicated in striation to begin with. Given the pervasive insistence of computers on State power and striation, there is perhaps no more relevant technology of which one can say, with Audre Lorde, that "the master's tools will never dismantle the master's house" (1984, 110).

Politically, the goal of this study is to expand on a cultural opening that generally has been discounted in public discourse. In today's left, political analysis of computation largely focuses on one of two political possibilities. The first, expressed in liberal writings like those of Joseph Trippi and Markos Moulitsas, comes close to a kind of technological determinism: it suggests that the Internet is inherently democratizing, and we simply need to have faith that global computerization will produce democracy as a necessary side-effect. Trusting that the computer makes our political efforts qualitatively different from earlier ones, advocates of this position suggest that computer-based tools for fundraising, organizing, and citizen journalism will have a transformative effect on the public sphere: because the old media conglomerates will inevitably dissolve in the face of ubiquitous Internet access, we need do little more than use the computational tools engineers provide for us—as well as, no doubt, creating a few of our own—to effect significant, anti-authoritarian political change. In its best form—McChesney (2007), for example—this position embodies an admirable vision of citizen participation in the creation of the polis, something like a genuine liberal position. In its worst form—say, Friedman

(2005)—a similar position can degenerate into something very close to techno-progressivist neoliberalism, in which the computer is inherently effecting such massive social changes that we are virtually powerless over them, and at the same time need not worry about them, since they are almost inevitably going to make society more egalitarian, more resistant to authoritarian control and centralization.

A second view, more prominent within academic and creative thought about computing, suggests that there actually are problems inside of the contemporary computing infrastructure, but that it is "*through* protocol that one must guide one's efforts, not against it" (Galloway 2004, 17). Adumbrating this position, Galloway and Wark, especially, describe the actions of hackers, artists, creative writers, and programmers who work diligently to exploit gaps in the system and to re-use the system, especially the computational system, for anti-authoritarian ends. Wark's "hacker class" is wider than just those (e.g., Kevin Mitnick) understood to be hackers in the most literal sense; nevertheless, Wark writes that "*A Hacker Manifesto* is among other things an attempt to abstract from the practices and concepts" of "groups, networks, and collaborations such as Adilkno, Ctheory, EDT, Institute for Applied Autonomy, I/O/D, Luther Blisset Project, Mongrel, Nettime . . ." (Wark 2004, n.31). These artists and creative programmers (and mailing lists and critical communities) are extremely diverse entities, but it is fair to say that they generally adhere to Galloway's dictum: "through protocol, not against it."

This, too, is a laudatory goal, perhaps even more so than the first form of resistance articulated above; but I wonder what authorizes Galloway's prohibition: "*not* against" protocol. I am all for resistance through protocol; what I want to articulate is the case precisely for resistance *against* what Galloway calls protocol, and what is more generally thought of as computerization. My point is not to simply raise a kind of Luddite anti-technologism according to which we should simply dispose of all computers; my point is to raise the question whether the shape, function, and ubiquity of the computing network is something that should be brought under democratic control in a way that it is not today. I do not think computing is an industry like any other, or even a communications medium like any other; rather, it is a name for the administrative control and concentration powers of our society—in a sense, precisely what Foucault would call our governmentality. It seems more than reasonable to insist that such governmental powers must remain in the hands of a widespread citizenry, one that encompasses both majorities and minorities, communities and individuals. It is not exactly the "concentration of media ownership," but the concentration of computing power within institutions, to which I am encouraging resistance. Thus to Galloway's dictum I offer this simple emendation: resistance "through protocol, *and* against it."

In this way the goal of this study is to point out how pervasive the discourse of computationalism has become throughout our powerful institutions, especially where these touch on the third rails of true political authority. Trying to broaden the space from which informed leftist thought can insist that the question of how much computer technology is used, and how and where it is used, raises questions that must be open to the polis and not simply decided by technocrats. To a degree, this position has started to be articulated with regard to legal notions of intellectual property and even, perhaps to a lesser extent, to the kinds of knowledge generated within medical fields and biological research (where the question of who owns and who has access to genetic information is becoming more and more heated).

I don't think we can know at this historical juncture which of these modes of resistance might or might not be successful; nor do I see any reason to suppose they are anything but complementary, even if there is no doubt that differences will exist among them. But I will confess to being concerned about just where (because he does not say) a writer like Galloway derives the imperative in his statement that we *must not* resist against what he calls protocol. Again, resisting through protocol is a laudable goal; actually working to democratize media and information technology is a laudable goal (as for example in democratized projects like Wikipedia, and open source and free software, etc.); but it seems to me we can leave it to technocrats and capitalists to insist that we as the citizenry have no right or power to determine how technologies change, adapt, and function in society. No doubt there are a whole range of technical questions that can be left to specialists. The ubiquity of computer technology is not one of them.

It can be no coincidence that the computer emerges at just a moment when the public ideology of human enslavement has been changed by intense social effort. We address computers as our slaves, and never think of the power and satisfaction we feel precisely in knowing how perfectly the machine bends to our will. We exercise and intensify mastery over the machine at the individual and the social levels; we experience frustration when the real world fails to live up to the striated and rigid computational model. Yet we continue to look to the computer for solutions to this problem, itself largely created and intensified by the computer. We don't see people who use computers extensively (modern Americans and others around the world) breaking out everywhere in new forms of democratic action that disrupt effectively the institutional power of capital (see Dahlberg and Siapera 2007, Jenkins and Thorburn 2003, and Simon, Corrales, and Wolfensberger 2002 for close analysis of some of the more radical claims about democritization), yet our discourse says this is what computers bring. Our own society has displayed strong tendencies toward authoritarianism and perhaps even corporate fascism, two ideologies strongly associated with rationalism, and yet we continue to endorse even further tilts in the rationalist direction. This book is written in the hope that this historical imbalance between rationalism and "anti-rationalism" has gone about as far as it can go it the rationalist direction. Perhaps, despite appearances, there is a possible future in which computers are more powerful, more widespread, cheaper, and easier to use—and at the same time have much less influence over our lives and our thoughts.

PART ONE

COMPUTATIONALISM
AND COGNITION

CHAPTER TWO

Chomsky's Computationalism

Mᴏʀᴇ than any other figure, Noam Chomsky defined the intellectual climate in the English-speaking world in the second half of the 20th century. References to Chomsky's work dwarf those to the work of his closest competitors ("Chomsky Is Citation Champ," 1992); not only did Chomsky redefine the entire academic discipline of linguistics, but his work has been something close to definitive in psychology, philosophy, cognitive science, and even computer science. While it is well known that Chomsky's work has been influential in these fields, a stronger argument is possible: namely that Chomsky's embrace and defense of a particularly powerful ideology made his work useful for an intellectual and cultural politics that was looking for a home. In this sense, despite Chomsky's immense personal charisma and intellectual acumen, it is both accurate and necessary to see the Chomskyan revolution as a discourse that needed not so much an author as an author-function—a function "tied to the legal and institutional systems that circumscribe, determine, and articulate the realm of discourses" (Foucault 1969, 130).

Scholars have offered any number of plausible explanations for Chomsky's rise to prominence, not least his own personal brilliance and the incisiveness of his linguistic theories. Yet it seems reasonable to set aside some of these explanations and to think carefully about just what the times were and just what was the content of Chomsky's writing that made it seem not merely compelling but revolutionary. In what sense was the world ready and waiting for this particular Chomsky to emerge? A few scholars have begun to trace certain political movements within the English-speaking academy in the 1950s and early 1960s that point toward the existence of a directed search for a particular ideological view that would help to guide intellectual work toward a goal we have now come to recognize as neoliberalism, and that would condition in a profound manner the intellectual climate established in leading universities (see Amadae 2003; Edwards 1996; McCumber 2001; Reisch 2005). In a deliberate and also largely covert effort to resist the possibility of communist/Marxist encroachment on the U.S. *conceptual* establishment (which points at something far broader than institutional philosophy), individuals, government entities including the military and intelligence bodies (De Landa 1991), and private foundations like the RAND Corporation, promoted values like objectivity and rationalism over against subjectivity, collectivity, and shared social responsibility.

Dovetailing precisely with the emerging availability of computing machinery in universities and with the waning productivity of the first wave of computing theorists (Turing, von Neumann, Shannon, et. al.), Chomsky offered the academy at least two attractive sets of theses that, while framed in terms of a profoundly new way of understanding the world, in fact harkened back to some of the most deeply entrenched views in the Western intellectual apparatus. First, as a general background, Chomsky insists that the only reasonable locus for analysis of cognitive and linguistic matters is the human individual, operating largely via a specific kind of rationality (a view that Chomsky would later come to call "Cartesian rationalism"; Chomsky 1966); second, specifically with regard to the substance both of cognition and of language, Chomsky argues that the brain is something very much like one of the most recent developments in Western technology: the computer.

What is vital to see in this development is not merely the presence of these two views but their conjunction: for while one can imagine any number of configurations according to which the brain might be a kind of computer without operating according to classical rationalist principles (a variety of recent cognitive-scientific approaches, especially connectionism [see Bechtel and Abrahamsen 2002 for a thorough overview], offer just such alternatives), there is a natural ease of fit between the computationalist view and the rationalist one, and this fit is what proves so profoundly attractive to the neoliberal academy. This helps to explain why the Chomskyan program, like many programs of high computationalism, is so often found along the most institutionally conservative and even rightist political perspectives (while Chomsky's real-world politics are widely understood to be radically left, his institutional politics are often described exactly as authoritarian, and Chomsky himself is routinely described as engaged in "empire building"; see Harris 1993), and why it is defended with a doctrinal tenacity usually reserved for religious orthodoxies.

We begin with Chomsky because his views combine and serve as a discursive source for the perspective that the most fundamental of human phenomena—cognition and language—can be effectively reduced to computation. They are also divorced sufficiently from contemporary computing projects to help us to isolate computationalism's discursive and cultural functions. This is remarkable enough on its own, but what is especially telling is that the Chomskyan perspective does not emerge in isolation; rather, it accompanies a highly striated perspective on institutions and politics that has remained a hallmark of computationalism to the present day; it aligns itself with the most powerful and conservative forms of institutional authority; and it continues to be defended and occupied, institutionally, by the most traditionalist, individualist, and high-rationalist actors. Thus it is almost always the case that partisans of the Chomskyan revolution are opposed to anti-individualist, socially embedded, and/or interpretive perspectives.[1] Chomsky's work and its profound alignment—even identification—with computationalism helps to define these connections and provide a paradigm for the form they take throughout discursive fields where authority and mechanism are primary concerns.

Computationalism and the Chomsky Hierarchy

One way of cashing out what differentiates generative linguistics from its predecessors—that is, one way of understanding the substance of the "Chomskyan revolution in linguistics" (see especially Harris 1993, and Huck and Goldsmith 1995; and also Hymes and Fought 1981; Joseph 2002; and Newmeyer 1996)—is just that human language is in principle computable. This is not mere metaphor; whatever its precise meaning, it is a *rhetorical* commitment that is clear in Chomsky's most notable early publication, the 1957 monograph *Syntactic Structures* (itself excerpted from a much longer unpublished work that was published in somewhat modified form in 1975 as *The Logical Structure of Linguistic Theory*), and that remains central in Chomsky's terminology to this day.[2] Despite the evident and at times radical shifts in Chomskyan theory, the term *computation* remains among the few permanent elements throughout his linguistic work.

Despite being one of his earliest published works, *Syntactic Structures* follows the argumentative and rhetorical forms that have become characteristic of Chomsky's research. In *Syntactic Structures,* Chomsky wants especially to argue for the mental reality of an entity (though not one that can be locally identified) called the *language organ* that exists in a material sense somewhere (the term will later become the "faculty of language" to emphasize that Chomsky does not mean there will be found a physically separate part of the brain devoted to processing language): "syntactic investigation of a given language has as its goal the construction of a grammar that can be viewed as a device of some sort for producing the sentences of the language" (11). "The ultimate outcome of these investigations," Chomsky writes, "should be a theory of linguistic structure in which the descriptive devices utilized in particular grammars are presented and studied abstractly, with no specific reference to particular languages." Given that few linguists and philosophers had until that point suspected that such a "device" might exist, and that it might actually determine linguistic function outside of reference to particular languages, one might wonder what drove Chomsky's intuition and what would cause him to suspect that language might be characterized in this way—in such a way that what many linguists consider the fundamental aspects of languages (their grammars) could be explained away in terms of an abstract "device" now called syntax.

What device did Chomsky have in mind? It has long been noted that Chomsky accepted funding for about a decade from several parts of the U.S. defense establishment. The writing of *Syntactic Structures* itself was "supported in part by the U.S. Army (Signal Corps), the Air Force (Office of Scientific Research, Air Research and Development Command), and the Navy (Office of Naval Research); and in part by the National Science Foundation and the Eastman Kodak Corporation" (7). This has led some to speculate on the sources of Chomsky's lifelong insistence on the autonomy of intellectual and social practices, and also led to a division with those whom one would think to be Chomsky's natural allies, the generally left-thinking intellectuals of the U.S. academy. What has not been thought about so much, though, is just why the military was interested in Chomsky's work—what did both the military and Chomsky think the results of his work might be, and how would they benefit the military?

The structure of *Syntactic Structures* provides some answer. Chapter 3 of the book, "An Elementary Linguistic Theory," is often read quickly as presenting a simplistic straw man, a formal theory based on logical principles just so counterarguments to it can be incorporated into the final theory. But the elementary linguistic theory is no arbitrary simple candidate: it is the logical structure that forms the foundation of contemporary computer science: the finite-state automata developed by Markov and von Neumann (1966) but introduced into U.S. computer science exactly via Chomsky's research. What Chomsky describes is not a theory but a "machine":

> Suppose that we have a machine that can be in any one of a finite number of different internal states, and suppose that this machine switches from one state to another by producing a certain symbol (let us say, an English word). One of these states is an initial state; another is a final state. Suppose that the machine begins in the initial state, runs through a sequence of states (producing a word with each transition), and ends in the final state. Then we call the sequence of words that has been produced a "sentence." Each such machine thus defines a certain language; namely, the set of sentences that can be produced in this way. Any language that can be produced by a machine of this sort we call a finite state language; and we can call the machine itself a finite state grammar. (18–19)

This is no straw man. This is what early computer scientists, especially those unfamiliar with the history of 20th-century logical work that produced the computer, believed computers might do. The "device" of which Chomsky speaks so often in his early work can be most accurately understood as a computer program, as no less a prominent computational linguist than John Goldsmith (2004) has recently suggested.

In the 1950s, the main U.S. centers for the study of automated communications and information systems were established in Cambridge, Massachusetts (especially the Psycho-Acoustic and Electro-Acoustic Laboratories, PAL and EAL respectively). Spanning the intellectual distance between Harvard and MIT, this nexus is also the site of Chomsky's remarkable contribution to computer science, one that coincides with his early linguistics work, overlaps with it in significant intellectual ways, and has been largely unexamined outside of engineering circles. It is precisely the connection between this work and his linguistic theory proper, and the relative obscurity of these strands of thought with regard to each other, that seems especially trenchant for the investigation of computationalism as an ideology of institutional power.

The thinkers at PAL and EAL were especially concerned with the physical aspects of speech production. They were examining every aspect of human linguistic and mental activity to find formalizable phenomena, because what is formalizable can by definition be performed by a Turing Machine. Paul Edwards reports on a telling moment in the history of these laboratories:

> [George] Miller himself marks the year 1956, when he returned to Harvard, as the great transition. In that year his studies of language, information theory,

and behavior crystallized into a new research paradigm. In an unpublished essay, Miller recounts his experience of the second Symposium on Information Theory, held at MIT on September 10–12, 1956. There he had his first realization, "more intuitive than rational, that human experimental psychology, theoretical linguistics, and the computer simulation of cognitive processes were all pieces from a larger whole."

At the symposium, Shannon and others gave papers on coding theory in engineering. [Alan] Newell and [Herbert] Simon, fresh from the 1956 Dartmouth Summer Seminar on artificial intelligence organized by John McCarthy, presented their Logic Theory Machine. Noam Chomsky discussed an early version of transformational-generative (TG) grammar in his "Three Models of Language." (TG grammars would rapidly replace the Markov-chain model of Shannon and Miller with their more powerful formal-mechanical model. Miller recalls Newell told him "Chomsky was developing exactly the same kind of ideas for language that he and Herb Simon were developing for theorem proving.") (Edwards 1996, 228–9)[3]

In our current climate it is remarkable to think of such diverse figures working together on similar problems, but in the ferment of Cambridge in the 1950s we find nearly the entire set of figures and views that would rise to prominence in later decades. Although Chomsky disclaims any direct interest in computer science, his work was in some ways developed in opposition to the behaviorism he saw not in just the views of Skinner and Quine, but also, in the emerging mainstream of computer science. Chomsky distances himself from these views—those of figures like McCarthy, Newell and Simon, who might think of themselves as inspired by Chomskyan theory—to put his system outside the lineage of which it is exemplary.

This is to say that where nascent AI researchers like Newell and Simon understood themselves to be building psychological models that could account for what Chomsky calls linguistic competence—and thus took inspiration from Chomsky's work—Chomsky disclaims all of this research as treating the brain as a "black box" because its functions are being simulated but not directly represented in a digital computer. This is exactly the view known in analytic philosophy as *functionalism,* a view that through Jerry Fodor and Hilary Putnam derives inspiration from Chomsky despite being the apparent opposite of the view Chomsky offers; this topic is discussed at length in the next chapter.

What sparked engineering interest in Chomsky's views, what other people saw in his views, may be best understood through the PAL laboratory and George Miller, since Chomsky made his contribution to computer science in direct and indirect collaboration with Miller. In a series of papers still widely anthologized today in computer science textbooks (Chomsky 1956, 1959a; Chomsky and Miller 1958; Chomsky and Schützenberger 1963), Chomsky developed a theory of logical kinds of grammars that develop out of von Neumann's work on automata (von Neumann 1966), itself emerging from the logical work of the early Wittgenstein (1922), Carnap (1937), and others who are now recognized as part of the early canon of analytic philosophers. This theory is known even today as the Chomsky Hierarchy, and the desire to find logical hierarchies in analog and social phenomena like language and thinking seems especially strong in this work (see Davis 1958; Davis and Weyuker 1983).

The goal of the work now known as the Chomsky Hierarchy is to establish a system in which the term *language,* here identified exactly with syntax, can be applied both to logical formalisms like those used by computers and also to so-called natural languages.[4] At this point in history, computer languages were much more mathematical and logic-based than they are today; some of them closely resembled pure mathematical equations. Although there are aspects of logical systems that look a lot like human language, it was clearly tendentious, even in the 1950s, to say that the two systems are the same kind of thing.[5] So Chomsky specifies his terms this way:

> A grammar is a set of rules—preferably a finite set, if we expect finite automata to learn them—that specify the grammatical strings of symbols. Now there are a great many different ways to state a set of rules. The rules as stated in the traditional grammar books do not lend themselves to logical analysis, and so it is natural to search for some alternative method of description that will be more compatible with our modern methods of describing communication processes in general. For example, one possible method for describing a grammar is in terms of a program for a universal Turing machine. (Chomsky and Miller 1958, 92–93)

Even this brief passage equivocates consistently between whether "a grammar" is something that an automaton should or should not be able to use. In other words, are the logical rules instanced by systems like Peano logic (one of the systems developed in the Frege-Turing-Gödel heritage) the same kinds of rules that structure natural languages? Even Chomsky does not think so: "the rules as stated in the traditional grammar books do not lend themselves to logical analysis," he writes, despite the fact that such a grammar *is* a set of finite rules. Is a system of finite rules a grammar in the sense that a "traditional grammar" is? Rather than answering this question, the ideological burden of Chomsky's work on CFGs is to establish the existence of a *hierarchy which can contain both natural and logical languages to a single system.* This is so that "finite automata" can learn them—again, an expectation that seems to stem from beliefs about technology rather than from observation of languages, even on Chomsky's account.

If throughout his intellectual life Chomsky has endured others seeing what they want to in his work, it seems clear that what happens in this case is not just computer scientists but an entire community of technologically-minded intellectuals seeing in Chomsky's work precisely the potential to do what Chomsky disclaims—to bring human language under computational control. Surely it is no leap to think that this is exactly what the defense-industrial establishment sees in Chomsky's program, which attracts the attention of precisely the logicians, computer scientists, and technicians who are looking for someone to lead them down the glory road to "machines speaking." By the time funding for such projects has largely dried up in the late 1960s—perhaps in the face of the pullback from Vietnam and Chomsky's outspoken opposition to it—Chomsky writes that "machine translation and related enterprises . . . seemed to me pointless as well as probably quite hopeless," but that he is "surprised" to "read repeated and confident accounts of how work in generative grammar developed out of an interest in computers, machine translation, and related matters. At least as far as my own work is concerned, this is quite false" (Chomsky 1973, 40).

What is false for Chomsky nevertheless seems true for the field as a whole and for the logico-philosophical and ideological structures that underlie it. It was precisely computers and the ferment around them that were the main foci of labs like PAL and EAL, to Chomsky's dismay, because "technological advances . . . seemed to me in some respects harmful in their impact, in that they tended to direct research toward problems suggested by the available technology, though of little interest and importance in themselves" (Chomsky 1973, 40). Chomsky's "hierarchy" papers appear in *Information and Control,* one of the first journals to publish cybernetic-style work in what was to become mainstream computer science. The suggestive title of the journal echoes terms that are important to Chomsky's later work, again exactly pushing the metaphor between a computer's logical "language" and natural languages. Taken together, the ideological burden of the CFG essays is to legitimate the application of the word *language* to logical systems,[6] despite the obvious fact that logical systems have historically been understood as quite different from human languages.

The Nature of Form in Formal Linguistics

Of course, Chomsky's influence was felt much more strongly in mainstream linguistics than in computer science; in mainstream linguistics, where Chomsky's program has been known variously as "generative linguistics" or "transformational grammar," among other appellations, the connection between computers and Chomskyan linguistics has rarely been made overt. Chomsky's logic papers and the Chomsky hierarchy are rarely mentioned in linguistics *per se,* and computerization is rarely mooted as a test of Chomsky's theories. Yet from the outset the idea of computerization has been notably close to the heart of Chomsky's program, not merely because Chomsky's work was housed for years in MIT's office of Machine Translation, but for some of the cultural reasons we have been discussing.

What, after all, is a "transformation," in Chomsky's terms? One of the most plausible accounts is that it is precisely an algorithm, which is to say, a structure that is logically identical to (and often actually is) a computer program; as John Goldsmith, a leading practitioner of both computational linguistics (CL) and mainstream linguistics, has recently put it, "generative grammar is, more than it is anything else, a plea for the case that an insightful theory of language can be based on algorithmic explanation" (Goldsmith 2004, 1). The kinds of transformations Chomsky documents from his earliest work onward (Chomsky 1957), ones which "invert" sentence structure, derive *wh*-questions, or make active sentences into passive ones, are all logical formulae that do not simply resemble computer programs: they are algorithms, the stuff of the computer that Alan Turing, just prior to Chomsky and in some ways coterminous with him, had identified as the building blocks for an entire exploded mechanism of calculation.

Goldsmith, in terms that are meant to be helpful both for the study of computers and languages, writes:

> Loosely speaking, an algorithm is an explicit and step-by-step explanation of how to perform a calculation. The classical ancient world developed a number of significant algorithms, such as Euclid's algorithm for finding the greatest common divisor of two integers M and N. It is a process of continuing to divide one integer by another, starting with M and N, and holding on to the remainder, but each time dropping the dividend; once we find that the remainder is zero, the greatest common divisor is the last divisor in the operation. This remarkable path to the discovery of the greatest common divisor that bears Euclid's name has another important property that most people today take to be an essential part of being an *algorithm:* it is an operation that is guaranteed

to work (that is, to be finished) in a finite amount of time (that is, a finite number of calculations)—though the specific value of the finite limit is likely to depend on the particular input that we choose to give to the algorithm. (Goldsmith 2004, 4)

The emphasis on finitude, operability, precise definition, and guaranteed completion are all hallmarks of both contemporary computing science and of Chomskyan linguistics, just as they were for Turing's discovery and implementation of the computer itself. Because the operation is well-defined, bounded, and finite, and at the same time can be instantiated in a substance which can carry out such operations a (theoretically) infinite number of times, it solves what is for Chomsky the unique puzzle of human language (unique because it has not been, for other students of language, its chief unexplained quality): how can human beings "produce or understand an indefinite number of new sentences" (Chomsky 1957, 15)? This apparently mathematical quality of human language use and production has been among Chomsky's chief concerns from the beginning, despite the intuitions of other linguists that it is an arbitrarily mathematical way of setting the problem: students of art or literature, for example, are rarely puzzled by the unbounded nature of human creativity that produces their objects of study.

For Chomsky, the fact that human beings can produce a theoretically infinite number of sentences means there must be an engine somewhere inside the human mind that is capable of generating infinitely many structures, and the only object we know of that can do this—or do this in a principled manner—is the logical engine we today call a computer, but which can just as easily be understood as an algorithm, in the exact sense that a simple algorithm known as a Turing Machine can ultimately be said to be the logical equivalent of any existing computer. Somewhere inside the human brain there must be a physical or logical engine, call it the language organ, whose job is to produce mathematical infinity, and the advent of this ability—also happens to be the crucial disjunction that separates humans from nonhumans and perhaps even intelligence from nonintelligence (see Chomsky 2005; Hauser, Chomsky, and Fitch 2002). (Although his remarks on the topic are more scattered, presumably there must be a similarly infinite computational engine enabling cognition.)

Goldsmith, following Zellig Harris (2002) and others, has argued that Chomsky's work was much less original than it seemed, in that several other researchers, not least among them Chomsky's teacher, Harris himself, were articulating ideas of algorithm and transformation not entirely dissimilar from those of Chomsky (see Goldsmith 2004, 5–8). Plausibly, the cause for this brief proliferation of theories in the 1950s was the other major intellectual development of the time, which was of course the development and proliferation of computers and computer programming. Unlike so much of human cultural production, computational objects must be precisely defined and these definitions must be consistent, or the program will not work. The promise of a theory of language that could eliminate exactly what had troubled almost every student of language to that day—namely, the inability to fully formalize linguistic practice, or to come up with fully automatic schemes for language-to-language translation—spread through the intellectual community like wildfire. Notably, the thinkers who were most struck by these theories were almost exactly the same ones who were so possessed by computers: they were generally white, highly educated males, and rarely female or people of color. They were also, for the most part, not linguists.

It remained for a generation of white men who were not trained in Bloomfieldian and other anthropological theories of language (for despite Chomsky's famous attack on Skinner and Bloomfield's adoption of some behaviorist principles, the fact is that the study of language as a human, social phenomenon remained prominent until the Chomskyan revolution) to pick up Chomsky's theories and turn them into the mainstream of the discipline. Although there are many exceptions, it is still true that Chomskyan approaches have tended to attract white men (and also men from notably imperial cultures, such as those of Korea and Japan), and that women and minority linguists have tended to favor non-Chomskyan approaches. As in literary studies and other humanistic disciplines, the name often used for Chomskyan linguistics—*formal linguistics*—gestures at precisely the concern that defines the concerns for its adherents and defines its problems for others. Chomsky, like all computationalists, is convinced that pure form is something that can be studied in isolation from use, context, and social meaning, whereas followers of other schools may be profoundly interested in form but also consider it inseparable from the rest of the object of study, whether we call that context, content, or meaning.

Formal linguistics shares critical features with other explicit formalisms. At the same time, as a cultural formation, it is unusually explicit about its concerns and goals, even if not always according to the kinds of terms suggested here. It would be unfair to say that formal linguistics is simply linguistics that is interested in anything called linguistic form, where form means something like syntax. Almost all linguists are interested in form. Formal linguistics sets itself up as the champion of what might be termed a crucial core insight of Chomskyan linguistics as a whole, one that has sometimes colloquially been called a "belief in syntax": this is the view that syntax as a set of algorithmic rules is both strongly constitutive of human language as such, and also separable from the study of semantics, pragmatics, or other non-syntactic features of language. In this regard, syntax refers not, as it is sometimes understood, to all the grammatical principles of a given language, all the principles that would have to be listed in a full grammar for the language. Rather, syntax refers to the restricted set of logical rules that are necessary to generate all the sentences of a given language. Such algorithms may have little to do with the grammar *per se* of a given language, and are rarely if ever explicitly understood or invoked by native language speakers. They are largely unconscious and automatic, and reflect the operation of the computer inside the human mind that performs all linguistic operations—the Language Organ.

Thus, at the same time that Jerry Fodor, Hilary Putnam, and other analytic philosophers were working out the theory of philosophical functionalism, Chomsky and a different (if at times overlapping) set of followers were working out in rapid succession a series of theories of human language that saw a specialized kind of computer inside the human brain. This computer operated not on the simpler members of the Chomsky hierarchy (Context-Free Grammars, and the more complex Phrase Structure Grammars that take something like natural language sentences as their basic objects); but building off of these models, they take some kind of *ur*-linguistic structures, largely (but not entirely) independent of word meanings, and generate the actual sentences of natural languages from them. The level at which the computer is operating—sometimes called Deep Structure, later limited to "D Structure" or the initials DS and then explicitly not to be labeled Deep Structure—closely resembles what Fodor calls the Language of Thought, an internal, inaccessible and generally logical rule-system that allows what we see of thought or language to be built on top of it.

In the early heyday of Chomskyan linguistics, this program was carried out, in the main, by white men and a few women who got excited about linguistics by Chomsky's program itself, rather than by prior training in or exposure to linguistics. They considered the Boas-Sapir-Bloomfield tradition of linguistic investigation to be old hat and outmoded (to the degree they were even aware of it), whereas Chomsky represented the new thing—that is, in some sense at least, Chomsky's work carried with it the penumbra of technological newness. It also offered mechanic clarity: it worked hard to clean up the messiness of language as we see it (which Chomsky notoriously dismisses as "performance") in favor of a clean internal computer that Chomsky views as language itself (Chomsky's "competence"). Formal linguists tended to focus on English and to a lesser extent other European languages; dismissed the project of data collection, which had been a hallmark of the anthropological linguistics of Boas and Sapir; focused on introspective data as the most relevant source material for analysis; and, despite their overt pursuit of something like linguistic universals, also dismissed out of hand both the data collected by Joseph Greenberg and his students about existing language universals, and tended to work from the assumption that all languages would likely turn out to be like English at the Deep Structure level.

To some linguists, the Chomskyan revolution represents the greatest disaster that had happened to the study of language in nearly two hundred years. Despite Chomsky's overt leftist politics, Chomsky's effect on linguistics was to take a field that had been especially aware of cultural difference and the political situations of disempowered groups and, in some ways, to simply dismiss out of hand the question of whether their practices might have much to offer intellectual investigation. One of Chomsky's earliest and most devoted followers, who went on to become one of his most ardent critics, Paul Postal, recalls that his early 1960s attempt to apply generative principles to Mohawk in his dissertation, which might have been thought especially interesting since it would demonstrate the applicability of generative grammar to a language that does not, on the surface, look much like English, was "considered slightly comic for some reason" by other generativists.[7] In other words, Chomsky took one of the few actually leftward-leaning academic fields in U.S. culture and, arguably, swung it far to the right. By arguing strenuously that linguistic phenomena could be separable into form and content, essentially out of his own intuitions rather than any particular empirical demonstration, Chomsky fit linguistics into the rationalist tradition from which it had spent nearly a hundred years extricating itself.

The early generativists did not merely display a bias toward English; they presumed (no doubt to some degree out of lack of exposure to other languages) that its basic structures must reflect the important ones out of which the language organ operated. The arrogance and dismissal of generativists toward other approaches, especially in the 1960s, can hardly be overstated. This was a scientific revolution; it was making clear and straight what until that point had been fuzzy and multivariate; it was cleaning up what had been dirty. Despite the multiple revisions of the Chomskyan program through the years, and its concomitant accommodation of data and structures from "traditional" linguistics that it had earlier thought to eliminate (e.g., case, inflection, voice), it retains this self-description of its project as uniquely scientific in comparison with other programs of linguistic research.

Even some of Chomsky's closest adherents have been surprised by the latest (and perhaps final) version of his theory, though, which on at least one reading entails the jettisoning of all that had come before. Explicitly, the Minimalist Program (first widely disseminated in the final two chapters of Chomsky 1995) resuscitates much of traditional grammatical analysis, like case, eliminates all talk of levels of structure, transformations, generation, and even the fully autonomous existence of syntax, while it retains what has arguably been the core of Chomsky's work all along: the notion that the language organ (now the faculty of language, FL) is a computer and that it operates on linguistic objects without the messiness of performance data. Thus FL is a "computational system that relates form and meaning" (Chomsky 1995, 378). FL possesses features that are "unexpected [in] complex biological systems, more like what one expects to find (for unexplained reasons) in the study of the inorganic world" (168). Chomsky has been frequently criticized for assuming, without strong empirical evidence, that such a fundamental feature of human cognition should be so unlike other biological systems and similar to what he admits are "inorganic" systems; arguably it is just the ability of computers and other algorithmic processes, like formal languages themselves, to separate form and content that Chomsky finds so unacceptable in other living systems and so attractive in the inorganic.

Here, then, we can clearly see that what formal linguists mean by form is something much more ideologically loaded than would be a straightforward concern with structure of any sort; as in the critique of formalism in the study of literature, the pursuit of pure form is yoked to a range of other social and political concerns so closely as to make them appear almost identical. Among the most thoughtful and sympathetic surveys of the formalist tendency in recent linguistics is Frederick Newmeyer's *Language Form and Language Function* (1998). Newmeyer is, in the broadest terms, a generativist himself, although his turn in recent years toward examination of work outside the Chomskyan tradition distinguishes him somewhat from the most orthodox members of that tradition. Newmeyer follows much recent terminology in using the word *functionalist* to describe linguists who are broadly interested in the Boas-Sapir-Bloomfield traditions and who largely reject Chomskyan approaches; it is critical not to confuse functionalism in analytic philosophy (the view that what we call human intelligence might be realized in any number of physical systems, especially computers, as detailed in Chapter 3) with linguistic functionalism, which can be understood either as the view that most parts of linguistic structure have the origins in language use (although this origin may be heavily deferred and not even evident in the direct analysis), or simply as linguistics that generally views context and content as essential, inseparable and nonautonomous parts of language.

Newmeyer is one of the few writers to have attempted to explicate the use of the term *formal linguistics* to describe the Chomskyan tradition. He writes that the "formalist (structuralist, generativist) orientation" is one of the two broad contemporary approaches to linguistics, crucially aligning Chomskyan with the structuralism it typically eschews (despite its clear use of structuralist principles). As Newmeyer points out, some contemporary functionalists overtly take up methods from linguists who we now take to be structuralists (Saussure, Jakobson, Prague school linguists, and Bloomfield himself; see Hymes and Fought 1981). Nevertheless, the term *formal linguistics* is a common substitute for generative linguistics, despite any number of apparently contradictory facts: for not only do Chomsky's more recent approaches not necessarily seem to put autonomous linguistic form at the forefront, but there are any number of nongenerative, nonfunctionalist form-centered linguistic methods that are typically not taken to be part of formal linguistics: these include the well-known programs of Lexical-Functional Grammar (LFG), Generalized Phrase Structure Grammar (GPSG), and Head-Driven Phrase Structure Grammar (HPSG). Each one of these programs has been typically accepted by some linguists as a promising and in some ways "saner" alternative to Chomskyan generativism, and to adopt what is useful in the Chomskyan formalisms without much of the baggage; yet despite their plausibility, none of these programs has attracted the intellectual energy of Chomsky's own program.

Again, within common professional parlance, the phrase "formal linguistics" is not taken to refer to HPSG, LFG, or GPSG, despite the clear commitment of such theories to form as such. These theories typically remain agnostic as to some of the deeper conceptual-ideological entailments of the Chomskyan theories, but also typically do not take advantage of a transformational "faculty of language"—that is to say, an internal computer—and also remain relatively agnostic as to the interaction of the human language faculty with the other parts of human cognition. Perhaps it is for personal reasons, but none of these theories, despite probably being more reasonable than Chomsky's own rapidly changing outlook, has been widely adopted by the linguistics community, in part because none are taken to speak to the deep "belief in Syntax" that binds together all of Chomsky's programs.

Another way of understanding this belief in syntax is as a belief in pure, autonomous form that stands apart from the human world of performance. Arguably, Chomsky's own personal magnetism combines with the powerful contemporary ideological commitment to pure form that lives with special emphasis in the world of computers, and what attracts people to Chomsky's linguistics is exactly the combination of conceptual forces that define rationalism and that may seem, on the surface, to have little to do with each other: a belief that thinking itself is nothing but the movement of form, and that there is also a kind of powerful authority outside of formal manipulation, a God-like (or theological) authority who solves the "problem" created by the view that thinking is pure form. That Chomsky is attracted to the rationalist tradition is not news: his own partial reading of this tradition, which focuses in particular on Descartes and significantly overlooks the politics of other figures in the tradition like Hobbes and Machiavelli, is evident from his own 1966 volume *Cartesian Linguistics: A Chapter in the History of Rationalist Thought*. That Chomsky is deeply interested in the operations of a supreme and transcendent authority is evident not merely from his political writings, but no less from his conduct in linguistics itself, where he is understood as a supremely dominant authority figure, accepting acolytes and excommunicating them with equal ease.

Thus what is commonly called formal linguistics cannot be taken in any plain sense as a commitment to the study of language form; rather, it is almost transparently a pursuit of something like strong rationalist authority within language itself, or rather a desire to take language as such out of the operation of human cognition and its embedding in both the social and individual worlds, and to make them supremely subordinate to an external, godlike authority. The scholars who pursue Chomskyanism and Chomsky himself with near-religious fervor are, almost without exception, straight white men who might be taken by nonlinguists to be "computer geeks." Like computer evangelists (such as Kurzweil, Negroponte, and Rheingold 2000), they are full of fervor about what their work will eventually demonstrate (although it has not yet achieved those demonstrations), and almost incredibly dismissive of approaches that find empirical problems in their formalisms or attempt to pursue similar goals while maintaining one eye on "the world." The world is of little interest to computationalists, who, despite the obviousness (to them) of the theory they have adopted, with regard to the rest of society have something to prove: arguably, what they have to prove is that the mind itself, and the language in which it expresses itself, is not caught up in the messiness of the world, and that those of us who think mind, world, and language are intertwined "all the way down" are mistakenly committed to a voluntarist romanticism, falsely believing that mind and world could alter what we say and what we mean.

Formalism is visible in one other place in contemporary linguistics, and that is precisely in the field of CL taken both narrowly and broadly. In the broad pursuit of CL, which is almost indistinguishable from Chomskyan generativism but nevertheless gives itself a different name, the computer and its own logical functions are taken as a model for human language to begin with, so that computer scientists and Artificial Intelligence (AI) researchers use what they have learned to demonstrate the formal nature of human language. A significant percentage of books with CL in the title are committed to just this program, rather than to the computer processing of language itself. On the other hand, books like Robert Berwick's *Acquisition of Syntactic Knowledge* (1985) attempt to demonstrate how human beings learn syntax (but really the Syntax-with-a-capital-S in which some Chomskyans believe) by explicitly adopting the "program metaphor," again here for the Language Organ as a whole rather than for individual transformations:

> This book . . . uses the most sophisticated model we have of a complex time-changing process, a computer program, as its model for language growth. Think of the process that learns a grammar as a computer program that "writes" a grammar as its output. The amount of information required to "fix" a grammar on the basis of external evidence is identified with the size of the shortest program needed to "write down" a grammar. The term *program* here is deliberately ambiguous, denoting either a computer program for producing a grammar, given some input data, or a developmental program in an ontogenetic sense. (5–6)

There is little doubt that a computer can be used in this way, but it is highly debatable what such an effort ultimately shows: as we have seen, the fact that a computer or computer program can emulate a physical process does not necessarily tell us anything about the nature of that physical process.

The other widespread use of the word *formal* in contemporary linguistics is, again, one that can be easily misconstrued by the casual observer. Textbooks and research volumes in CL and in Computer Science use the phrase "formal language" itself in an ambiguous fashion. Based on the Chomsky hierarchy, such works presume to begin with that logical systems like Context-Free Grammars, Markov Algorithms, and even Turing Machines themselves are languages—again, arguably simply because this label has been applied to them from the early days of Chomsky's logic papers. Textbooks like *Models of Computation and Formal Languages* (Taylor 1998) and *Foundations of Computational Linguistics* (Hausser 2001) take such formal objects as obvious models for human language and then proceed to examine how much of human language can be understood from this viewpoint, while rarely if ever paying close attention to the linguistic phenomena that conform only imperfectly at all to logical models.

After all, there is little doubt that human languages can realize logical forms, or that some parts of linguistic practice appear logical on the surface: this is the observation that licenses almost all linguistic approaches that are interested in form. But human language can be used to work mathematical and overtly logical systems like the formal logic taught in contemporary philosophy classes, and even programming languages themselves: the fact that language is capable of simulating these systems cannot be taken as strong evidence that language *is* such a system. The parts of language that escape formalization are well understood and have long been recognized as problems for pure and purely autonomous theories of form; these are exactly the phenomena that Derrida calls iterability, and the presence of idioms. Iterability in this narrow sense points to the fact that any linguistic object can apparently be repurposed for uses that diverge from what appear to be the syntactic compositional elements of a given object. Thus while the phrase "snow is white," so often invoked by logicians, appears to have a single, stable worldly denotation, in practice it can be used to mean an almost infinite number of other things, and in fact such a bald declarative statement would rarely, in human language practice, be used simply to express its apparent denotative meaning. Even obvious and repeated phrases like "hello" and "goodbye," via processes of iteration and citation, often bear much more meaning than they would seem to do from the syntactic view, and can be iterated for other purposes, if we can even say what "the meaning" of words and phrases are in any given context.

Closely related to the phenomenon of iterability, but more widely acknowledged and studied by generativists, is the question of idiomaticity, when an object with a particular syntactic form is habitually repurposed and used in such a way so as to partially or completely ignore the syntactic principles out of which the object is constructed. How is it, for example, that the phrase "to kick the bucket" entails no metaphorical bucket and no metaphorical kicking? Surely we are not decomposing this idiom into its syntactic parts when we hear or use it, but there is no marker or other cue in the object to tell us to reject the plain syntactic use of all its parts: as is not the case in some idiomatic uses (e.g., "hoist by his own petard"), the construction and all its constituent parts are all actively used, productive parts of English. For a purely formalist account, both idiomaticity and iterability must be seen as paralinguistic operations, outside of the core operations of the syntax that is the internal computer called the faculty of language (which is not to deny that some linguists have developed admirable formal analyses of there phenomena). Of course, the history of philosophy, linguistics taken broadly, and even contemporary approaches to these subjects, offers alternate views, including the ones advocated by Derrida himself, according to which such phenomena are not only not troubling, but also at least in part are constitutive of human language.

A plausible alternative to the Chomskyan view, then, and one held by something like the majority of working linguists—and therefore based more fully on material facts about language in use than on *a priori* introspection—is that there is no engine of linguistic structure, even at the level of the noun–verb distinction, locatable in the brain, nor is there reason to suppose that language and cognition evolved separately. Instead, they all evolved together, as a package of cognitive and linguistic capabilities whose computational features, to the degree they are at all constitutive, make up only a small and likely indistinguishable fraction of the whole—a whole that has become so imbricated in our cognitive, linguistic, and social histories that we speakers have only ever dreamed of separating them into two different "kinds" called form and content.

Cartesianism and Computationalism

In the mid-1960s, in response to his first flush of fame and to the burgeoning internal challenges to his work from spirited students like George Lakoff, Paul Postal, and James McCawley, Chomsky published two volumes that firmly cemented his place in contemporary intellectual life, far beyond linguistics proper and into fields as diverse as philosophy, psychology, and the new field of cognitive science. The first of these, *Aspects of the Theory of Syntax* (1965), is justly famous as Chomsky's first major attempt to develop "meaning-preserving transformations," but its even more powerful impact comes from what it shares with the second volume, *Cartesian Linguistics: A Chapter in the History of Rationalist Thought* (1966), which is the overt rhetorical emphasis on rationality as the defining characteristic of human nature, and the situation of generative procedures in an explicit historical intellectual frame.

In the first chapter of *Aspects* and even more explicitly in *Cartesian Linguistics,* Chomsky outlines in the most explicit way in his career so far his identification with a particular strand of Western thought and the particular way in which it characterizes the idea of an automaton—an abstract machine, or a linguistic computer in which the human mind forms. It is Chomsky himself who chooses to develop the particular reading of Western intellectual history on which his theory rests, and it represents a particular and unusual take on that history. Now Chomsky situates himself in the tradition of what until recently had been almost thoroughly discredited work from the 17th century:

> The "Cartesians," with no living tradition, represented an even more advantageous historical anchor for Chomsky. The critics of *Cartesian Linguistics* were strident, but tardy; for by the late 1960s, Chomsky had in effect vanquished the former students of Bloomfield for dominance in the field. Henceforth his most serious rivals were to be his own former students and associates. The period of Chomsky's interest in the "Cartesians" coincides with his most strident remarks about Saussure. By this time Chomsky's agenda had become just the opposite of what it had been in his 1963 article: to lump Saussure and the neo-Bloomfieldians in one great "modern linguistics" demonology, framed by the Descartes-to-Humboldt tradition and its generative revival. (Joseph 2002, 151)

Joseph focuses primarily on Chomsky's role in linguistics, but it is clear that his place in Western philosophical thought at this moment was every bit as important. What Chomsky finds in his resurrection of Descartes is precisely a way to use the computational mind to forestall the assault on rationality that he sees expressed in thinkers like Quine.

While it is convenient and accurate to think of both the Bloomfieldians and the structuralists (including figures like Kenneth Pike, but also Chomsky's mentor Roman Jakobson) as the main targets of Chomsky's linguistic assaults, it is especially revealing to consider how Chomsky sees the intellectual tradition from the Cartesian perspective. The last linguist of note for Chomsky is the early 19th-century German linguist Wilhelm von Humboldt (1767–1835), praised at length in *Cartesian Linguistics* for his view that "a language is not to be regarded as a mass of isolated phenomena—words, sounds, individual speech productions, etc.—but rather as an 'organism' in which all parts are interconnected and the role of each element is determined by its relationship to the generative processes that constitute the underlying form" (Chomsky 1966, 26). By ascribing the keyword *generative* to Humboldt—despite arguing in *Syntactic Structures* and elsewhere that this concept is essentially new to Chomsky because of its specific formal mechanisms—Chomsky wants to show that he is part of a great intellectual tradition that should not be easily gainsaid by contemporary critics.

Remarkably, despite his repeated insistence that issues of linguistics and politics should be clearly separated, Chomsky praises Humboldt for seeing exactly the connection between the two spheres that Chomsky himself occasionally advocates:

> we should note that Humboldt's conception of language must be considered against the background provided by his writings on political and social theory and the concept of human nature that underlies them. Humboldt has been described as "the most prominent representative in Germany" of the doctrine of natural rights and of the opposition to the authoritarian state. His denuncia-

tion of excessive state power (and of any sort of dogmatic faith) is based on his advocacy of the fundamental human right to develop a personal individuality through meaningful creative work and unconstrained thought . . . . The urge for self-realization is man's basic human need (as distinct from his merely animal needs). One who fails to recognize this "ought justly to be suspected of failing to recognize human nature for what it is and of wishing to turn men into machines." (Chomsky 1966, 24–5)[8]

The danger of men becoming machines is precisely what is at stake in Chomsky's theory, as is political authoritarianism, and Chomsky is right to draw our attention to it. But Chomsky's version of intellectual history is selective enough to deserve further scrutiny.

One reason Chomsky reaches out to Humboldt's anti-authoritarian writings is because Humboldt has come down to us in a much less savory form that Chomsky does not discuss. Humboldt was the most famous advocate of the view that the races and the languages they spoke were part of an historic progression, so that some cultures and peoples were seen to be primitive forms. Much of Humboldt's work was devoted to developing typologies of human groups, according to which Indo-European languages in particular represented a true advancement from the languages spoken by others around the world.[9] Whether we call this Hegelianism or Romanticism or outright racism, it forms a critical part of the background of Humboldt's entirety of views, and it is curious that Chomsky leaves this out while stressing the connection of Humboldt's ethics with his linguistic views.

The notion of a "doctrine of natural rights" espoused by Humboldt also exposes the fundamentally libertarian bent of Chomsky's intellectual views. Natural rights views like Humboldt's, and even Chomsky's to the extent that they emerge from a particular conception of human creativity, are historically connected not so much with anti-authoritarian or working-class-based political movements, and certainly not with antiracist and gender equality movements, as they are with radical individualist conservatism, something like the "objectivism" associated today with Ayn Rand. This is consistent with Chomsky's leanings in the field of ethical philosophy and with his other intellectual-historical identifications.

Thus, rather than identifying with the intellectual traditions that have for a hundred years or more in the West been associated with left-leaning politics, Chomsky reaches back to a more primal conservatism and, by omission, annihilates all that has come in between. These omissions may be more telling than Chomsky's inclusions, for what they primarily overlook is the contribution of anthropology and politics to the study of non-Western languages. The names one does not read in Chomsky are not just the post-Humboldt, anti-Hegelian 19th-century linguists William Dwight Whitney and Max Müller, but perhaps even tellingly, the early 20th-century linguist-anthropologists Franz Boas and Edward Sapir and the linguists associated with them. For in these writers the study of language was implicated, as it is today in the work of cultural studies, with particular systems of global political domination and intellectual hegemony. These critiques, in particular, are exactly the ones Chomsky needs to push outside not just linguistic study but raw philosophical consideration, precisely because this has been a desideratum of the Cartesian program to which he claims to subscribe, especially when viewed from its radical libertarian-conservative frame.

It may be surprising too to learn that Chomsky's principal contribution to computer science—perhaps even one of the chief goals for which he was receiving funding—is explicitly called a "hierarchy," that especially exact and abstract trope of ordered, striated power. Chomsky's political work has long been opposed to just such formations, strongly favoring distributed and rhizomatic syndicates to empires and kingdoms.[10] But the hierarchy is critical for keeping logical (and so computational) languages on the same plane with natural languages, the ones Chomsky continues to have in mind. This strong ambivalence in Chomsky's thought—one that has been noticed, at least on occasion, by commentators including Joseph (2002)— itself deserves thorough attention, in that it embodies exactly the deepest and most explicit political tension in our own society. In his overt politics, Chomsky opposes the necessity of hierarchies in the strongest way, while his intellectual work is predicated on the intuitive notion that language and cognition require hierarchies. For Chomsky there must be no connection between these two spheres, despite the obvious (but structural and unconscious) ways in which they seem to connect. This is consonant with a core tenet of dominant Western modernity, which is that the way the rational part of the mind construes the world must be all there is to understanding the world.

By rational we have to mean something more than just related to the ego, although these two ideas have also become conflated in our culture. We tend to think that our conscious selves are identical with our rational selves, and our rational selves, as the name "rational" suggests, subsist exactly in the following of rules. The literal foundation of the word *rational* on the mathematical process of deriving ratios emphasizes its relation not just to calculation but to striation, accounting, State indictment of the political subject (rather than society itself) as alone responsible for its welfare. Even if what we do with our rationality is to pursue goals based on irrational beliefs and desires, which may be said to emerge from unconscious motivations, the means we use to pursue those goals are thought to be rational. This is the plan-based view of cognition which becomes rampant in all the fields associated with the computer model of the mind, and which in its waning years this program has come to doubt (which makes sense, in that it has long been doubted in more general philosophical consideration; see especially Suchman's [1987] *Plans and Situated Actions,* written in opposition to the plan-based view crystallized in George Miller, Galanter and Pribham's [1960] *Plans and the Structure of Behavior;* see Dreyfus [1992] for a detailed critique of the plan-based view).

George Miller himself perhaps best embodies the view that was about to sprout from Chomskyan computationalism into philosophical functionalism. In the early 1960s, in no small part due to the reception of Chomsky's writings, the Center for Cognitive Studies (CCS) was established at Harvard by Miller and Jerome Bruner. The CCS should be remembered as the first major center to use the words *cognitive science,* and once again it is fascinating to note who else backed this project:

> Over the years [the CCS] became a gathering place for those scientists who were most active in the blending of psychology, linguistics, computer modeling, philosophy, and information theory that Miller and Bruner were backing. Noam Chomsky, Nelson Goodman, Benoit Mandelbrot, Donald Norman, Jerrold Katz, Thomas Bever, Eric Lennenberg, and Joseph Weizenbaum were only a few of the dozens of visitors who spent a year or more at the Center between 1960 and 1966. More than $2 million in grant money flowed into the Center's coffers, mostly from the Carnegie Corporation, the National Institutes of Health, and ARPA. (Edwards 1996, 234)

So not only was this a project with an unusually high amount of military-industrial support (especially for a project that is largely philosophical rather than directly practical), but it was also one in which some of the main figures soon abandoned much of the core ideology on which it was founded. Goodman never was a strong computationalist; Katz turned from generativism to Platonism, in no small part due to work with one figure not mentioned here but of profound significance for philosophical computationalism, Jerry Fodor; Weizenbaum publicly dissented from the computationalist view and went on to write a compelling volume about its problems (in *Computer Power and Human Reason,* 1976); and even Miller himself later wrote that reflection had shown him that "how computers work seems to have no real relevance to how the mind works, any more than a wheel shows how people walk."[11] Of these figures, and in an interesting manner, only Chomsky can be said to remain committed to the computationalism that drove him to work with CCS. It is precisely politics and ideology, rather than intellectual reason, that gives computationalism its power. So some of the world's leading intellects have been attracted to it, precisely because of its cultural power; and so many of them have defected from it (just as so many have defected from Chomskyan generativism) because there exists a structure of belief at its core, one implicated not in technological progress but in the cultural structures of subjectivity.

Despite its strict reliance on formal mechanisms and models, what really excited nascent cognitive science researchers about Chomsky's intuitions was that he provided a means to connect the bridge between physical mechanism and mental process that has haunted philosophical thought since Descartes. Chomsky rejected the prevailing behaviorism of at least some of his contemporaries, paving the way for Miller, Bruner, Marvin Minsky (1967) and others to peer inside the black box and to make mental process accessible to formal theorization. Part of the historical frame is that

> *Syntactic Structures* offers an impressive general outline of how linguists could begin to talk meaningfully about meaning, and it clear in retrospect that many linguists found this outline to be the single most compelling feature of Chomsky's program. Three of his most prominent recruits, in particular—Paul Postal, Jerrold Katz, and Jerry Fodor—soon set to work on an explicit incorporation of semantics into the *Syntactic Structures* model. (Harris 1993, 50)

This moment of ferment gives birth not just to cognitive science as a discipline but to the doctrine that would come to be known as functionalism, which by the 1980s had become "the prevailing view in philosophy, psychology, and artificial intelligence . . . which emphasizes the analogies between the functioning of the human brain and the functioning of digital computers" (Searle 1984, 28).

Whether or not one finds this idea credible, it is notable that despite the general objections of some of the closest former workers in the field, by the 1970s the view that the brain itself must be something like a digital computer had become widely adopted throughout the academy. It is not even always clear what was meant by the comparison so much as that it had to be true, had to be that in some way the machine we had created was also a model of a more originary creation still in some ways beyond our understanding. But it is still remarkable the degree to which philosophers in particular took hold of this idea and ran with it, and perhaps even more remarkable is the degree to which, just as Chomsky's ideas became a cultural lightning rod in linguistics—on my argument, exactly because of the political forces to which they were and are tied—their extension in philosophy perhaps even more clearly came to define the boundaries of the field, and in a sense, thought itself.

This same moment (the one that also spawned the so-called linguistics wars; Harris 1993) coincides with important periods in the work of both Putnam and Fodor. Putnam, in the late 1950s and early 1960s, expounded the views we can call orthodox functionalism or, in philosophy-internal terms, machine-state functionalism. Fodor, a linguistics student of Chomsky's and then a philosophy graduate student under Putnam, at first did not espouse functionalist views of the mind. Instead, Fodor's work begins with the specific investigation of meaning in a generative frame. Working with another follower of Chomsky who would go on to become a well-known analytic philosopher, Jerrold Katz, Fodor wrote a key paper (Katz and Fodor 1963) whose goal was to show that semantics could be fit into the generative framework (both Katz and Fodor, along with linguists like Paul Postal, Edward Klima, and Robert Lees, were in the initial group of students Chomsky and Morris Halle attracted to their MIT Research Laboratory of Electronics in the early 1960s; see Harris 1993, 68). The paper appeared, like Chomsky's review of Skinner, in the prestigious linguistics journal *Language*, and then Fodor and Katz republished the paper in an extremely influential volume called *The Structure of Language: Readings in the Philosophy of Language* (Fodor and Katz 1964). The contributions to this volume give the key to the linguistic origins of analytic functionalism: for alongside some of Chomsky's early papers on the nature of grammatical rules, Zellig Harris's papers on transformational analysis, and technical papers by Postal, Klima, Halle, Fodor, and Katz, we find some of the central work by Quine that appeared just after *Word and Object* (1960), along with important papers by Quine's logical precursors, Rudolf Carnap and Alonzo Church, both on the relationship of logic to semantics.

We know this moment in philosophy as "the linguistic turn," in part due to a collection edited by Richard Rorty by that name (Rorty 1967), which stressed the ordinary-language tradition of Wittgenstein and Austin that Fodor and Katz exclude (although they are careful not to disparage it as well). There can be little doubt that there was at least one linguistic turn in philosophy in the 1960s, and for at least some philosophers—Rorty, Stanley Cavell, and John Searle, for example, although each in different ways—this meant a turn exactly to the ordinary language tradition of Austin and the late Wittgenstein. In this tradition central philosophical problems were seen as linguistically embedded conceptual biases that philosophy could only "cure," not solve. To some extent, the ordinary language tradition tried to accommodate the Chomskyan vision, and one could argue that both Quine's writings and Putnam's career show evidence of this synthesis. But for the analytic followers of Chomsky, especially Katz and Fodor, the linguistic turn meant something else. It meant a turn away from behaviorism toward deeper philosophical explanation; it meant a physicalist explanation for mental phenomena. It entailed a particular conception of mental function based on a conception of linguistic function that was in turn derived explicitly from Chomsky's views. It meant a conception of language that could allow mental contents to be formalized precisely because they use formal mechanisms for expression, what Fodor would formulate as the Language of Thought (Fodor 1975).

The Language of Thought is not just any language. It is a language built on exactly the kind of mechanism Fodor and Katz had worked out in the early writings at MIT and that feature prominently in many of the essays in Katz and Fodor (1964). It is a language for which the all-important issue is the attaching of concepts—mental contents—to the meaningless labels we call words. The labels must be meaningless because it is the contents that contain the meaning, on this view. There is something about this view that Fodor has never been able to accept—whether it is the Wittgensteinian maxim that "meaning is usage," or the recently popular view of meaning as conceptual role, Fodor has always set himself most strongly against views that strip meaning away from its primary place inside the concept, inside the mind, inside the person.

Several of Fodor's early papers, including papers with Katz, emphasize just this connection between their linguistic research and what was to emerge as Fodor's philosophy of mind. In a paper characteristically called "What's Wrong with the Philosophy of Language?" that appeared in 1962, Fodor and Katz set themselves against the currently popular version of this argument, based largely on Austin and Cavell (also see Fodor and Katz 1963, and Fodor 1964 for attacks on this school). A system of description that includes recursive rules, exactly the principle to which Chomsky continues to stick, emerge as the hallmark of a "genuine scientific theory" of language because it "systematically and economically interconnects a wide variety of observable events by representing them in terms of laws stated with theoretical concepts" (281). Further, "wherever a semantic theory seeks to assign meaning interpretations to sentences, it seems reasonable to suppose that it will treat complex sentences by resolving them into their constituent parts and making the relevant assignments part by part" (283).

Compositional analysis and the systematic representation of psychological laws remain the salient features of Fodor's work from early to late, along with an anti-behaviorist intuition about psychology and the commitment to modularity—in some ways, exactly the commitments of Chomskyan theory. By turning these methods and their concomitant linguistic analyses to the terms of philosophical theory, these thinkers could mount a new assault on the traditional mind/body problem armed with a clear and yet paradoxical tool out of computer science. The brain was not exactly a computer and the mind was not exactly software, but the hardware/software model is still the best metaphor we have for describing the brain, so much so that thinking and computation are almost indistinguishable.

Chomsky's fairest biographer, Robert Barsky, makes clear how fortuitous it was that Chomsky arrived first in Zellig Harris's classroom and then at Harvard (and through connections made there with Roman Jakobson, to MIT; see Barsky 1997, 86). His high school classmate Hilary Putnam also took Harris's courses, heard Chomsky and Harris speak, and felt gripped by their ideas (Barsky 1997, 58). When we speak of the "Chomskyan revolution in linguistics," we seem as much to be pointing to exactly the functionalist revolution in philosophy as we do to the actual work in generative linguistics of the 1960s and 1970s, which is today largely unread outside of the discipline. Chomsky's mark endures not there, precisely, but in the new mechanical-rationalist position he licensed in the heart of Western philosophical practice. Thus Chomsky says of his Skinner review, "it wasn't Skinner's crazy variety of behaviorism that interested me particularly, but the way it was being used in Quinean empiricism and 'naturalization of philosophy,' a gross error in my opinion. That was important, Skinner was not."[12] What offended Chomsky was what he saw as the antirationalism of those philosophers at Harvard and elsewhere who had resisted his ideas, unlike the Bloomfieldian linguists whom he seemed to effortlessly displace. Presenting his ideas in 1958 and 1959 at the Texas Conferences on Problems of Linguistic Analysis in English, and at the same time in Cambridge, Chomsky was surprised to find that although some, like Robert Lees, Morris Halle, and Robert Stockwell, went along with him, "W. V. O. Quine 'lost interest' in him."[13]

Despite a lack of overt acrimony, it is clear that Quine represents exactly an instance of a discourse that Chomsky needed to displace in Western philosophy. From this perspective, if from no other, Chomsky's willingness to look inside the mind for connections to something like computational operations butted up against Quine's speculative rejection of meaning as a subject for scientific inquiry (for Quine, famously, meaning was something about which there could be no "fact of the matter"). Chomsky's conception of language exists in interactive tension with a rationalist conception of the mind that takes its inspiration from a notion of individual human creativity. Quine's largely holistic thought risks coming close to an antiindividualism that offends Chomsky's most basic humanist intuitions. As Chomsky sees, and as Fodor and Putnam have both considered, the computational view of language fits hand-in-glove conceptually and historically with the archetypal individualist story of Western rationalism, and it becomes increasingly clear that both generativism and functionalism share this rationalist-individualist commitment above all else, and owe their institutional success precisely to the desire to buttress this commitment against the "attack" of the socially and politically oriented research that had come to inform much of the English-speaking academy.

CHAPTER THREE

Genealogies of Philosophical Functionalism

ONE OF THE MOST striking developments in the cultural politics of mid-to-late twentieth-century intellectual practice in the West, and particularly in the U.S., was the rise and at least partial fall of a philosophical doctrine known as *functionalism*. A term with application in nearly every academic discourse, functionalism has a specific meaning within contemporary analytic philosophy: as proposed by Hilary Putnam and subsequently adopted by other writers, functionalism is a "model of the mind" according to which "psychological states ('believing that p,' 'desiring that p,' 'considering whether p,' etc.) are simply 'computational states' of the brain. The proper way to think of the brain is as a digital computer." This is not simply a metaphor: "according to the version of functionalism that I originally proposed, mental states can be defined in terms of Turing machine states and loadings of the memory (the paper tape of the Turing machine)" (Putnam 1988, 73). Many of its advocates give this view the straightforward name "the computer model of the mind" (e.g., Block 1990; Schank 1973). According to functionalism, the brain just *is* a digital computer, or something similar enough to one such that if we could discern its physical structure in sufficient detail, we would discover a binary mechanism, probably electrochemical in nature, that constitutes mental representations, exactly as a computer can be said to create representations.

Today, what we might call orthodox functionalism no longer holds sway in analytic philosophy, although its influence has also not vanished. In retrospect, the heyday of functionalism coincides remarkably with a series of social and intellectual developments with which it is not usually connected. Functionalism has its roots in explicit political doctrine, a series of cultural beliefs whose connection to the philosophical doctrine *per se* is articulated not as individual beliefs but as connected discourse networks, ranging from the history of philosophy and linguistics to the history of military technology and funding. Functionalism emerges, explicitly and in public, along with a new academic discipline called cognitive science, a discipline connected much more directly to computerization than is widely understood. Put most clearly: in the 1950s both the military and U.S. industry explicitly advocated a messianic understanding of computing, in which computation was the underlying matter of everything in the social world, and could therefore be brought under state-capitalist-military control—centralized, hierarchical control. The intellectuals who saw the promise of computational views did not understand that they were tapping into a vibrant cultural current, an ideological pathway that had at its end something we have never seen: computers that really could speak, write, and think like human beings, and therefore would provide governmental-commercial-military access to these operations for surveillance and control.

Language and Analytic Functionalism

In the wake of Chomsky's insight that human language might be characterized in computational terms, philosophers became eager to incorporate and elaborate his views into standard analytic practice. The preeminent U.S. philosopher during Chomsky's early career, W. V. O. Quine, rarely addressed computational issues; and it is just as Quine assumes something like that status of analytic orthodoxy that two younger philosophers, Hilary Putnam and Jerry Fodor, emerge into view and eventually become the successor generation to Quine in the analytic canon. The critical nexus of philosophers and linguists who emerge in Quine's wake—and in ambivalent relationship to him—all studied with Chomsky at MIT and many completed their PhDs there; several then migrated to Harvard. Thus many of the figures one most associates with the early elaboration of Chomsky's views in philosophical terms, including Paul Postal and Jerrold Katz, also work closely with Fodor. Just as *Aspects of the Theory of Syntax* emerges in 1965, creating a well-known controversy over Defense Department funding of Chomsky's work, functionalism takes firm hold in analytic journals, and Fodor switches from linguist-philosopher to full-time philosopher.

Putnam eventually migrated to Harvard and remained there for the rest of his career, often working somewhat closely with Quine. Putnam's views change many times over the years, and he quickly moved away from orthodox functionalism, so his analyses are especially relevant to understanding the contexts and consequences of functionalism as a doctrine. At the same time, Fodor has remained extremely committed to functionalist doctrine for most of his career, so that he almost appears as Chomsky's philosophical doppelganger (during his later career Putnam often refers to a hypothetical synthesis of Fodor's and Chomsky's views as "MIT mentalism," despite their continued disavowal of philosophical identity; see, e.g., Putnam 1988). Fodor worked at MIT for much of the time that his work was most explicitly devoted to functionalism, and it is these views (and his late partial dissent from them) that are of particular cultural interest. The explicit connections made by philosophers between functionalism and other cultural views situate this intellectual practice with particular strength within a political sphere that is often thought to be not a *context for* but the *subject of* philosophy. On this view, functionalism can be seen as an extension of computationalism into modern subjectivity itself, so that its cultural value is of not secondary but of primary importance. Functionalism, then, may have originated as an explicit doctrine with a single individual's flash of intellectual insight, but it gains strength and force precisely for ideological reasons, and it remains important to us today for the same reasons.

The figures most associated with functionalism in an historical sense are the Harvard philosopher Hilary Putnam and his student and later MIT philosopher Jerry Fodor. Putnam is especially known for his writings of the 1980s and 1990s, when through at least two turns in his thought he went from functionalism to what he called "internal realism" and then to a modified form of pragmatism. But it was Putnam himself, in a series of highly influential papers of the early 1960s (that is, just as Chomsky's work was starting to be read widely outside of linguistics, and especially in analytic philosophy, where his views were arguably as influential as they were in linguistics), who first and most explicitly posed the functionalist thesis that "the proper way to think of the brain is as a digital computer" (Putnam 1988, 73). These papers appear slightly out of chronological order in volume two of Putnam's collected papers (Putnam 1975), but the earliest of them, "Minds and Machines," was printed in a volume edited by Sidney Hook in 1960.[1] That essay and the 1964 "Robots: Machines or Artificially-Created Life?" are among the clearest statements of purpose of the computationalist doctrine, and it seems no accident that they were also formulated geographically and socially right among the community of emerging cognitive-science researchers at Harvard. Putnam today sees the essays as expressing the same computationalist doctrine (i.e., "MIT mentalism") that both Chomsky and Fodor share, although in most of their writings Chomsky and Fodor are careful to try to distinguish their positions from the one Putnam critiques.

In "Minds and Machines," Putnam puts forth not merely the intuition that brains and digital computers are the same thing, but also the idea that "the various issues and puzzles that make up the traditional mind-body problem are wholly linguistic and logical in character" (Putnam 1960, 362)—which coincides in many ways with the grammatical intuition that Chomsky has put forward in the CFG and early generative grammar work. There exists (in some abstract space of possible constructions, never precisely formulated) a logico-linguistic hierarchy and human linguistic capability exists on it somewhere, as do formal systems like first-order logic. In addition, there exists (in that same abstract space) a Turing machine whose operation is directly related to that of the brain; Chomsky's approach and language show that he had read Turing (1936, 1937, 1950), and he was no doubt influenced by Turing's mathematical and logical work as well.[2]

Putnam's "Minds and Machines" proceeds along lines inspired at least in part by Wittgenstein and by Turing. Putnam wants to show that the traditional philosophical mind/body problem is soluble, in a Wittgensteinian sense—a problem that is an artifact of our language and that philosophical analysis can clear up, in the sense of "dissolve." Putnam seems to be endorsing Turing's method in "Computing Machinery and Intelligence," namely, rejecting the question "can machines think?" by replacing it with a question about the way machines and human beings each use language. Since it explicitly invokes the operations of Turing machines at length and the way in which they use language to refer to themselves as entities, it is hard not to see the article as in some sense a response to and elaboration of Turing (1950).

To bridge the gap between Turing's somewhat Berkeleyan method and contemporary analytic ones, Putnam turns in "Minds and Machines" to exactly the nub of *Syntactic Structures* and Chomsky's CFG work, the assertion that human and logical languages are the same kinds of things. More precisely, Putnam endorses in a somewhat peculiar way exactly Chomsky's writings and intuitions on the subject, extracting from them exactly the lesson about "machine languages" that Chomsky claims not to take from his own writings:

> It is important to recognize that machine performances may be wholly *analogous* to language, so much so that the whole of linguistic theory can be ap-

plied to them. If the reader wishes to check this, he may go through a work like Chomsky's *Syntactic Structures* carefully, and note that at no place is the assumption employed that the corpus of utterances studied by the linguist was produced by a conscious organism. Then he may turn to such pioneer work in empirical semantics as [Paul] Ziff's *Semantic Analysis* (1961) and observe that the same thing holds true for semantic theory. (Putnam 1960, 383; emphasis in original)

But the difference between Ziff's approach and Chomsky's is that Ziff is not trying to prove that machine grammars and linguistic grammar are isomorphic. In almost all of his later work, it is this central thesis that Putnam comes to doubt in the functionalist program. Later, Putnam comes to doubt not just the accuracy of the program, but its role in the larger project of philosophy and in culture in general; by the early 1980s, Putnam comes to wonder whether functionalism is part of a program to separate political and cultural concerns from philosophical practice, despite the rejection of just such a division in almost every other philosophical tradition than ours.

Fodor's Mind

As a student of both Chomsky and Putnam, Jerry Fodor articulated the most elaborated version of functionalism in the analytic literature. Developing out of his work on the compositionality of meaning with Katz (Fodor and Katz 1962), Fodor also followed up on Putnam's essays of the early 1960s in creating the most explicit version of functionalism, which Fodor variously (and often simultaneously) calls the Representational Theory of Mind (RTM), the Language of Thought (LOT), and the Computational Theory of Mind (CTM) (see Fodor 1975, 1981, 1983, 1987, 1990, 2000). Fodor writes that CTM is "the best theory of cognition that we've got; indeed, the only one we've got that's worth the bother of a serious discussion" (Fodor 2000, 1). Although it took some years for this model to develop its full terminology, it is implicit in Fodor's early linguistic work and explicit as early as Fodor (1975). It is also fair to say that Fodor's philosophical position is one of the central conceptual lightning rods in analytic philosophy. Along with Chomsky himself (and no doubt due in some part to the close proximity of their views), Quine, and Putnam, Fodor remains one of the most heavily cited philosophers in the field. Many of these publications take issue with Fodor; the question from a cultural perspective is whether there is something specific about Fodor's position that helps to explain why it attracts so much attention in the first place.

Fodor's style, rhetoric, arguments, and interests are all quite different from those of Chomsky. But there is a similarity in the way they each seem to have a central "core intuition" that they articulate repeatedly in work after work (a pattern which is not followed in this manner by many other prominent philosophers and theorists). In Fodor's case this core intuition has to do with what he calls the *compositionality* of thought, and specifically with an intuition about the nature of world–language relations. Fodor also has a deep and admittedly emotional reaction to certain kinds of intellectual views, which he calls at various times "holist" or "relativist" and associates with philosophers like the later Putnam, Quine (to some extent), the later Wittgenstein, and Searle, among others. What Fodor and Chomsky characteristically share, and what helps to expose the cultural investments of the rest of their views, is their deep belief in a rationalist psychology and their disdain for views that put too much weight on meanings that are produced outside the observable human mechanism.

Fodor's most explicit articulations of his rationalist views—before he started to call them into question himself—are found in the 1987 volume *Psychosemantics: The Problem of Meaning in the Philosophy of Mind* and the 1990 collection *A Theory of Content*. In important ways these volumes follow exactly the argument taken by Putnam in "Minds and Machines" and other early functionalist papers, although of course the argument has become much more sophisticated by the mid-1980s. Rhetorically, these volumes present themselves as the latest and best statements of a position that is to be articulated again and again, and while this is true to a large extent, it also represents Fodor's most fully articulated presentation of the archetypal machine-in-the-mind story. Like much of Fodor's other writing, they use an engaging and colloquial style that is meant to indicate the author's investment in issues of the moment—"I don't write for posterity" is the way he puts it (Fodor 1990, vii). But they also engage with longstanding philosophical questions, especially the mind-body problem.

One remarkable instance of cultural situating occurs in Fodor's use of Sherlock Holmes to demonstrate "a bit of reconstructive psychology, a capsule history of the sequence of mental episodes which brought Holmes first to suspect, then to believe, that the Doctor did it with his pet snake" in *A Theory of Content* (1990, 20). The Holmes passage Fodor cites without direct attribution comes from Conan Doyle's "The Speckled Band":

> I instantly reconsidered my position when . . . it became clear to me that whatever danger threatened an occupant of the room could not come either from the window or the door. My attention was speedily drawn, as I have already remarked to you, to this ventilator, and to the bell-rope which hung down to the

bed. The discovery that this was a dummy, and that the bed was clamped to the floor, instantly gave rise to the suspicion that the rope was there as a bridge for something passing through the hold, and coming to the bed. The idea of a snake instantly occurred to me, and when I coupled it with my knowledge that the Doctor was furnished with a supply of the creatures from India I felt I was probably on the right track . . . (20; ellipses in Fodor's text)

Fodor comments:

What is therefore interesting, for our purposes, is that Holmes's story isn't *just* reconstructive psychology. It does a double duty since it also serves to assemble *premises* for a plausible inference to the *conclusion* that the doctor did it with the snake . . . . Because this train of thoughts is tantamount to an argument, Holmes expects Watson to be convinced by the considerations that, when they occurred to him, caused Holmes's own conviction. (21; emphasis in original)

That is, as we have already seen several times, the same sort of argument from general patterns of causal inference, develops into an elaborate and highly technical theory of mental representation. So it isn't any surprise that Fodor concludes, "Conan Doyle was a far deeper psychologist—far closer to what is essential about the mental life—than, say, James Joyce (or William James, for that matter)" (21).

Both Joycean literary Modernism and Jamesian philosophical pragmatism were in part reactions precisely to the presumption in 19th-century writing that thoughts and the "mental life" itself followed an orderly (which is to say, orthodox rationalist) pattern, and this observation was supposed to proceed, in part, from some fairly careful and rigorous introspection. While Conan Doyle never insisted that he was providing an accurate representation of cognition-as-process, it is such a representation to which the Modernist phrase "stream of consciousness" explicitly refers. The Modernists thought on at least some level that they were providing an account of what it is like to think. Their account differs markedly from Conan Doyle's, and it is plausibly grounded in psychological observation and introspection:

This is now a description of my feeling. As I was saying listening to repeating is often irritating, always repeating is all of living, everything in a being is always repeating, more and more listening to repeating gives to me completed understanding. Each one slowly comes to be a whole one to me. Each one slowly comes to be a whole one in me. Soon then it commences to sound through my ears and eyes and feelings the repeating that is always coming out from each one, that is them, that makes then comes slowly then to be to one who has it to have loving repeating as natural being comes to be a full sound telling all the being in each one such a one is ever knowing. (Stein 1990, 264)

This is Gertrude Stein from her 1908 *Making of Americans,* not necessarily one of her most radically nonlinear works. In addition to its clearly not representing cognition along the same lines as Conan Doyle, the passage doesn't represent language in a way that is especially useful to Chomskians—in that widespread violations of apparent "syntactic rules" (among other violations) are employed as compositional method, while language still retains many of its meaningful functions. Why should we not believe that Stein captures something "essential" about cognition in her writing—something that the matter-of-fact, "common sense," rigorously deductive presentation of psychological process displayed by Sherlock Holmes, fails to capture? This does not even have to be attributed to artistic intuition: Stein studied psychology seriously at Harvard, taking courses with William James in particular as an undergraduate.

Fodor's theory, in general, requires that there be what he calls a Language of Thought (LOT), a kind of internal simulacrum of our external language that differs from ours in that its reference is determined entirely in the brain. For a variety of technical reasons, it looks as if Fodor could mount his theory without that feature, so the Appendix to *Psychosemantics* is called "Why There Still Has to Be a Language of Thought." What is important to LOT is what has always been important to Fodor: "LOT claims that *mental states*—and not just their propositional objects—*typically have constituent structure*" (Fodor 1987, 136; emphasis in original). In later work Fodor comes to call this view a compositional or *atomic* (as opposed to *holist*) view of meaning–mind relations (see especially Fodor 2000 and Fodor and Lepore 1992). In *Psychosemantics,* Fodor outlines what he calls a "schematic formulation of LOT":

> There is, in your head, a certain mechanism, an *intention* box . . . . What you do is, you put into the intention box a token of a mental symbol that *means* that P. And what the box does is, it churns and gurgles and computers and causes and the outcome is that you behave in a way that (*ceteris paribus*) makes it true that P.
>
> So, for example, suppose I intend to raise my left hand (I intend to make true the proposition that I raise my left hand). Then what I do is, I put in my intention box a token of a mental symbol that means "I raise my left hand." And then, after suitable churning and gurgling and computing and causing, my left hand goes up. (Fodor 1987, 136)[3]

This alone is not sufficient to characterize a LOT theory; "what makes the story a Language of Thought story, and not just an Intentional Realist story, is the idea that these mental states that have content also have syntactic structure—constituent structure in particular—that's appropriate to the content that they have" (137).

An Intentional Realist story (roughly, the view that beliefs about things in the world have psychological reality) does not satisfy Fodor, perhaps due to his commitment to the metaphor that twice forms rhetorical climaxes in the presentation: "churning and gurgling and computing and causing." At least the first two of these terms are meant as rhetorical overkill that stress the mechanical nature of the "intention box": *churn* refers either to the mechanical work of a butter churn or the churning of gears and *gurgle* to hydraulics, whether organic or artificial. It is the third and fourth terms that appear key: these are Fodor's keyword, *compute;* the philosophical keyword, *cause.* For an Intentional Realist, who might be represented here by John Searle or the post-functionalist Putnam, a person's intentions toward the world are real, but they do not necessarily have a structure that requires a particular kind of mechanism in order to have physical cause in the world (see Searle 1983, 1984, 1992). Mind and world are both made of the same kind of stuff, but it is not easy to explain the relation of the mental to the physical. The LOT theorist goes much further, and ends up jettisoning much of the Intentional Realist's notion of mind–world relations. The syntax machine provides systematicity that the Intentional Realist can't generate: "Linguistic capacities are systematic, and that's because sentences have constituent structure. But cognitive capacities are systematic too, and that must be because *thoughts* have constituent structure. But if thoughts have constituent structure, then LOT is true" (151).

The differences between the Intentional Realist stance and the LOT stance end up putting many other thinkers on one side of a debate on which Fodor sees himself having few clear allies—in a sense, picturing himself as the isolated individual at the heart of the rationalist picture of cognition and of culture. Among his few allies are Chomsky, of course, since it is Chomsky's account of syntax that fuels Fodor's main computational intuition.

> Computers are a solution to the problem of mediating between the causal properties of symbols and their semantic properties. So if the mind is a sort of computer, we begin to see how you can have a theory of mental processes that succeeds where—literally—all previous attempts had abjectly failed; a theory which explains how there could be nonarbitrary content relations among causally related thoughts . . . . In computer design, causal role is brought into phase with content by exploiting parallelisms between the syntax of a symbol and its semantics. But this idea won't do the theory of mind any good unless there are mental symbols: mental particulars possessed of both semantic and syntactic properties. (Fodor 1987, 19)

The traditional Cartesian problem is how mind-stuff can affect world-stuff; rather than accepting that somehow mind and world are one (a view sometimes called monism), Cartesians insist that mind-stuff is somehow special, rational, willing, conscious. This position is known today as dualism, and although one does not usually think of Fodor or Chomsky as dualists, their shared explicit Cartesianism points in just this direction. Mind is special: it causes physical reality. What is in the mind is *intention*: cause.

This sounds like a religious view, and there are suggestions in the writings of both Chomsky and Fodor that go along with the religious leanings of the thinkers that Chomsky sees as his intellectual forebears (Descartes himself, and the monks who wrote the Port Royal *Grammar* that Chomsky discusses at length in Chomsky 1966). In Fodor's case, there is a tendency to adopt what Putnam critically names a "God's-eye view" of the world, nowhere more explicit than in the Epilogue to *Psychosemantics,* titled "Creation Myth," where Fodor steps back from the LOT problem to explore Intentional Realism more directly. Since Intentional Realism is accepted by many of the philosophers with whom Fodor has his most serious disagreements, it is not altogether clear why this defense is necessary in the first place. To address it, Fodor phrases the mind-body question this way: "how is embodied intelligence possible?" Since "embodiment implies mortality, and mortality constrains the amount of information that a mind can come to have" (Fodor 1987, 130), this frame makes it seem especially critical to "solve" the mind–world relations that, whatever philosophers say, human beings clearly are able to master.

From a Wittgensteinian perspective, sometimes problems like this one can be created in the language that frames them; after all, cats, to use Fodor's favorite example, are able to learn a great deal of species-specific behavior in a single generation (which is added to a much smaller store of innately "coded" behaviors, so that a cat raised in isolation does not learn many critical behaviors). To solve the problem in the form he has posed it, Fodor puts himself in the position Putnam warns us about:

> Here is what I would have done if I had been faced with this problem in designing *Homo sapiens.* I would have made a knowledge of commonsense *Homo sapiens* psychology *innate;* that way nobody would have to spend time learning it. And I would have made this innately apprehended commonsense psychology (at least approximately) *true,* so that the behavioral conditions that it mediates would not depend on rigidly constraining the human behavioral repertoire or on accidental stabilities in the human ecology. Perhaps not *very much* would have to be innate and true to do the job; given the rudiments of commonsense Intentional Realism as a head start, you could maybe bootstrap the rest. (Fodor 1987, 132; emphasis in original)

The chapter is called "Creation Myth" precisely because it is ideologically and rhetorically appealing to put oneself in the sovereign position for the kind of theory Fodor advocates. Much like the computer scientists today who run simulations of biological and complex natural processes not for predictive but for philosophical purposes, there is a satisfying closure, an answer to the question of final cause, written right into the texture of this story. The atomic story is the story of command and control—manage the units by identifying them and labeling them. What emerges from their combined product is Statist and individualist, because there is an individual who combines the state and the person in one—namely, the familiar and authoritarian figure of the King, God as King, or what Derrida reminds us to think of as the transcendental signifier. That our culture longs for such a figure is a deep part of computational ideology, despite its failure to find mechanical deliverance either in a mental computer or in real ones.

Despite his philosophical incisiveness, Fodor is clear that his project ultimately derives from emotional sources that admit of direct ideological reading:

> I hate relativism. I think it affronts intellectual dignity. I am appalled that it is thought to be respectable. But, alas, neither my hating it nor its affronting intellectual dignity nor my being appalled that is thought to be respectable shows that relativism is false. What's needed to show that it is false is to take away the arguments that purport to show that it is true. The argument, par excellence, that purports to show that relativism is true is holism. So this book is an attempt to take away holism. Hate me, hate my dog. (Fodor 1990, xii)

This is from *A Theory of Content,* and the clear focus in that volume on the atomic nature of content shows the strong tie between that view and computationalism. What does "relativism" mean to Fodor? In its philosophical instantiation it comes from, among others, Quine, Donald Davidson (who holds an anti-Cartesian view known as "anomalous monism"), Richard Rorty, and the later Putnam. Inside the field this appears innocuous enough, but in a larger context the forces of relativism would seem to align exactly with the philosophical and literary enemies Fodor obliquely names, and that Chomsky shares: deconstruction, cultural studies, feminism and race-oriented studies, historicism, identity politics, postcolonialism—because within the larger cultural frame this is how these theories line up. It may or may not be the case that Fodor endorses these approaches; intellectually, his work taps into a powerful current that has these cultural developments as its nemesis (in this sense, as with Chomsky and generative grammar, the functionalist doctrine is a discourse that has an author-function, in Foucault's terminology, more importantly than it is ascribed to Fodor as a particular author; see Foucault 1969).

By the mid-1990s, Fodor was starting to have doubts about the functionalist enterprise (and, *a fortiori,* mainstream cognitive science), and his writings begin to show these doubts in rhetorically interesting ways. They also begin to dovetail with the work of Chomsky's former student and Fodor's former collaborator Jerrold Katz, who suggests that Fodor and Chomsky misunderstand both the linguistic and Cartesian consequences of their own theories (see Katz 1990, 1996, and 1998; and Katz and Postal 1991). These doubts begin to emerge in Fodor's mediation on one of Putnam's most famous thought problems, *The Elm and the Expert* (1994), but they are especially telling in *Concepts* (1998a) and *The Mind Doesn't Work that Way* (2000), the latter of which is a surprising and somewhat scandalous attack on Stephen Pinker's profoundly rationalist *How the Mind Works* (1997), which on its surface purports to popularize the machine nativism of Chomsky and Fodor (and so which Fodor and Chomsky were both quick to repudiate; also see Fodor 1998b).

In *The Mind Doesn't Work That Way,* Fodor reacts to the cognitive psychology he sees presumed in recent evolutionary theory and that informs Pinker's work. Fodor agrees with at least some of these biological arguments, which he calls the "New Synthesis," but

> standard accounts of New Synthesis cognitive psychology . . . often hardly feature what seems to me to be overwhelmingly its determining feature, namely, its commitment to Turing's syntactic account of mental processes. Leaving that out simplifies the exposition, to be sure; but it's *Hamlet* without the Prince. I propose to put the Prince back even though, here as in the play, doing so makes no end of trouble for everyone concerned. Much of this book will be about how the idea that cognitive processes are syntactic shapes the New Synthesis story; and why I doubt that the syntactic theory of mental process could be anything like the whole truth about cognition, and what we're left with if it's not. (Fodor 2000, 6)

This passage displays the familiar rhetorical elements present in much of Fodor's writing, including literary allusion that is striking in both its cultural valence and its specific invocation of royal hierarchy (in that *Hamlet* is often discussed in terms of character without mentioning Hamlet's royal standing).

Even more characteristic of Fodor's recent thought, though, is the pinpoint focus on "Turing's syntactic account of mental process." We have to understand that Turing himself provided no such thing: if anything, Turing (1950) is a neobehaviorist argument about why we should *not* look inside the black box of human thinking to find computer-like structures. What Turing provided, and then what Chomsky elaborated in particular into a thesis about human language processing became, with Fodor and Putnam's help (along with other interested contributors), what appeared to be an entirely new philosophical doctrine about how the mind processes language. This doctrine is based not in any specific observation but rather, much as the behaviorism Chomsky attacked, in philosophical intuition. It turns out, in fact, to connect to a specific and particularly valued stream of cultural thought. If we were discussing English history we would be calling it "Tory history" as opposed to "Whig history." If we were discussing literary criticism we would be calling it the "formalists" vs. "culturalists." In the linguistics tradition proper, its opponents are figures like Boas, Sapir, Bloomfield, Hymes, Labov; in philosophy its opponents are Heidegger, the late Wittgenstein, Dewey, Rorty, Habermas, Derrida. What do these figures share? To put it schematically, they share a conviction that surface politics do in fact penetrate throughout the intellectual sphere, that direct engagement with cultural history and its hierarchies of power are necessary concomitants to intellectual practice, especially when it advances into core areas of human practice like language and thought.

In the 1950s, with the quiet but enormous military-industrial promotion of computers) and widespread utopian depictions of future computerization (Edwards 1996), it is at least conceivable that, well-meaning intellectuals could have tried on extreme versions of the without appreciating their full cultural significance. It seems clear that some academics who signed on to the functionalist program ultimately defected from it precisely along these lines, and sometimes (as in cases like Weizenbaum, Putnam, and Winograd) seeing the cultural-philosophical entailments of anti-holist philosophies. As Fodor's later work has tended toward engagement with properly "classical" philosophical issues—in his case of course focusing ever more closely on compositionality and atomism, and Hume's associationism (see Fodor 2003; Fodor and Lepore 2002)—the cultural commitments of his philosophical orientation have emerged more clearly. In a *festschrift* for Fodor (Loewer and Rey 1991) that features contributions from many leading analytic philosophers, another leading philosopher of mind, Daniel Dennett, matches Fodor's typical rhetoric in an essay called "Granny's Campaign for Safe Science" (Dennett 1991).

Invoking the "notional Granny" Fodor references in his writings (and perhaps Fodor's real grandmother, featured in black-and-white photograph opposite the Table of Contents in Loewer and Rey 1991, vi) to help explain "what is the thread tying together all of Jerry Fodor's vigorous and influential campaigns over the years," Dennett finds a somewhat surprising answer. "Jerry Fodor is a Granny's boy, a romantic conservative whose slogan might well be 'What is good enough for Granny is good enough for science'" (Dennett 1991, 87). What informs this view is a particular view of science: "He, like Noam Chomsky, has had a subtler game plan: saving Granny's Cartesianism by outsciencing Science, by turning Granny's cherished views into redoubtable science itself: Cognitive Science" (88). But Fodor's is no ordinary cognitive science; it is opposed to all contemporary computational research programs, while implicitly endorsing some kind of scientific procedure from his own core metaphorical intuition that "to believe is to be in a computational relation to a representation" (91). "Safe science is 'classical science,' Fodor has always insisted, but with Granny urging him on, he admits that the safest science is *no science at all.*"

What Granny endorses are exactly those tenets of Intentional Realism which Fodor sees from God's perspective in the "Creation Myth." They have to not be "real" just in the sense that they have phenomenal reality for social beings, but *real to the eventual physical science of the brain.* Some science must eventually find "I want to eat that piece of pie" in our brains, somehow, even though no conceivable science has proposed how we might find it. This is beyond the philosophical commitment that Intentional Realism seems to entail. The strength not of Fodor's commitment to this view, but to the philosophical community's interest in Fodor's commitment, is precisely the ideological strength of the State's investment in this view—in the view that the mind itself can be subjected to order, or in Deleuze and Guattari's terminology, striated. That such views are particularly implicated in the modern Western self-conception comes out in the specific representations that Fodor has sometimes instanced as being "conceptually atomic" and therefore in some sense *innately available* to the brain. While this may or may not be what Fodor means to say, it is how the examples have been taken, and Fodor continues to use such examples in his recent work: Fodor's view is that in particular the term "belief has a functional essence . . . Ditto, *mutatis mutandis,* 'capitalism,' 'carburetor,' and the like" (Fodor 1998a, 8). It is the second example that is explicit, because Fodor's views have sometimes been understood to mean that *carburetor* is an innate concept. *Carburetor* is the perfect cultural example, in its specific evocation of the Fordist ordering of production and its suggestion that the modern vehicle itself and its processes of production are an essential part of human being. What Fodor adds in to the equation as he begins to dissent from functionalism, then, is *capitalism,* and it is hard to imagine a more apposite way of indicating the political heritage within which his line of thought turns out to be profoundly implicated.

The Cultural Politics of the Computer Model
of the Mind

While Fodor has clearly been a lightning rod in contemporary philosophical activity, the doctrine with which he is associated has been widely available in philosophical practice, and its distribution there is no less ideological. No aspect of this story is more revealing than the way in which Fodor's PhD advisor and Chomsky's high school classmate Hilary Putnam rises to prominence in part on a wave of functionalist doctrine, and then to a second prominence by developing extremely thorough arguments to pull that doctrine apart.

Putnam's early functionalist papers already display a different rhetorical approach than much of Fodor's writing. To be more accurate, Putnam's career prior to and including the functionalist papers displays a different set of grounding concerns. Perhaps it is enough to say that Putnam is always concerned about foundations; this is important because Putnam's early decades of philosophical writing are dedicated to defining a Realist interpretation of mathematics, according to which—much like Katz's later interpretation of Chomsky's linguistics—"the much-touted problems in the philosophy of mathematics [are], without exception . . . problems internal to the thought of various system builders" (Putnam 1967, 43). In summarizing his mathematical thought in the late 1960s, he writes: "I don't think mathematics is unclear; I don't think mathematics has a crisis in its foundations; indeed, I do not believe mathematics either has or needs 'foundations'" (43; also see Putnam 1979, 43–59).

Putnam uses realism throughout his career as a way of getting at concrete experience and the self-understanding of persons while admitting that such accounts are always subject to a radical perspectivalism that becomes coincident with what Putnam at times calls "Realism-with-a-capital-R": a kind of doctrine of the ultimate reality of things that moves from Kantian open-mindedness toward concepts to a belief in super-real Platonic forms. Putnam takes this position out of sympathy with Kant and other figures who see ethics and metaphysics as deeply intertwined, in a way that demands human commitment:

> I don't think it is bad to have pictures in philosophy. What is bad is to forget they are pictures and to treat them as "the world." In my picture, objects are theory-dependent in the sense that theories with incompatible ontologies can both be right. Saying that they are both right is not saying that there are fields "out there" as entities with extension and (in addition) fields in the sense of logical constructions. It is not saying that there are both absolute space-time points which are mere limits. It is saying that various representations, various

languages, various theories, are equally good in certain contexts. In the tradition of James and Dewey, it is to say that devices which are functionally equivalent in the context of inquiry for which they are designed are equivalent in every way that we have a "handle on." (Putnam 1982, 40–1)

This passage could not be clearer about computers in particular and their role in philosophy, because however we understand them, we have yet to find ways in which computers are actually "devices which are functionally equivalent in the context of inquiry for which they are designed" with regard to human beings.

To speak of how and why human beings were designed is, of course, to step exactly into religious terrain that technological thought characteristically claims to avoid. Here again, Putnam's thought shows an overt attention to cultural context that both Fodor and Chomsky strenuously deny. In one of his most compact and elegant statements-of-purpose—one composed just at another turn in his philosophical thought toward an even more ethically-based stance—Putnam puts thought about the computer at the center of the contemporary philosophical situation. This volume, *Renewing Philosophy* (1992), starts off with a penetrating discussion of the project of Artificial Intelligence from a perspective that can only be said to be in harmony with the explicitly Heideggerian critique of Dreyfus (1992) and Haugeland (1985). It begins with a brief rhetorical glance at reconciling Putnam's deeply held religious beliefs with philosophical practice, suggesting that in his early years Putnam "didn't reconcile" the two parts of his thought (the religious believer, and the atheistic practitioner of scientific materialism; Putnam 1992, 1). Over the course of his career, Putnam comes to accept a position he associates with the late Wittgenstein, Dewey, William James, Quine, and to some extent Derrida—which is to say just those thinkers who form the "opposite flank" to Fodor's atomists. The project of "renewing philosophy" requires a reconsideration of those issues that have been properly thought "religious" and those thought "scientific" so that we do not accept the position that "science, and only science, describes the world as it is in itself, independent of perspective" (x).

Putnam draws our attention precisely back to Hobbes and the historical context of the view that "thinking is appropriately called 'reckoning,' because it really is a manipulation of signs according to rules (analogous to calculating rules)" (3). Putnam writes that the view "seemed so evident to [him] (and still seems evident to many philosophers of mind)" was this:

If the whole human body is a physical system obeying the laws of Newtonian physics, and if any such system, up to and including the whole physical universe, is at least metaphorically a machine, then the whole human body is at least metaphorically a machine. And materialists believe that a human body is just a living body. So . . . materialists are committed to the view that the human body is—at least metaphorically—a machine. It is understandable that the notion of a Turing machine might be seen as just a way of making this materialist idea precise. Understandable, but hardly well thought out.

The problem is the following: a "machine" in the sense of a physical system obeying the laws of Newtonian physics need not be a Turing machine. (4)

Putnam offers some intriguing logical results to support this conclusion, but in a sense it is clearly available to empirical investigation, since many sorts of extremely sophisticated cellular and molecular "machines" are in no sense capable of universal computation in Turing's sense (instead, they are properly analog machines, devoted to one or several tasks but not generally applicable to others).

Among the reasons that Putnam rejects functionalism in *Renewing Philosophy* is that a half-century of computer research has failed to produce anything like a simulation of inductive reasoning and of human language understanding. In addition he is concerned about the view that there is some kind of formalizable "symbol processor" in the brain. This is exactly where the computational view itself tends to lead:

The view that language learning is not really learning, but rather the maturation of an innate ability in a particular environment . . . leads, in its extreme form, to pessimism about the likelihood that human use of natural language can be successfully simulated on a computer—which is why Chomsky is pessimistic about projects for natural language computer processing, although he shares the computer model of the brain, or at least of the "language organ," with AI researchers . . . . Similarly, the optimistic view that there is an algorithm (of manageable size) for inductive logic is paralleled by the optimistic view of language learning: that there is a more or less topic-neutral heuristic for learning, and that this heuristic suffices (without the aid of an unmanageably large stock of hard-wired-in background knowledge, or topic-specific conceptual abilities) for the learning of one's language, as well for the making of inductive inferences in general. Perhaps the optimistic view is right; but I do not see anyone on the scene, in either AI or in inductive logic, who has any interesting ideas as to how the topic-neutral learning strategy works. (15–6)

Putnam's target is exactly the computational metaphor itself: it is simply misleading in its application to both language and cognition, even if it does provide interesting results in some areas (much as extremely complex computer simulations can help in predicting weather, but they do not lead us to conclude that weather itself is a digital process or even a computational one).

Putnam's argument against the computer metaphor is tied to his thoughts about the place of computation in thinking. Fodor still writes that "thinking is computation" (Fodor 1998a, 9).[4] Putnam sees this view as explicitly tied to the formalism of the early Wittgenstein (the Wittgenstein of the *Tractatus*, 1922), and Putnam puts himself instead on the side of the Wittgenstein of the late writings published as the *Philosophical Investigations* (1953), *Of Certainty* (1972), and *Culture and Value* (1984), among others. Putnam writes that he once disagreed with Wittgenstein's views, especially the famous counter-semantic dictum that "meaning is use":

> At one time, I myself had the hope that what Wittgenstein refers to as the use of words, or . . . the technique of usage, could be completely surveyed and analyzed in a functionalist way; that is, that all the various referring uses of words could be neatly organized and depicted by something like a computer program. In *Representation and Reality* (1988), I explained my reasons for thinking it overwhelmingly likely that this cannot be done. (Putnam 1992, 166)

The reason is exactly the one Putnam originally had rejected, and arguably the same view about language that joins Wittgenstein, Derrida, and even Quine himself in a relativist triumvirate—on which Putnam comments throughout his works of this period (Putnam 1981a, 1983, 1988, 1990, 1992; also see Golumbia 1999; and Staten 1984). Putnam writes that

> what Wittgenstein is telling us is that referring uses don't have an "essence"; there isn't some one thing which can be called referring. There are overlapping similarities between one sort of referring and the next, that is all. This is why, for example, Wittgenstein is not puzzled, as many philosophers are, about how we can "refer" to abstract entities . . . . Stop calling three an "object" or an "abstract entity" and look at the way number words are used, is his advice. (Putnam 1992, 167–8)

Both words and computational rules are implicated in this thinking, but just as critically, so are what we traditionally call "religious" and ethical discourses, the entire range of relations that language and mind have to what we call the world.

Without a doubt, the world is just what the computationalist view wants to exclude—from cognition, from language, and perhaps as importantly to the self. Computationalism, when harnessed by the power of State philosophy, underwrites an extremely specific and contemporary notion of the self that is tied closely to the kind of subjectivity displayed by powerful leaders in our society. Instrumentalist reason is now the highest form of reason; means are everything, because the ends will be taken care of by themselves (by market-driven Providence, manifest in a technological nature). The self is not part of the world, but must attain mastery over it; subjects who cannot attain mastery have earned their almost-inevitable fate. To attain mastery is to understand that not all discourses are equally privileged; discourses are hierarchical, and at the top of the hierarchy is Science.

To separate discourses like Science and religion as having reliably different relations to the world is to misunderstand precisely the role of human thinking—which is not to say human reason—in the world. It is to fall victim to precisely what all these so-called relativist thinkers have been trying to tell us:

> Wittgenstein . . . would not have regarded talk of certain discourses being "cognitive" and other discourses being "non-cognitive" as helpful, [and] he would not have regarded the question as to whether religious language refers as helpful either . . . . The use of religious language is both like and unlike ordinary cases of reference: but to ask whether it is "really" reference or "not really" reference is to be in a muddle. There is no essence of reference. (Putnam 1992, 168)

Thus the problem comes in believing, with science-oriented thinkers like Chomsky, the early Wittgenstein, Fodor, and *a fortiori* the many contemporary computationalists who think computers are "very close to being able to speak our language," or with religious fundamentalists who often describe their own relation to language as being essential or direct, that there is any sort of direct reference relation at all.

What is there instead? Putnam is right that the answer is not relativism and it is not religion, any more than it is Artificial Intelligence or Fodorian future science. What there is instead of reference is exactly what all the thinkers that Fodor and Chomsky and others conceptualize as the enemy posit. It is also that what Putnam refuses to see is the point of Derrida's writings, just as it is for Putnam in at least some of his phases, and what it is for Heidegger in "The Question Concerning Technology." As Putnam paraphrases Wittgenstein, "we have no other place to stand but within our own language game" (Putnam 1992, 172). This "language game," so well known in the *Investigations,* is not some arbitrary game we can choose to play, exactly; it is the nature of language itself, and the exact reason that computers will always remain external to the world of language (for "play" in this sense, see Derrida 1967). The logical "languages" that Chomsky wants to put on a hierarchy with English and other natural languages do not play the game; they do not have "play," in Derrida's famous way of putting it.

> §559. You must bear in mind that the language game is so to say something unpredictable. I mean it is not based on grounds. It is not reasonable (or unreasonable).
>
> It is there—like our life. (Wittgenstein 1953)

"In German," writes Putnam,

> the next-to-last sentence reads "Nicht vernünftig (oder unvernünftig)." . . .
> the German word *vernünftig* has a different flavor from the English *reason-*
> *able.* . . . In German the word *vernünftig* connects with *Vernunft*, and this
> particular notion of Reason was given pride of place by Kant, who contrasted
> Reason in that sense with mere understanding, *Vernunft* with *Verstand*. . . . I
> am inclined to read Wittgenstein in §559 as saying that the language game is
> like our life in that neither the language game nor our life is based on *Ver-*
> *nunft*, which is a direct denial of the heart of Kant's philosophy. (Putnam
> 1992, 174)

The computer is limited in principle to ratiocination: exactly and only those
actions that can be defined by rules. There is no more precise way of summarizing the characteristically Western self-image than the "logical man"
in one sense embodied by Mr. Spock or the "Grammatical Man" of a mass-
market title on the subject written at the height of functionalist confidence
(Campbell 1982). But while the ideal is Mr. Spock, the reality is Kirk: blind
obedience, hierarchical order, the State as discovering techno-militarists,
putting itself in the God's-eye seat of judgment over all cultures, even if its
best (Kantian) hope is to never violate the needs of those beneath it. Kirk's
gender, his relation to gender, and his race, the State, and the state of being
the colonizer, are inextricably bound to these definitions, despite the wish
to make them autonomous. The sense that we are the primitive being, that
the Id (or, in more accurate translations of Freud, as suggested by Deleuze
and Guattari 1983, "it") is part of us, that our language might be outside
the idealized realm of the rational, that our category of *the animal* might
include precisely some of the most important features we use to define our
selves—all these ideas are present in Wittgenstein and anathema to computationalism.[5]

It is no accident that Putnam, along with other thorough critics of formalist technological theories in general—Ellul, Ong, Derrida—turns to explicitly religious thoughts in the course of analysis of formalism. Formalism
and computationalism join biological reductionism in the political philosophy we might call objectivism—the belief in a quasi-platonic "world out
there" that transcends the human social world. The most explicit objec-
tivist view in contemporary culture is associated with Ayn Rand, whose
total obedience to self-interest mimics closely the rationalist religious views
of Descartes, Hobbes, and Machiavelli—the transcendent self, transcendent God, and even Derrida's transcendent logocentrism seem best understood as facets of this same socio-politico-conceptual ideology (see especially
Saul 1992). The "relativism" of which these views are always accused by
objectivists is nothing of the sort. It is an insistence on the materiality of the

social world—on the fact that it is we humans, in part through their language, who make their world meaningful for ourselves. Putnam is exactly right to caution us in *Representation and Reality* that functionalism is exactly a kind of mentalism, "the tendency to think of concepts as scientifically describable ('psychologically real') entities in the mind or brain" (Putnam 1988, 7). The problem with mentalism is that, like it or not, it walks hand-in-hand with objectivism about concepts and reference, that "the totality of objects in some scientific theory or other will turn out to coincide with the totality of All the Objects There Are" (120).

While in some ways there are strange bedfellows among the constellation of views collected under the headings of mentalism, instrumentalism, functionalism, objectivism, computationalism, and fundamentalist religious belief-cum-repressed capital consumerism, it is also remarkable how closely aligned are these forces in contemporary culture. Even though they will not connect it, the most aggressive capitalist companies that rely especially strongly on computational methods (Wal-Mart, McDonald's) overlap closely with the Christian heartland. Sometimes the same individuals (often enough the managers and owners) embrace all the same doctrines—fundamentalist Christianity, Objectivism, and instrumentalism often sit easily together. Among the less socially privileged it is more common to adopt one or another of these doctrines—to be absorbed into computer instrumentalism, or into fundamentalism—but even at this level social pressures are hierarchical. Putnam is right to see that what ties these views together is ultimately a doctrine that can only be called religious in nature: what he calls a "God's-Eye View." This view says we can accurately map out all of human reality—which must ultimately include social reality—in objective terms. But as Putnam shows, building on Gödel's incompleteness theorem (itself a signal part of the history of computation), "it is part of our notion of justification in general (not just of our notion of mathematical justification) that reason can go beyond whatever reason can formalize" (Putnam 1988, 118; also see Putnam 1977). Instead, "the important thing . . . is to find a picture that enables us to make sense of the phenomena from within our world and our practice, rather than to seek a God's-Eye View" (109). This is exactly what Derrida means when he says that "a 'madness' must watch over thinking":

> I must try to write in such a way that the language of the other does not suffer in mine, suffers me to come without suffering from it, receives the hospitality of mine without getting lost or integrated there. And reciprocally, but reciprocity is not symmetry—and first of all because we have no neutral resource here, no *common measure* given by a third party. This has to be invented at every moment, with every sentence, without assurance, without absolute guardrails.

Which is as much as to say that madness, a certain "madness" *must* keep a lookout over every step, and finally watch over thinking, as reason does also. (Derrida 1995, 363)

We do not know how to formalize this "madness," this "irreason" that nevertheless has a long tradition even within Western Enlightenment thought, as something like counter-Enlightenment. Most importantly, we do not want to know how: it is critical not to our self-understanding but to our social practice itself that we as social beings can escape whatever formalization we manufacture. No doubt ratiocination characterizes a part of human thinking, but thinking encompasses that which exceeds formalization (which is to say almost everything in a perfectly matter-of-fact matter: very little of the social fabric is usefully understood in formal terms). Both Kant's view of the centrality of reason, and Wittgenstein's view of the centrality of "forms of life," must be accurate (as the poststructuralist reinterpretation of Kant suggests), despite the difficulty we have in holding these opposites in our heads at once. That is the human thing: that we can work along such conflicting but apparently reasonable lines. There is nothing mysterious about the fact that computers have trouble following such conflicting tendencies. More remarkable is our persistent expectation that they can or should—which is to say, our persistent belief that we can "ultimately" isolate mind away from its particular embodiment (see Lakoff and Johnson 1999), and no less its social matrix.

PART TWO

COMPUTATIONALISM
AND LANGUAGE

CHAPTER FOUR

Computationalist Linguistics

THE IDEA THAT the human brain might just be a computer, to be actualized via the Promethean project of building a computer that would replicate the operations of a human brain, entailed a real (if, in part, *sub rosa*) investigation of what exactly was meant by "the human brain" and more pointedly "the human mind" in the first place. Such questions have been the substance of philosophical inquiry in every culture, not least among these the Western philosophical tradition, and engagement with these analytic discourses could not likely have produced any kind of useful working consensus with which to move forward.[1] Rather than surveying these discourses, then, and in a fashion that comes to be characteristic of computationalist practice, the figures we associate with both the mechanical and intellectual creation of computers—including Turing, von Neumann (1944), Shannon, and Konrad Zuse (1993)—simply fashioned assertions about these intellectual territories that meshed with their intuitions. These intuitions in turn reveal a great deal about computationalism as an ideology—not merely its shape, but the functions it serves for us psychologically and ideologically.

Perhaps the easiest and most obvious way to show that a computer was functioning like a human brain would be to get the computer to produce its results the same way a human being (apparently) does: by producing language. This was so obvious to early computer scientists as hardly to need explicit statement, so that in Turing's 1950 paper "Computing Machinery and Intelligence," his now-famous Test simply stipulates that the computer can answer free-form English questions; Turing does not even suggest that this might be difficult or, as arguably it is, altogether intractable. Philosophers and linguists as widely varied as Putnam and Chomsky himself might suggest that the ability to use language is thoroughly implicated in any notion of intelligence, and that the bare ability to ask and answer free-form English questions would inherently entail part or even all of human intelligence, even if this was all the machine could do. From one perspective, Turing's Test puts the cart before the horse; from another it masks the difficulty in defining the problem Turing wants to solve.

On grounds both philosophical and linguistic, there are good reasons to doubt that computers will ever "speak human language." There are substantial ways in which this project overlaps with the project to make computers "display human intelligence," and is untenable for similar reasons. Perhaps because language *per se* is a much more objective part of the social world than is the abstraction called "thinking," however, the history of computational linguistics reveals a particular dynamism with regard to the data it takes as its object—exaggerated claims, that is, are frequently met with material tests that confirm or disconfirm theses. Accordingly, CL can claim more practical successes than can the program of Strong AI, but at the same time demonstrates with particular clarity where ideology meets material constraints.

Computers invite us to view languages on their terms: on the terms by which computers use formal systems that we have recently decided to call languages—that is, programming languages. But these closed systems, subject to univocal, correct, "activating" interpretations, look little like human language practices, which seems not just to allow but to thrive on ambiguity, context, and polysemy. Inevitably, a strong intuition of computationalists is that human language itself must be code-like and that ambiguity and polysemy are, in some critical sense, imperfections. Note that it is rarely if ever linguists who propose this view; there is just too much in the everyday world of language to let this view stand up under even mild critique. But language has many code-like aspects, and to a greater and lesser extent research programs have focused on these. Much can be done with such systems, although the ability to interact at even a "syntactically proper" level (seemingly the stipulated presupposition of Turing's test) with a human interlocutor remains beyond the computer's ability. Computers can aid human beings in their use of language in any number of ways. At the same time, computers carry their own linguistic ideologies, often stemming from the conceptual-intellectual base of computer science, and these ideologies even today shape a great deal of the future direction of computer development.

Like the *Star Trek* computer (especially in the original series; see Gresh and Weinberg 1999) or the Hal 9000 of *2001: A Space Odyssey,* which easily pass the Turing Test and quickly analyze context-sensitive questions of knowledge via a remarkable ability to synthesize theories over disparate domains, the project of computerizing language itself has a representational avatar in popular culture. The *Star Trek* "Universal Translator" represents our Utopian hopes even more pointedly than does the *Star Trek* computer, both for what computers will one day do and what some of us hope will be revealed about the nature of language. Through the discovery of some kind of formal principles underlying any linguistic practice (not at all just human linguistic practice), the Universal Translator can instantly analyze an entire language through just a few sample sentences (sometimes as little as a single brief conversation) and instantly produce flawless equivalents across what appear to be highly divergent languages. Such an innovation would depend not just on a conceptually unlikely if not impossible technological production; it would require something that seems both empirically and conceptually inconceivable—a discovery of some kind of formal engine, precisely a computer, that is dictating all of what we call language far outside of our apparent conscious knowledge of language production. In this way the question whether a computer will ever use language like humans do is not at all a new or technological one, but rather one of the oldest constitutive questions of culture and philosophy.

Cryptography and the History of Computational Linguistics

Chomsky's CFG papers from the 1950s served provocatively ambivalent institutional functions. By putting human languages on the same continuum as formal languages, Chomsky underwrote the intuition that these two kinds of abstract objects are of the same metaphysical kind. Chomsky himself dissented from the view that this means that machines would be able to speak human languages (for reasons that in some respects have only become clear quite recently); but despite this opinion and despite Chomsky's explicit dissent, this work served to underwrite and reinforce the pursuit of CL. More specifically, and famously, Chomsky's 1950s work was funded by DARPA specifically for the purposes of Machine Translation (MT), without regard for Chomsky's own repeated insistence that such projects are not tenable.[2] Given Chomsky's tremendous cultural influence, especially over the study of language, it is remarkable that his opinion about this subject has been so roundly disregarded by practitioners.

In at least one way, though, Chomsky's work fit into a view that had been advocated by computer scientists (but rarely if ever by linguists) prior to the 1950s. This view itself is quite similar to Chomsky's in some respects, as it also hinges on the equation between formal "languages" and human languages. The intellectual heritage of this view stems not from the developers of formal languages (such as Frege, Russell, Husserl, and possibly even Peano and Boole), who rarely if ever endorsed the view that these rule sets were much like human language. Most famously, formal systems like Peano logic emerge from the study of mathematics and not from the study of language, precisely because mathematical systems, and not human languages, demand univocal interpretation. Formal logic systems are defined as systems whose semantics can be rigidly controlled, such that ambiguity only persists in the system if and when the logician chooses this condition. Otherwise, as in mathematics, there is only one meaningful interpretation of logical sentences.

The analogy between formal languages and human languages stems not from work in formal logic, since logicians usually saw the far gap between logic and language. But the early computer engineers—Turing, Shannon, Warren Weaver, even the more skeptical von Neumann (1958)—had virtually no educational background in language or linguistics, and their work shows no sign of engaging at all with linguistic work of their day. Instead, their ideas stem from their observations about the computer, in a pattern that continues to the present day. The computer does not just run on formal logic, via the Turing machine model on which all computers are built; famously, among the first applications of physical computers was to decode German military transmissions. Because these transmissions were encoded language and the computer served as an almost unfathomably efficient decoder, some engineers drew an analogy between decoding and speaking: in other words, they started from the assumption that human language, too, must be a code.

Two researchers in particular, Shannon and Weaver, pursued the computationalist intuition that language must be code-like, and their work continues to underwrite even contemporary CL programs of (Shannon's work in particular remains extremely influential; see especially Shannon and Weaver 1949; and also Shannon 1951 on a proto-CL problem). Weaver, a mathematician and engineer who was in part responsible for popularizing Shannon's views about the nature of information and communication, is the key figure in pushing forward CL as an intellectual project. In a pathbreaking 1955 volume, *Machine Translation of Languages* (Locke and Booth 1955), Weaver and the editors completely avoid all discussion of prior analysis of language and formal systems, as if these fields had simply appeared *ex nihilo* with the development of computers. In the foreword to the volume, "The New Tower," Weaver writes:

> Students of languages and of the structures of languages, the logicians who design computers, the electronic engineers who build and run them—and especially the rare individuals who share all of these talents and insights—are now engaged in erecting a new Tower of Anti-Babel. This new tower is not intended to reach to Heaven. But it is hoped that it will build part of the way back to that mythical situation of simplicity and power when men could communicate freely together. (Weaver 1949, vii)

Weaver's assessment is not strictly true—many of the students of language and the structures of language have never been convinced of the possibility of erecting a new "Tower of Anti-Babel." Like some computationalists today, Weaver locates himself in a specifically Christian eschatological tradition, and posits computers as a redemptive technology that can put human beings back into the prelapsarian harmony from which we have fallen. Our human problem, according to this view, is that language has become corrupted due to ambiguity, polysemy, and polyvocality, and computers can bring language back to us, straighten it out, and eliminate the problems that are to blame not just for communicative difficulties but for the "simplicity and power" that would bring about significant political change.

Despite Weaver's assessment, few linguists of note contributed to the 1955 volume (the only practicing linguist among them is Victor Yngve, an MIT Germanicist who is most famous for work in CL and natural language processing, referred to as NLP). In an "historical introduction" provided by the editors, the history of MT begins abruptly in 1946, as if questions of the formal nature of language had never been addressed before. Rather than surveying the intellectual background and history of this topic, the editors cover only the history of machines built at MIT for the express purpose of MT. The book itself begins with Weaver's famous, (until-then) privately circulated "memorandum" of 1949, here published as "Translation," and was circulated among many computer scientists of the time who dissented from its conclusions even then.[3] At the time Weaver was president of the Rockefeller Foundation, and tried unsuccessfully to enlist major figures like Norbert Wiener, C. K. Ogden, Ivor Richards, Vannevar Bush, and some others in his project (see Hutchins 1986, 25–27). In contemporary histories we are supposed to see these figures as being short-sighted, but it seems equally plausible that they saw the inherent problems in Weaver's proposal from the outset.

Despite the widespread professional doubt about Weaver's approach and intuition, his memorandum received a certain amount of public notoriety.

"An account appeared in *Scientific American* in December 1949 . . . This in turn was picked up by the British newspaper the *News Chronicle* in the spring of 1950, and so appeared the first of what in coming years were to be frequent misunderstandings and exaggerations" (Hutchins 1986, 30). Such exaggerations continue to the present day, when prototype or model systems confined to narrow domains are publicly lauded as revolutions in MT. Despite the real limitations of the most robust MT systems in existence (easily accessed today via Google's translation functions), there is a widespread sense in the popular literature that computers are close to handling human language in much the same way humans do.

Weaver's memorandum starts from a cultural observation: "a multiplicity of languages impedes cultural interchange between the peoples of the earth, and is a serious deterrent to international understanding" (15). Such a view can only be characterized as an ideology, especially since Weaver provides no support at all for it—and it is a view that runs at odds with other views of politics. The view becomes characteristic of computationalist views of language: that human society as a whole is burdened by linguistic diversity, and that political harmony requires the removal of linguistic difference. We might presume from this perspective that linguistic uniformity leads to political harmony, or that political harmony rarely coexists with linguistic diversity—both propositions that can be easily checked historically, and which both arguably lack historical substance to support them.

Like Vannevar Bush in his famous article proposing the Memex (Bush 1945), Weaver reflects in large part on the role computers have played in the Allied victory in World War II. Not only is there concern about the tremendous destructive power loosed by the hydrogen bomb, which fully informed Bush's desire to turn U.S. scientific and engineering prowess toward peaceful ends; there is a related political concern expressed in terms of linguistic diversity which has been exposed by the computational infrastructure used in the service of Allied powers in World War II. Both the exposure and discovery of atomic power and of computational power seem to have opened an American vision into an abyss of power, an access to what Deleuze and Guattari would call a War Machine that worries those previously neutral and "objective" scientists. Of course computers and computation played a vital role in the development of atomic power, and in the writings of Weaver and Bush (and others) we see a kind of collective guilt about the opening of a Pandora's Box whose power can't be contained by national boundaries or even political will—and this Pandora's Box includes not just the atomic bomb but also the raw and dominating power of computation.

The most famous part of Weaver's memorandum suggests that MT is a project similar to cryptanalysis, one of the other primary uses for wartime computing. Since cryptanalysis seems to involve language, it may be natural to think that the procedures used to replicate the German Enigma coding device (via Turing's work with the aptly named "Bombe" computer at Bletchley Park) might also be applicable to the decoding of human language. Of course, in actuality, neither Enigma nor the Bombe played any role in translating, interpreting, or (metaphorically) decoding language: instead, they were able to generate statistically and mathematically sophisticated schemes for hiding the intended linguistic transmission, independent in every way of that transmission. Neither Enigma nor the Bombe could translate; instead, they performed properly algorithmic operations on strings of codes, so that human interpreters could have access to the underlying natural language.

Weaver's intuition, along with those of his co-researchers at the time, therefore begins from what might be thought an entirely illegitimate analogy, between code and language, that resembles Chomsky's creation of a language hierarchy, according to which codes are not at all dissimilar from the kind of formal logic systems Chomsky proves are not like human language. Thus it is not at all surprising that intellectuals of Weaver's day were highly skeptical of his project along lines that Weaver dismisses with a certain amount of hubris. In the 1949 memorandum Weaver quotes correspondence he had with Norbert Wiener (whose own career reveals, in fact, a profound knowledge of and engagement with human language).[4] Weaver quotes from a private letter written by Wiener to him in 1947:

> As to the problem of mechanical translation, I frankly am afraid the boundaries of words in different languages are too vague and the emotional and international connotations are too extensive to make any quasimechanical translation scheme very hopeful . . . . At the present time, the mechanization of language, beyond such a stage as the design of photoelectric reading opportunities for the blind, seems very premature. (Wiener, quoted in Weaver 1955, 18)

Weaver writes back to Wiener that he is "disappointed but not surprised by" Wiener's comments on "the translation problem," in part for combinatorial (i.e., formal) reasons: "suppose we take a vocabulary of 2,000 words, and admit for good measure all the two-word combinations as if they were single words. The vocabulary is still only four million: and that is not so formidable a number to a modern computer, is it?" (18). Weaver writes that Wiener's response "must in fact be accepted as exceedingly discouraging, for, if there are any real possibilities, one would expect Wiener to be just the person to develop them" (18–19). Rather than accepting

Wiener's intellectual insights as potentially correct, though—and it is notable how exactly correct Wiener has been about the enterprise of CL—Weaver turns to the work of other computer scientists (especially the other contributors to the 1955 volume), whose computational intuitions have led them to experiment with mechanical translation schemes.

Weaver's combinatoric argument fails to address Wiener's chief points, namely that human language is able to manage ambiguity and approximation in a way quite different from the way that computers handle symbols. The persistent belief that philosophical skeptics must be wrong about the potential for machine translation is characteristic of computational thinking from the 1950s to the present. Only Claude Shannon himself—again, a dedicated scientist and engineer with limited experience in the study of language—is accorded authority by Weaver, so that "only Shannon himself, at this stage, can be a good judge of the possibilities in this direction"; remarkably, Weaver suggests that "a book written in Chinese is simply a book written in English which was coded into the 'Chinese Code'" (22). Since we "have useful methods for solving any cryptographic problem, may it not be that with proper interpretation we already have useful methods for translation?"

This perspective seems to have much in common with Chomsky's later opinions about the universal structure of all languages, so that "the most promising approach" to Weaver is said to be "an approach that goes so deeply into the structure of languages as to come down to the level where they exhibit common traits" (23). This launches Weaver's famous metaphor of language as a kind of city of towers:

> Think, by analogy, of individuals living in a series of tall closed towers, all erected over a common foundation. When they try to communicate with each other, they shout back and forth, each from his own closed tower. It is difficult to make the sound penetrate even the nearest towers, and communication proceeds very poorly indeed. But, when an individual goes down his tower, he finds himself in a great open basement, common to all the towers. Here he establishes easy and useful communication with the persons who have also descended from their towers.
>
> Thus may it be true that the way to translate from Chinese to Arabic, or from Russian to Portuguese, is not to attempt the direct route, shouting from tower to tower. Perhaps the way is to descend, from each language, down to the common base of human communication—*the real but as yet undiscovered universal language*—and then re-emerge by whatever particular route is convenient. (23, emphasis added)

This strange view, motivated by no facts about language or even a real situation that can be understood physically, nonetheless continues to inform computationalist judgments about language. Both Chomsky's pursuit of a Universal Grammar and Fodor's quest for a "language of thought" can be understood as pursuits of this "real but as yet undiscovered universal language," a language that is somehow at once spoken and understood by all human beings and yet at the same time inaccessible to all contemporary human beings—again, positing an *Ursprache* from which mankind has fallen into linguistic and cultural diversity that are responsible for political disunity.

Even to Weaver, it is obvious that everyday language is not much like a conventional code. This prompts him to suggest two different strategies for using mechanical means to interpret language. First, because "there are surely alogical elements in language (intuitive sense of style, emotional content, etc.) . . . one must be pessimistic about the problem of *literary* translation" (22, emphasis in original). In fact, Weaver only proposes that a computer would be able to handle "little more than . . . a one-to-one correspondence of words" (20). In "literary translation," "style is important," and "problems of idiom, multiple meanings, etc., are frequent" (20). This observation is offered with no argumentative support whatsoever, but for the idea that "large volumes of technical material might, for example, be usefully, even if not at all elegantly, handled this way," even though, in fact, "technical writing is unfortunately not always straightforward and simple in style" (20). As an example, Weaver suggests that "each word, within the general context of a mathematical article, has one and only one meaning" (20).

Weaver's assertion, as most linguists and literary critics know, does not mesh well with the observed linguistic facts. Many of the most common words in English are grammatical particles and "auxiliary verbs" such as "of," "do," "to," "have," and the like, which turn out to be notoriously difficult to define even in English dictionaries, and extraordinarily difficult to translate into other languages. Because each language divides up the spheres of concepts and experience differently, there is rarely a stable, one-to-one correspondence between any of these common words and those in other languages. One of Weaver's favorite off-hand examples, Mandarin Chinese, poses some of these problems for mechanical translation. Because Chinese does not inflect verbs for tense or number, it is not possible to distinguish infinitive forms from inflected or tensed forms; there is no straightforward morphological distinction in Chinese, that is, between the English expressions *to sleep* and *sleep*. The Chinese speaker relies on context or time expressions to determine which meaning might be intended by the speaker, but there is no process of internal "translation" according to which we might determine which of these forms is "meant." The mechanical translator from English to Chinese would either have to automatically drop the helper verb "to," or presume that all English forms are equivalent to the uninflected Chinese verb. Neither option is accurate, and no Chinese text, no matter how controlled its domain, "avoids" it.

In his famous debate with John Searle, Jacques Derrida challenges Searle's extension of J. L. Austin's speech-act distinction between performative, constative, and other forms of linguistic expression, arguing that any instance of language might be understood as performative, or citational, or "iterative" (Derrida 1988; Searle 1977). Here we see an even more potent and influential version of Searle's position, that some parts of language can be broken out as the purely logical or meaningful parts, leaving over the "stylistic" or "literary" elements. But what Wiener tried to argue in his response to Weaver is that all language is literary in this sense: language is always multiple and polysemous, even when we appear to be accessing its univocal parts.

The crux of Wiener's and Weaver's disagreement can be said to center just on this question of univocality of any parts of language other than directly referential nouns. This disagreement rides on the second suggestion Weaver and other computationalists make, and which continues to inform much computational work to this day: namely that *human language is itself broken* because it functions in a polysemous and ambiguous fashion, and that the solution to this is to rewrite our language so as to "fix" its reference in a univocal manner. One reason Weaver writes to Ogden and Richards is because of their work earlier in the century on a construct called "Basic English," one of many schemes to create universal, standard languages (the effort also includes Esperanto) whose lack of referential ambiguity may somehow solve the political problem of human disagreement. Wiener points out in his letter to Weaver that "in certain respects basic English is the reverse of mechanical and throws upon such words as *get* a burden which is much greater than most words carry in conventional English" (quoted in Weaver 1949, 18). Weaver seems not to understand the tremendous importance of particles, copulas, and other parts of language that have fascinated linguists for centuries—or of the critical linguistic role played by ambiguity itself. Most English-speakers, for example, use words like "to," "do," "have," "get," "like," "go," and so forth with tremendous ease, but on close question often cannot provide precise definitions of them. This would lead one to believe that precise semantics are not what human beings exclusively rely on for language function, even at a basic level, but of course this observation may be unsettling for those looking at language for its deterministic features.

Weaver's principal intuition, that translation is an operation similar to decoding, was almost immediately dismissed even by the advocates of MT as a research program. In standard histories of MT, we are told that this approach was "immediately recognized as mistaken" (Hutchins 1986, 30), since the "computers at Bletchley Park were applied to cracking the cipher, not to translating the German text into English" (30). This conclusion emerges from engineering investigation into the problem, since few linguists or philosophers would have assented to the view that languages are codes; nevertheless, even today, a prominent subset of computationalists (although rarely ones directly involved in computer language processing) continue to insist that formal languages, programming languages, and ciphers are all the same kinds of things as human languages, despite the manifest differences in form, use, and meaning of these kinds of systems. Surely the mere fact that a particular word—language—is conventionally applied to these objects is not, in and of itself, justification for lumping the objects together in a metaphysical sense; yet at some level, the intuition that language is code-like underwrites not just MT but its successor (and, strangely, more ambitious) programs of CL and NLP.

From MT to CL and NLP

Weaver's memo continues to be held in high esteem among computational researchers for two suggestions that have remained influential to this day. Despite the fact that MT has produced extremely limited results in more than 50 years of practice—as can be seen using the (generally, state-of-the-art) mechanisms found in such easily accessed tools as Google and Babelfish—computationalists have continued to suggest that machines are not just on the verge of translating, but of actually using human language in an effective way. It is often possible to hear computationalists without firm knowledge of the subject asserting that Google's translator is "bad" or "flawed" and that it could be easily "fixed," when in fact, Google has devoted more resources to this problem than perhaps any other institution in history, and openly admits that it represents the absolute limit of what is possible in MT.[5]

With time and attention, CL and NLP projects have expanded in a range of directions, some more fruitful than others. While observers from outside the field continue to mistakenly believe that we are on the verge of profound progress in making computers "speak," a more finely grained view of the issues suggests that the real progress in these fields is along several much more modest directions. Contemporary CL and NLP projects, proceed along several different lines, some inspired by the work originally done by Weaver and other MT advocates, and other work inspired by the use of computers by linguists. Contemporary CL and NLP includes at least the following areas of inquiry: *text-to-speech synthesis* (TTS): the generation of (synthesized) speech from written text; *voice recognition:* the use of human language for input into computers, often as a substitute for written/-keyboarded text; *part-of-speech tagging:* the assignment of grammatical categories and other feature information in human language texts; *corpus linguistics:* the creation and use of large, computer-based collections of texts, both written and spoken; *natural language generation* (NLG) or *speech production:* the use of computers to spontaneously emit human language; *conversational agents:* the computer facility to interact with human interlocutors, but without the ability to spontaneously generate speech on new topics; *CL of human languages:* the search for computational elements in human languages; *statistical NLP:* the analysis of human language (often large corpora) using statistical methods; *information extraction:* the attempt to locate the informational content of linguistic expressions and to synthesize or collect them from a variety of texts. The visible success in some of these programs (especially ones centered around speech synthesis and statistical analysis, neither of which has much to do with what is usually understood as *comprehension;* Manning and Schütze [1999] provides a thorough survey) leads to a popular misconception that other programs are on the verge of success. In fact, the extremely limited utility of many of these research programs helps to show why the others will likely never succeed; and the CL/NLP programs that avoid a hardcore computationalist paradigm (especially statistical NLP) help to show why the main intellectual program in these areas—namely, the desire to show that human language is itself computational, and simultaneously to produce a "speaking computer" and/or "universal translator"—are likely not ever to succeed. The work of some researchers relies exactly on the statistical methods once championed by Weaver to argue that some contemporary conceptions of language itself, especially the formal linguistics programs inspired by Chomsky, rely far too heavily on a computationalist ideology.

Two of the most successful CL programs are the related projects of TTS and voice recognition: one using computers to synthesize a human-like voice, and one using computers to substitute spoken input for written input. In neither case is any kind of engagement with semantics or even syntax suggested; contrary to the suggestions of Weaver and other early CL advocates, even the apparently formal translation of written language into spoken language, and vice versa, engages some aspects of the human language system that are at least in part computationally intractable. The simpler of the two programs is voice recognition; today several manufacturers, including Microsoft, IBM, and a specialist company, Nuance, produce extremely effective products of this sort, which are useful for people who can't or prefer not to use keyboards as their main input devices. These programs come equipped with large vocabularies, consisting mainly of the natural language terms for common computer operations (such as "File," "Open," "New," "Menu," "Close," etc.), along with the capability to add a virtually unlimited number of custom vocabulary items. Yet even the best of these systems cannot "recognize" human speech right out of the box with high accuracy. Instead, they require a fair amount of individualized training with the user. Despite the fact that software developers use statistical methods to pre-load the software with a wide range of possible variations in pronunciation, these systems always require user "tuning" to ensure that pitch, accent, and intonation are being read correctly. Unlike a human when she is listening to another human being, the software cannot necessarily perceive word boundaries consistently without training. In addition, these systems require a huge amount of language-specific programming, much of which has not been proven to extend to languages and pronunciation styles that are not anticipated by the programmer. There is no question of "comprehension" in these systems, despite the appearance that the computer does what the speaker says—anymore than the computer is understanding what one types on a keyboard or clicks with a mouse. The voice recognition system does not know that "File—Open" means to open a file; it simply knows where this entry is on the computer menu, and then selects that option in just the same way the user does with a mouse.

TTS systems, also widely used and highly successful, turn out to present even more complex problems as research objects. Because the voice recognition user can control her vocabulary, she can ensure that much of her input will fall into the range of the software's capability. TTS systems, unless the vocabulary is tightly controlled, must be able to pronounce any string they encounter, and even in well-controlled language practices like English this may include a vast range of apparently nonstandard usages, pronunciations, words, and spellings. In addition, for TTS systems to be comprehensible by human beings, it turns out that much of what had been understood (by some) as paralinguistic features, like prosody, intonation, stops and starts, interruptions, nonlexical pauses, and so forth, must all be managed in some fashion, or otherwise produce speech that sounds extremely mechanical and even robotic. Most such systems still today sound highly mechanical, as in the widely used Macintosh speech synthesizer or the systems used by individuals like Stephen Hawking, who are unable to speak. Even these systems, it turns out, do not produce speech in a similar manner to human beings, but rather must use a pre-assembled collection of parts in a combinatorial fashion, often using actual recorded samples of human speech for a wide range of applications that directly generated computer speech can't manage.

Among the best-studied and most interesting issues in TTS is the question of intonation. While in some languages formalized tones (such as Chinese, Thai, and Vietnamese) are a critical feature of language "proper," other levels of intonation—roughly, the tunes we "sing" while we are speaking, such as a rising intonation at the end of questions—are found in all languages. Human speakers and hearers use these tonal cues constantly in both production and reception, but the largely analog nature of this intonation and its largely unconscious nature have made it extremely difficult to address, let alone manage, in computational systems. One contemporary researcher, Janet Pierrehumbert, has focused on the role of intonation in a general picture of phonology, and while she makes extensive use of computers for analysis, her work helps to show why full-scale TTS poses significant problems for computational systems:

> Intonational phrasing is an example of "structure." That is, an intonation phrase specifies that certain words are grouped together, and that one of these words is the strongest prosodically. The intonation phrase does not in and of itself specify any part of the content. Rather, it provides opportunities to make choices of content. For each intonation phrase, the speaker selects not only the words, but also a phrasal melody. The phonetic manifestations of the various elements of the content depend on their position with respect to the intonational phrasing. (Pierrehumbert 1993, 261)

The intonational phrase is among the most common and analog aspects of speech (analog in the sense that there is no hard-and-fast binary role for when a particular intonational melody does or does not have a specific meaning, but are also interpreted with remarkable skill and speed by human listeners). In the most obvious cases, such as brief questions and brief declarative statements, it is possible to create stereotypes that are recognizable by human beings, but computational systems fail to make the consistent alterations in such presentations that are characteristic of human speech. A human being has a range of melodies for asking questions, each of which may contribute to meaning in a more-or-less fashion; a computer has no background position from which to "choose" any of these analog options, but rather is likely to choose a hard-coded intonation phrase in these most stereotypical cases. The result is highly mechanical, even if recognizable by human beings.

Of course it is tempting, especially from the computationalist perspective, to see these intonational phenomena as paralinguistic, but Pierrehumbert has shown conclusively (as many linguists have also known for hundreds of years) that such phenomena are critical to all spoken language (and even in our interpretation of some written language) and that they reach deeply into the nature of phonetics itself. Intonation and phonetics are in part "suprasegmental": they are meaningful units that are larger than the apparent span of words (at least, in the way English orthography creates word boundaries, which as Wiener points out, is not consistent across all languages). Even the most apparently straightforward of phonetic facts, such as the pronunciation of individual speech sounds, turn out to be seriously conditioned by their place in suprasegmental melodies. While "there is no impasse as far as the human mind is concerned; it apparently recognizes the phonemes and the prosody together" (269), the need for discrete representations of any linguistic facts in a CL system makes it difficult to determine whether prosody or phonetics are the "base" representation on which to grow the other. Pierrehumbert calls the effects of prosody and intonation on human speech "nonlocal," using vocabulary from physics to suggest that the impact of such phenomena can't be assigned in a one-to-one correspondence with apparent linguistic tokens. "Nonlocal" implies a kind of mystical action-at-a-distance that may not comport well with the physical nature of the mind; a less overdetermined term might be "analog."

The correspondence between apparently linguistic tokens and suprasegmental melodies is something that computational researchers have hardly learned how to manage for purposes of recognition, to say nothing of natural language generation. Because "melody is not provided by the lexical choice, but rather functions as a separate simultaneous channel of information" (277), it would be necessary to categorize this channel meaningfully for computational generation; yet we do not even have a proposed routine for capturing this phenomena, despite the everyday ease with which human language users access it. Yet for speech-to-text technology to work in either direction (TTS systems and voice recognition), this phenomenon would have to be well understood and modeled not just for English but for other languages that use tone and melody in a variety of ways. For this reason, some TTS systems use what are essentially recordings of human voices speaking certain strings with "natural" (but generally unanalyzed) intonation, which are then simply played back by the system when the token is accessed.

Neither TTS nor voice recognition addresses what most in the general public assume to be the main tasks for CL and NLP, despite the clear need for these programs to handle such phenomena. Instead, putting aside the difficulties in this aspect of speech production, most CL and NLP research from the 1960s until recently has bypassed these issues, and taken the processing of written text in and of itself as a main project. (Even in Turing's original statement of the Test, the interlocutors are supposed to be passing dialogue back and forth in written form, because Turing sees the obvious inability of machines to adequately mimic human speech as a separate question from whether computers can process language.) By focusing on written exemplars, CL and NLP have pursued a program that has much in common with the "Strong AI" programs of the 1960s and 1970s that Hubert Dreyfus (1992), John Haugeland (1985), John Searle (1984, 1992), and others have so effectively critiqued. This program has two distinct aspects, which although they are joined intellectually, are often pursued with apparent independence from each other—yet at the same time, the mere presence of the phrase "computational linguistics" in a title is often not at all enough to distinguish which program the researcher has in mind.

SHRDLU and the State of the Art in Computational Linguistics

The two faces of CL and NLP in its strong mode are either (1) to make computers use language in a fully human fashion, generally via conversational agents that can interact "in the same way as a human being" with human or other language-using interlocutors; and (2) to demonstrate that human language is itself a computational system, and therefore can be made algorithmically tractable for computation. No doubt, the most famous computer system that pursues primarily the first goal is a system built in the late 1960s and early 1970s by Terry Winograd in the Artificial Intelligence laboratory at MIT, through the same program that funded Chomsky's work. Winograd's system, called SHRDLU (named for the second line on a linotype printer; see Winograd nd1), took advantage of the 20 years of research following Weaver's original memo on MT. Rather than starting with language, then, Winograd saw that a more feasible approach was to start with the world—or rather a world, one which a computer could conceivably be able to reason about—noting that this quality of "aboutness" (or what Searle and other phenomenologists call *intentionality*) seems to be a base feature of human language. Since a computer has such limited sensory access to the human world of experience, part of Winograd's project was to create an ingenious "model world"—a world of objects and actions that both human beings and computers might be able to speak about.

SHRDLU's model world persists as one of the most famous constructions in the history of computer science. Its world can be depicted in both physical space and simulated in the computer, such that the various programs contributing to SHRDLU can "perceive" objects in the model world in the same way they might be metaphorically said to perceive the elements of any running computer simulation. Rather than simply reading output devices, though, SHRDLU is constructed so as to provide answers in a limited (200-word) vocabulary of English. The model world consists of any number of a limited kind of objects: blocks of exactly three shapes (pyramids, blocks, and boxes). The blocks are colored, which provides SHRDLU with a range of real-world information about its model. It also "understands" some basic physical concepts of its world; and it can "learn" by having new terms defined in terms of words it already understands. SHRDLU also understands certain other actions, including actions it can take (moving blocks around), providing it with models of the most prominent grammatical categories (nouns, verbs, adjectives).

SHRDLU is able to produce remarkable conversations in what look like everyday written English transcriptions of conversations. Because it has physical extension, it is able to interact with the world of blocks, whether via a physical appendage or the internal simulation Winograd's system used. Through a complex and highly modularized series of computer programs, SHRDLU does something that looks like conversing:

Person: PICK UP A BIG RED BLOCK.
Computer: OK. (does it)
Person: GRASP THE PYRAMID.
Computer: I DON'T UNDERSTAND WHICH PYRAMID YOU MEAN.
Person: FIND A BLOCK WHICH IS TALLER THAN THE ONE YOU ARE HOLDING AND PUT IT INTO THE BOX.
Computer: BY "IT", I ASSUME YOU MEAN THE BLOCK WHICH IS TALLER THAN THE ONE I AM HOLDING.
Computer: OK. (does it)
Person: WHAT DOES THE BOX CONTAIN?
Computer: THE BLUE PYRAMID AND THE BLUE BLOCK.
Person: WHAT IS THE PYRAMID SUPPORTED BY?
Computer: THE BOX.
Person: HOW MANY BLOCKS ARE NOT IN THE BOX?
Computer: FOUR OF THEM.
Person: IS AT LEAST ONE OF THEM NARROWER THAN THE ONE WHICH I TOLD YOU TO PICK UP?
Computer: YES, THE RED CUBE.
Person: IS IT SUPPORTED?
Computer: YES, BY THE TABLE.
Person: CAN THE TABLE PICK UP BLOCKS?
Computer: NO.
Person: CAN A PYRAMID BE SUPPORTED BY A BLOCK?
Computer: YES.
Person: CAN A PYRAMID SUPPORT A PYRAMID?

Computer: I DON'T KNOW.
Person: STACK UP TWO PYRAMIDS.
Computer: I CAN'T.
(SHRDLU dialogue from Winograd nd2)

It isn't easy to capture the excitement SHRDLU created in 1968 and 1969 when Winograd first showed the system to other AI researchers. Winograd seemed to have started at just the right place, by replicating what looks like the linguistic behavior of a young human being who may not have mastery of the full range of linguistic expressions, but can demonstrate impressive knowledge of a limited set of world–word relations. This dialogue reads plausibly like an interaction between an adult and a child playing with blocks, although it lacks the inevitable digressions present in almost any child's speech.

Like many CL & NLP projects, SHRDLU gestures in two directions at once: it hints at building more complicated systems that could handle more human language; and it also presents a model of what might be going on in the human brain. Notably, however, this model is much less subtle than Chomsky's view of linguistic computation; instead, the system relies exclusively on expressions from formal logic. Nearly every linguistic operation SHRDLU can perform can be expressed in a logical equation, up to and including the assignment of variables to unknown terms, as in the following stretch of dialogue:

Person: DOES A STEEPLE
Computer interrupting: SORRY, I DON'T KNOW THE WORD
   "STEEPLE".
Person: A "STEEPLE" IS A STACK WHICH CONTAINS TWO GREEN
   CUBES AND A PYRAMID.
Computer: I UNDERSTAND.
Person: ARE THERE ANY STEEPLES NOW?
Computer: NO.
Person: BUILD ONE.
Computer: OK. (does it)
Person: CALL THE BIGGEST BLOCK "SUPERBLOCK".
Computer: OK.
Person: HAVE YOU PICKED SUPERBLOCK UP SINCE WE BEGAN?
(SHRDLU dialogue from Winograd nd2)

Here SHRDLU demonstrates variable assignment to an unknown term ("steeple"); demonstrates the ability to extrapolate from the single noun *steeple* to its plural steeples without explicitly asking for a pluralization rule; and assignment of a new term when this is explicitly assigned ("Call the biggest block 'superblock' ") when this requires analysis of the model world according to measurable criteria.

SHRDLU resembles the human linguistic facility so closely that many AI researchers took it to be a clear proof of concept for much more robust and usable CL systems. Underlying this view, though, is what can only be called a computationalist view of language itself. SHRDLU does not posit that it models a system that is part of human language, or a linguistic capability that human beings can also perform; rather, at least in its initial formulations, SHRDLU includes the posit that its mechanism is the fundamental operation of language, and that other linguistic operations are parasitic on, or additional to, this fundamental one. In this sense SHRDLU crosses the line between a CL research program and a model of human language capability. The programs that make up SHRDLU might be plausibly thought a simulation of the "modules" that make up the human language capability. Each module contains explicit definitions for the linguistic features it needs to "know about"; for example, SHRDLU includes explicit representations of linguistic entities like CLAUSE, PHRASE, WORD, ADJUNCT, TRANSITIVE VERB, INTRANSITIVE VERB, ADJECTIVE, and so on. Each of these categories has been hard-coded into the programming structure, so that any nonce word encountered by the system must be assigned to its relevant categories, using contextual clues.

In addition, the SHRDLU system contains explicit representations of phenomena like logical relations ("equals," "and," "or," "is a member of"), spatial relations ("on top of," "inside of"), phrasal types (question, declaration, request), and others. None of these systems are available for reflection or modification by the "speaker"; they are programmed in by the system beforehand. Phenomena that do not appear in SHRDLU's explicit representations can't be added to the system via conversation (as nonce words can be); instead they, too, must be programmed into the computer. Here already we encounter a significant difference between the SHRDLU system and the human one, because we simply don't know what the human equivalent of the SHRDLU *programming* environment is; and it would be tendentious to say the least to suggest that analogues for the modules in the human brain could be much like SHRDLU's modules.

Take one of the most problematic modules, namely, the one that realizes Boolean and other logical forms. It surely is the case that human children and adults can manipulate these concepts; yet it is also the case that some logical concepts can be among the difficult developmental stepping-stones for children, and that the use of logic by human beings does not seem to reflect a hard-coded "logic module" that is part of the Language Organ, simply because human beings are extremely inconsistent in their implementation of logical formulae. Much of formal logic, even in its simplest instantiations, is put off in our educational system until university. Surely if the human language organ relied heavily on hard-coded routines for critical functions like AND, OR, and NOT, it would be strange to find that they filter up to the actual human being so imperfectly. Some system of interference must be preventing the brain from accessing the logical computer operating inside of itself—which seems like an arbitrary and counterintuitive way for the biological organism to develop.

The human child, unlike the SHRDLU program, must create or realize its linguistic facility solely through conversation and introspection: positing a programmer to write routines comes dangerously close to endorsing a kind of intelligent-design view of the development of language. The child's grasp of logic is not simply an imperfectly matured system, but a part of a complex interaction between individual and environment whose configuration is not at all clear. This can be seen by considering the ways in which the SHRDLU sample dialog is actually quite different from a parallel conversation that an adult might have with a child about the same block world SHRDLU uses. Of course any given child might well have exactly the kind of conversation shown in the SHRDLU example; at the same time, it is fair to say that the SHRDLU conversation does not quite follow the typical course of a human interaction on the same subject.

Take the definition of new terms by ostension, using the example "steeple." Winograd's writing is compelling and his model is impressive, so it is easy to ignore the fact that what the computer has "learned" here is an ostensive formal definition that fails to capture exactly what would be relevant about the term "steeple" in English. While what SHRDLU understands as a steeple resembles an English-language steeple in shape and to a limited degree in function, it absolutely does not carry with it the connotations most English speakers would associate with the term (for example, that it is associated with some styles of church architecture, typically painted a neutral color, and not necessarily identical with any object of its relative shape and size). Both of the terms SHRDLU learns by definition in the dialogue, *steeple* and *superblock,* resemble English terms only by analogy. In fact, like all completely computer-based languages, or what should better be called formal systems, terms defined in SHRDLU's language are entirely contained within the world of form; they do not make reference to the larger world and its web of holistically defined and contextually malleable language uses. They make a perfect model of what Chomsky sometimes calls I-language (for "Internal Language," the pre-semantic formal code on which the language faculty operates), but only because despite appearances there is no "external reality" for them to deal with; there is no possibility of one of SHRDLU's interlocutors spontaneously using *steeple* in a wholly different manner from what has come before, or metaphorically applying it to something that is not at all a steeple, or analogizing superblock to apply to a different kind of object altogether.

For these reasons and other similar ones, Winograd himself abandoned the SHRDLU project and, under the influence of Heideggerian thought such as that found in Dreyfus's writings, began to think about the ways in which computers as machines interact with humans and function in the human world, and to see language as a practice that can only be understood in context. Language plays only a partial role in the social world in Winograd's revised vision:

> The world is encountered as something always already lived in, worked in, and acted upon. World as the background of obviousness is manifest in our everyday dealings as the familiarity that pervades our situation, and every possible utterance presupposes this. Listening for our possibilities in a world in which we already dwell allows us to speak and to elicit the cooperation of others. That which is not obvious is made manifest through language. What is unspoken is as much a part of the meaning as what is spoken. (Winograd and Flores 1987, 58).

Of course, despite the continued respect with which he is received in the computer world, Winograd's knowing dissent from computationalist dogma, and his specific and thorough knowledge of the CL research programs and its orientation, had little impact on the actual direction of CL and NLP. They could not, because these worlds are not driven by the scientific procedures according to which they claim to operate; rather, they are ideological programs driven by a furious need to show that computers can take over language, that language itself can be formalized, and that those parts of human experience that cannot be formalized, and so are difficult to control mechanically, are also of little value or interest.

CHAPTER FIVE

Linguistic Computationalism

DESPITE THE MANIFEST difficulties found everywhere in high computationalist attempts to make computers "speak," thinkers outside of
CL proper persist in believing that such a development is likely in the near
future. Few prominent CL researchers describe their projects as failures, or
spend much time explaining in their published works the significant limitations of fully algorithmic efforts to produce free-form speech, since it has
become quite clear that such efforts are no longer considered worthwhile
or even meaningful projects to pursue. This does not mean CL and NLP are
unsuccessful: on the contrary, the complexity they help to uncover in linguistic production has opened up new avenues for linguistic analysis, of
both the computational and conventional varieties. They have simultaneously revealed any number of limited-scope and domain-specific linguistic
tasks that are highly tractable to computational analysis.

Some computer games, for example, can list every statement that can be
made within the world of the game, so that fully automated characters can
speak them; yet the completely routine nature of such speech fragments is
never mistaken by linguists for the syntactic and semantic creativity everywhere evident in natural languages. Such computational mechanisms can
be extended, so that, for example, certain programs for natural language
generation can be used to produce what look like standard news stories
about limited domains: the statistics of a baseball game, for example, can
be used to generate terse game summaries that read much like what a

human writer might produce. Again, no serious linguistic researcher mistakes such productions for mimicking more than an important part of natural language; and critically, no serious linguistic researcher suggests that this success implies further success in free-form language production. On the contrary, such domain-specific success looks much more like the absolute limit of computational language production.

Somewhat remarkably, but in a strong testament to the power of computationalist ideologies, outside the sphere of professional CL researchers, we find a much less skeptical group of researchers who do, in fact, believe that much more significant strides in computer processing of language are just around the corner. Despite the repetition of such claims throughout the history of computers, these computationalists presume that CL researchers simply have not experimented with obvious strategies for comprehension and translation, or that insufficient processing power has been brought to bear on the problem. While the presence of professional computational linguists in industry today means that companies who focus on language products make such claims less often than in the past, they can still be found with unexpected frequency outside professional CL circles. Yet the views of professional computational linguists have a surprisingly restricted sphere of influence. They are rarely referenced even by the computer scientists who are working to define future versions of the World Wide Web, especially in the recent project to get the the web to "understand" meanings called the Semantic Web. They have little influence, either, over the widespread presumption among computationalists that the severe restrictions today's computers impose on natural language diversity are irrelevant to the worlwide distribution of cultural power.

Computationalism and Digital Textuality

During the last fifteen years, a small body of writing has emerged that is concerned with an idea called in the literature the OHCO thesis, spelled out to mean that texts are Ordered Hierarchies of Content Objects. This idea emerges in a particularly narrow band of academic scholarship situated somewhere between computer science and library science that is still notably representative of much computationalist thinking and research. It is also notably distant from mainstream philosophical practice of any sort, or from literary theory, or from textual criticism or linguistics, and suffers from this lack of contextualization. As proposed in a series of essays by DeRose, Renear, and others (Coombs, Renear, and DeRose 1987; DeRose et al. 1990; Renear 1995), and affirmed in later works by them and others, the OHCO thesis, and no less the stubborn pursuit of increasingly restricted versions of it, is supposed to have been a kind of first stab at a way to represent not merely the formal aspects of a text (in the sense that a word processor can represent any text that is typed into it), but textual semantics.[1]

Now largely abandoned in favor of a somewhat grudging admission that many semantic features cannot be definitively represented (a thesis called in Renear, Mylonas, and Durand [1996] "OHCO-3," "perspectives can be decomposed into OHCOs"), OHCO's initial acceptance within the scholarly text processing community is said to reflect normal scientific practice adjusting itself to the facts, and no doubt it does. But the particular shape taken by the initial OHCO thesis is highly revealing about a computational bias: a gut feeling or intuition that computation as a process must be at the bottom of human and sometimes cultural affairs, *prior to the discovery of compelling evidence that such a thesis might be correct.* In the practical world, this often translates to an assumption that the default methods already built into the computing architecture are largely satisfactory to represent the world of culture, with some minor modifications perhaps necessary "at the margins," and often despite the explicit statement of earlier technologists that these tools will not be appropriate for those tasks.

Recent work on the OHCO thesis suggests that its most restrictive versions are untenable just because of deep conceptual issues that emerged only through prolonged contact with real-world examples. While true in its own way, this theory-internal story plays down the rationalist cultural orientation of the computer sciences themselves. The literature on the OHCO thesis is surprisingly reticent about these underpinnings. Have observations about the structure of text or of language, or philosophical speculation, led well-known thinkers to propose something like OHCO? Renear (1995) approvingly cites an extract from Wittgenstein for an epigraph, an extract that tends toward Wittgenstein's late "healing" view of philosophical practice as a process of "clarifying," but he does not connect this to the OHCO question in the main text. Nor does Renear reflect on the fact that this Wittgenstein (1953) is one of the writers whose work would most immediately lead one to raise questions about any OHCO-like thesis.[2]

Despite being presented in a topic cluster in the philosophy journal *The Monist* about the philosophical implications of electronic publishing, Renear locates digital textuality in a tendentious frame. Renear develops a philosophical typology via three seemingly familiar positions, which he calls Platonism, Pluralism, and Antirealism. Platonism, to Renear, is the "view that texts are hierarchical structures of objects such as chapters, titles, paragraphs, stanzas, and the like, [and] is already implicit in the early efforts to theorize about the development of text processing software, and is implied in the SGML standard itself, which is a standard for defining hierarchical models for representing texts" (Renear 1995, §5.1.2). The idea that we draw such conclusions from the practice of computer engineers is quite odd, and no less so in that it requires an analysis of the Platonic texts that is itself tendentious and that Renear does not provide. Since SGML describes hierarchical objects, we would of course expect anything it characterizes to be hierarchical. But how do we get from here to the view that *text itself*, in the abstract, is hierarchical, much less that such a view is Platonic?

Despite the scantiness of the discussion in Renear (1995), it remains one of the only serious examinations in the OHCO literature of the thesis that text in the abstract is fundamentally hierarchical. The OHCO literature presumes the thesis is true, and then grudgingly admits accommodations; it only rarely pauses to touch down in the philosophical and conceptual literature which it claims to have engaged, which often anticipates the same issues. No recent philosophical work on language or textuality—whether in the Anglo-American or Continental traditions—provides good underpinnings for such a formalist view of language (and even Chomsky's formalism, arguably the most hierarchical of current linguistic theories, seems irreconcilable with anything like OHCO). Theories of literary editing, for example those of Thomas Tanselle (1992), Donald McKenzie (1999), Jerome McGann (1983, 1991), soundly reject any such theses and never support what Renear calls a Platonic orientation. So it would be difficult to say, as one might wish, that the original OHCO thesis is rooted in philosophical tradition, or editing tradition, or any tradition at all but the intuitions of particular computer scientists.

The lack of historical setting is no less problematic when we come to Renear's second philosophical faction, "Pluralism": and here, unlike Platonism, there really is not even a living philosophical position one could tenably identify with the name. Renear tells us that the pluralist emerges in response to a "real practical problem":

> Briefly the difficulty is that while the SGML world assumed that text encoders would always represent the logical structure of a text as a single hierarchical structure, there in fact turned out to be many hierarchical structures that had reasonable claims to be "logical." A verse drama for instance contains dialogue lines, metrical lines, and sentences. But these do not fit in a single hierarchy of non-overlapping objects: sentences and metrical lines obviously overlap (enjambment) and when a character finishes another character's sentence or metrical line then dialogue lines overlap with sentences and metrical lines. (Renear 1995, §5.2.1)

Once again, Pluralism emerges not in a philosophical or conceptual context but in a computational context, generated by "text encoders" of "the SGML world." Whether one also calls these researchers "library scientists," "computer scientists," "engineers," "programmers," etc., it is hard to grant that their basic intuitions about such a fundamental question as the nature of text should be taken seriously without deep engagement with the fields of research touching on the question, and in which the questions they raise are well-known and could hardly be said to have settled answers.

Unlike the classical position called Platonism and his relatively ad-hoc Pluralism, Renear's third classificatory term comes straight out of contemporary philosophy: Antirealism. Renear associates this term with Wittgenstein through the work of Alois Pichler, "a researcher at the Bergen Wittgenstein Archives who is the author of some very important and philosophically illuminating papers on transcription," who writes in an interpolated quote, apparently following Wittgenstein, that "texts are not objectively existing entities which just need to be discovered and presented, but entities which have to be constructed" (Pichler 1995, p. 774, quoted in Renear 1995, §5.3.1). Renear suggests that Antirealists like "Landow, Bolter, and Lanham do not really establish their claims," and "neither do Huitfeldt, Pichler, and the other post-modern text encoders."

Without reference to any background literature or recognizable positions—as to Platonism, Pluralism, Antirealism, or postmodernism— Renear then retreats from his original claim, and in fact grants the accuracy of what Huitfeldt sees as the two major components of the Antirealist view: "there are no facts about a text which are objective in the sense of not being interpretational," and "a text may have many different kinds of structure (physical, compositional, narrative, grammatical)" (quoted in Renear 1995, §5.3.7 and §5.3.9, respectively). To Renear, in fact, both of these claims "may be true"—in fact he "think[s] that they are true"—but there "is no path of compelling argumentation from either of them, or from both of them together, to the conclusion that 'texts are not objectively existing entities'" (§5.3.11). But in the end, "Antirealism may indeed be the appropriate attitude to take toward theories of textuality, but whether or not it is so I don't think Huitfeldt or Pichler have shown that there is any motivation for Antirealism in our experiences with text encoding" (§5.3.17). This is of course an argument that requires support, but it is nowhere to be found.

It seems remarkable that this discussion constitutes the core intellectual articulation of the contemporary discussion of computational textuality. There is literally so much intellectual work in world history that bears on the underlying questions raised by the OHCO literature that it is almost impossible to cite succinctly; and in this respect the shape of Renear's argument and no less of much of the arguments found in much other writing on the topic remains hard to fathom. Furthermore, this set of observations is not without influence or power, at first simply by displacing more reasonable and respectful models of textuality that might be usefully implemented, but also because of the ways in which it rides roughshod over so much valuable work of the past several hundred years from all over the world and in many different disciplines. In this respect the OHCO thesis represents a strong instantiation of a computationalist ideology, one according to which we should first assume worldly phenomena are computational (meaning that they work the way *we imagine* computers work), and then wait for exceptions (whether empirical or conceptual) to influence further iterations of our model.

Rather than the Platonism/Pluralism/Antirealism scheme that Renear offers, a more useful typology in this context can be found in the longstanding schism between Rationalism on the one hand, and something we might variously see as Empiricism, Pragmatism, or Antirealism on the other, which we will here call anti-rationalism. One place to put the stake in between these two camps is precisely language itself. According to the first camp, language is very precise and orderly, ultimately based on one-to-one correspondences with things in the real world which account for our ability to know—a means of cognition (rationality) than helps to explain our presence in the world. Putnam and other philosophers call this a "correspondence theory of truth," according to which a version of Metaphysical Realism is erected that makes the World almost transcendentally Real.[3]

According to the second camp, language is often very "imprecise" and "disorderly" (if these terms have any precise meaning), based in social and cultural accommodation and history, and more about people acting together (communication) than about cognition. To the degree that language and cognition are intertwined—and this degree is quite large—it becomes difficult to see whether language is "deformative" or "constitutive" of cognitive practices themselves. On this view (and reductively), there is the appearance everywhere of one-to-one correspondence between words and things, but this says nothing about the "actual fact" of such correspondences, whatever that actual fact might be. To both Kant and the late Wittgenstein—two thinkers whose views are certainly worth at least the respect of the OHCO writers—asking questions about "what *is*" in the sense of "what a text *is*" are going to seem highly problematic.[4] Whether or not there is some sort of ultimate reality of the way things are—what Kant would call the *noumena*—there simply is no human access to it, nor any human purpose in reasoning too much about how it might operate.

On what we are calling the anti-rationalist view, then, human language can never afford to be fully "pinned down": human beings can never allow the dictionary definitions of words to exhaust their semantic potential, despite our need to rely on semantic regularity much of the time. Thus, we should never expect schemes to regularize, normalize, segment, or even culturally control language to be wholly effective without implementing similarly effective controls on all other social behavior. It has always been a part of the rationalist dream in particular to "regularize" language and languages to purge them of ambiguity and other "problematic" features, without recognizing that such features are everywhere and indeed constitutive of language.

There is no less a strong cultural symmetry between strong rationalism and cultural prescriptivism about language *per se*, as in the French Academy, characterized not by the linguistic but by the cultural good that is supposedly done by maintaining supposedly linguistic norms for language's own sake. We can only be clear about what we mean, say the prescriptivists, if we stop giving in to our primitive need to play, and our social need to communicate even when we ourselves are unsure about what we want to say. We must put the planning, individualist mind where base urge had been. This is not what Freud meant by *"Wo Es war, soll Ich werden."* It is a particular presumption about how people will and can function in social reality, one that few of the anti-rationalists would share.

Each of these groups has exerted a fair amount of influence over the discussion of textuality, but even more broadly, each has exerted much influence over theories of language. More forcefully, neither one of these groups would implicitly endorse an off-hand distinction between *text* and *language,* in the sense that we might expect text to have structuring properties different from those of language *per se*. The very early Chomsky might well have liked it if language itself turned out to be composed of hierarchically arranged objects, and much of his work was directed at just this sort of demonstration. But Chomsky himself admits that performance, which is to say language in practice, is nothing but "error"—nothing but deviations even from the appearance of ordered hierarchy. If language itself could be characterized in terms of ordered hierarchies, or even (as OHCO-3 would have it), perspectives on ordered hierarchies, we should expect Chomsky's work to be much less controversial than it is. Chomsky's Minimalist Program dispenses with any attempt to systematically characterize hierarchies in language, despite his continued fascination with our apparent reliance on hidden hierarchical structures. Furthermore, Chomsky's opponents in contemporary linguistics—some of whom might be characterized broadly as anti-rationalists—base much of their work on the obvious ways in which language as such does not neatly conform to hierarchical structuring patterns. So if some version of OHCO is going to obtain, it has to be found in something special added into text that is not found in language—this despite the fact that it is not at all obvious how we distinguish between textual language and nontextual language.

From the perspective of the Text Encoding Initiative (TEI) and other language-oriented tools for computer markup, the last thing we should want to do would be to establish beforehand some kind of text/nontext distinction, since a good part of the point of TEI is to mark up *linguistic* data whose archival or transcription source is in turn oral data itself. Whether the source is modern oral history or indigenous and endangered languages, such spontaneous presentations offer no transparent generic "markup conventions" we could argue might be applied without radically altering "the text itself." To the degree that computing as a project pitches itself at the whole world and not just the modern office, it is the exception rather than the rule that our "source text" is a stable document with defined generic characteristics, let alone generic boundaries that might persist across time and space. (And of course, in cases where these are clear, the anti-rationalist has no strong objections to using these features for markup purposes.) Derrida has exactly this problem in mind in *Of Grammatology* (1976), where he demonstrates repeatedly that a hard-and-fast distinction between written text and spoken language is extremely difficult to maintain under philosophical pressure, and especially once we move beyond the "obvious" contemporary Western context and geography. Prior to questions of genre, form, editorial apparatus, and so on, Derrida can make us question whether we really understand what is at stake in the "clear difference" between marking words on paper and speaking them aloud.

This drives us back to that original intuition that formed OHCO in the first place: that it is possible, desirable, reasonable, or useful to try to *describe the structure of texts* in markup based on SGML. Remember that this is more than the straightforward truism that "computers can be used to mark documents": after all, we have nearly 50 years of text processing to prove that point. But it is instructive to think about what Microsoft Word does in this regard: it *does* mark every document as a hierarchical object with XML-like metadata, but it does not try to say much about the content of the document in that structure. Every document has a title; that title exists in a hierarchical relation to the document itself. It is not an inherent feature of nature that "documents" have titles; that is an imposition of our culture and our software architecture. It is a reasonable accommodation that still causes some problems for authors some of the time, especially as a document goes through multiple revisions. In this example, the Word document is an Ordered Hierarchy of Content Objects: but the hierarchy is formal, thin, and virtually silent about the truly unlimited content it can contain.

Throughout the Microsoft Word or WordPerfect document, text is explicitly marked with PostScript and other formatting-oriented markup languages. This markup is objective because it corresponds to enumerable features of the computer: the font, font size, and so on. If one chooses one can impose further quasi-semantic structures like headers and sub-headers, but the features for creating these are quite rich and flexible, offering more default options than the ones apparent in raw XML, and still often must be overridden by users in manual fashion. The situation is even more complex for typesetting software for books. And yet even this incredibly rich system of hierarchically ordered objects only minimally corresponds to the content of the text itself. It is not easy to imagine Microsoft Word adding value to text processing by adding a suite of semantically oriented tools that will aid the human being in writing his or her text. It is specifically human creativity in text production that the word processor is enabling, and over time it has seemed that in fact most writers prefer text processors to be as formal as possible—that is, to interfere as little as possible with the creation of text content, and to make alterations to text appearance straightforward and consistent. This does not make it sound like even text producers have been waiting for the capability to generate text in terms of the semantic categories it harbors—after all, we already have terrific ways of manipulating those categories, which we call writing and thinking.

Language Ideologies of the Semantic Web

Ordinarily, a discourse like the one on the OHCO thesis might simply pass unnoticed, but in the present context it is interesting for several reasons. Not least among these is the clear way in which the OHCO writers are proceeding not (only) from the Platonic philosophical intuitions which they say drive them, but instead or also from certain clear prevailing tendencies in our own culture and world. The first is, of course, the idea that computers should be promulgated and promoted into every aspect of social life: one sees this ideology in every sphere of commercial activity, and here it is vital not to disconnect computing as a cultural project from its existence as a commercial project.[5] From the side of the computing salesperson, computers are always being underutilized, could always do more, could specifically replace stubborn human workers who insist that their work can't be computerized. From the side of the computing worker, computers should be used more, in no small part because the concentration of knowledge and power in the computer guarantees job security which is by definition otherwise less strong.

In this sense, the OHCO thesis is an offshoot of one of the strangest and yet most typical episodes of our computer culture and especially the strength of computationalist ideologies over and above the capabilities of computers. The rush of excitement that accompanied the development of the Internet—before and then including the web—had students and scholars everywhere preparing plain-text and then HTML-marked text of (especially public-domain) literary and historical texts. These texts, often poorly edited, nevertheless started to look something like a digital archive of important cultural works, and once this appearance became manifest official institutional archivists became interested in the project and started talking a lot about standards—the same kinds of standards that had been proliferating through industry at the time and that continue to proliferate today. Standards-issuing bodies, often tied to industry, like ISO and even W3C, had already been suggesting that HTML should be "replaced" or "supplemented" by a structured data variant, and XML was developed by the W3C as a "simpler" and "less restrictive" offshoot of SGML. The goal of this movement was largely industrial and commercial. Its purpose was simple: to enable accurate point-to-point data transmission for commercial purposes, for example, across incompatible legacy databases communicating over the Internet. The main beneficiaries of the implementation of structured data on the web would be commercial and financial, because commercial and financial institutions are the ones being harmed by their inability to adequately mark up *data*—not really text—and to use the ubiquitous Internet as a means to avoid the use of private networks.

For this purpose, XML and its variants are really profoundly effective tools, but that does not altogether explain why the web-user community and academics have been so taken with XML. Again, XML really helps to deal with data; the easiest way to think of data is in terms of databases. A database consists of fields with relatively brief amounts of data, and these fields are labeled. The relation of field contents to label is vital and it is the one that XML most easily replicates. But little about language to begin with, let alone "texts in particular," let alone even *business documents,* resembles a database. Thus, even where it might well produce profit, vendors are having only limited success with software applications that parse business-related correspondence such as e-mails and provide semantic categorization that is usable by business decision makers. To some extent, the idea sounds intrusive, and the only actual implementation of such strategies is still much more keyword-based and involves monitoring employee e-mails for illegal and anticompetitive activities.

Related to this is the hard distinction between form and content that a database model of text implies. This idea is yoked to the implementation of the Semantic Web itself, suggesting somehow that the problem with the web so far and with HTML in particular has been its "blurring" of the form/content distinction.[6] Tags like <b> for bold and <i> for italic are today "deprecated" because they express formatting ideas in what should be a purely semantic medium, so that we should only use tags like <em> and <strong> instead. Of course it is much more ambiguous to the author what these tags will mean in display terms than <b> and <i>: there is nothing at all to prevent implementations where <em> is realized as bold text and <strong> as italic text. The main benefit of such implementations is ideological: it is like strong grammatical prescriptivism in language teaching, ridding the world of "bad" vernaculars. When we step back from such processes, even in formation, we often find astonishing creativity among the vernacular practice. With HTML, that conjecture doesn't need much proving out: we have the proof abundantly before us. Why has the web community in general moved toward a philosophical perspective that is bent on driving people away from their abundantly productive, if occasionally unruly, practices?

If businesses could profit by marking up the semantic parts of regular linguistic data there is little doubt they would. Amazon.com clearly uses features of semantic structuring in its selling and searching tools, but at the same time its extremely sophisticated system shows the real limits of such systems for people when they interact with text. As far as I know Amazon does not mark the *contents* of books with rich XML, although this clearly would be within its powers, beyond the *Books in Print*–based metadata it maintains for each book. Amazon does display something like the Library of Congress subject headings for books at the bottom of the page, a feature I suspect users often do not know to access. University libraries today display those same subject headings, through which mechanism we have finally come to understand that these subject headings are a cataloguer's dream run amok: for items can be categorized in many different ways, even when this categorization is restricted to a narrow domain, that it is virtually useless as a cross-reference tool. The problems with such categorization schemes are too manifold to discuss in detail, but suffice to say it is often more difficult to search for an anthropological study of matriarchy in rural China by searching on keywords like matriarchy, China, and anthropology than it is to search through the LoC category hierarchy for the multiple headings which would fit the subject.[7] Even having found an initial result, it is usually more effective to follow keyword searches and the references found within results than to follow the semantic subject headings, because they have been created by human beings and like all human linguistic products are highly variable as to production and interpretation.

For a project like the Semantic Web to work, something more than the statistical emergence of properties from projects like del.icio.us and other community tagging projects is going to be needed.[8] Despite their higher statistical frequency, these projects suffer even more greatly from the LoC problem, in that precisely what a tag is "supposed" to mean varies from person to person, and ultimately coalesces on what cognitive scientists would call category prototypes—so blogs get tagged with "politics" or "environment" as the most salient tags, precisely the words authors have already chosen as keywords.[9] This is apparent even in the standard historical understanding of the success of SGML and no less, arguably, of XML:

> The best use of SGML is generally made in big corporations and agencies that produce a lot of documents and can afford to introduce a single standard format for internal use. Besides IBM, early applications of the new technology include the projects developed by Association of American Publishers (AAP) and the U.S. Department of Defense. (Darnell 1997, §3.2)

The focus of XML and its associated technologies is data interchange among large organizations with standardized data objects. It is also useful for tagging and cataloging large catalogs of objects with discrete parts and labels (such as complex military vehicles, where SGML is routinely used in documentation procedures and integrated into the design and development process). These characteristics are precisely those that texts tend not to display, much as they are the ones that language and other creative human activities that are not bound by discrete limits tend to display. This is not a mystery unless baseball is a mystery (because it is analog) while computational simulations of baseball are explicable (because they are fundamentally based in binary computations).

This "truth" might sound like Antirealism or deconstruction, and it is certainly hospitable to both, but it is really not so radical, in the sense that few linguists or philosophers of whatever camp would object to it. Language is highly plastic and ambiguous, even when it appears to be solid and referential. We might be able to approximate schemes for representing certain aspects of linguistic structure, and perhaps semantic structure, as these exist in a given text, but these would always be both theoretical and partial, and they are by no means necessary. They are certainly not necessary to produce "marked-up digital text," in the sense that I am now writing a text in Microsoft Word that is 100 percent digital and yet in no way marked by human-usable *semantic* tagging. Future versions of Microsoft Word will decompose files into XML for storage, but this XML will continue to conform to the Word expectations—it will not look for an OHCO-style structure in the document, in the sense that there will be any sort of overarching structure describing the document semantics, and despite the Word document's structure literally *being* an OHCO.

This brings us to a more general set of questions, which have to do with the place and appropriateness of XML and similar semantic tagging schemes in humanities computing, and the role and function of digital humanities as a field. It has been quite astonishing to see the speed with which XML and its associated technologies have not merely spread throughout humanities computing, but have become a kind of conversion gospel that serves not merely as motivation but as outright goal for many projects. "Convert the texts to XML," "everything should be XML-compliant," "XML provides semantic searching"—to the degree that these cries have been heard within humanities circles they have been surprising. Humanities researchers don't produce databases: they produce language and texts. Language and texts are largely intractable to algorithmic computation, even if they are tractable to simulated manipulation on the computer. Such manipulation is a primary goal of the computing industry. Whatever one thinks of Microsoft Word, it clearly serves the text-processing (and text-computational) needs of scholarly researchers perfectly well, and will continue to do so. If and when rich semantic markup of text becomes useful for the general public—an event one has reason to anticipate only with great doubt—such tools will surely be incorporated into our everyday tools for text production by Microsoft and other major manufacturers.

Some humanities projects may benefit from extensive XML markup, but for the most part what archives do is limited, precisely because it turns out that best archiving practices show that minimal markup leads to longest life and maximum portability. Microsoft Word allows users to easily create "metadata" for any document via a series of preference dialogues that most users probably do not recognize as Metadata-with-a-capital-M. Thus the recent push in digital humanities for users to become deeply involved with XML markup seems strange. Such involvement is typical of programmer-level involvement with the computer—that is, it is programmers, rather than managers and creative people, who work with XML, even in large business and government organizations. Surely the last thing we want is to say that digital humanists must be programmers. It is great to have some programmers among us, but it is vital to have nonprogrammers as well. Certain trends in computer history suggest a move toward making programmatic capabilities more available to the user, and less restrictively available to programmers alone, exactly through demotic tools like HTML, BASIC, and Perl. The way to do this with XML, I would suggest, is to incorporate it into relevant applications rather than to insist that humanities scholars, even digital humanists, must by definition be spending the majority of our time with it.

Another reason the OHCO materials are interesting is that they, like the general set of XML recommendations from the W3C and associated bodies, are focused on language. There is a great deal of interest in language and what language can do for computers, on how programming languages can be more responsive to human language. What seems so strange about this is that it presents as settled a series of questions that are in fact the most live ones for investigation. We don't already know how language "works"; we are not even sure what it would mean to come to consensus about the question. In one area in which I do digital humanities work, the creation of digital archives for so-called Minority and Endangered Languages, I routinely face the assumption that XML is going to "mark up" "everything" about the relatively unknown research language. But in fact we almost always end up precisely not trying to do anything of the sort. It is hard enough just to archive "texts" made up of "sentences," and even this sort of markup implies analytical decisions that must be written up for future users of the archive. No doubt, some researchers may wish to create highly rich, structured-data-based applications driven off of this archival language data, but it would be a grave error to try to incorporate such markup into the archive itself. That would actually obscure the data itself, and the data is what we are trying to preserve in as "raw" a form as possible.

Language: despite its claims to global utility, the web is particularly monolingual. The irony of being offered a remarkable tool at the price of sacrificing one's language is exactly that with which many in the world are presented today. There are remarkable conceptual, practical, technical, and linguistic challenges in making the World Wide Web truly worldwide. But rather than working on this problem—in many ways part of a great refusal to recognize it—the W3C and digital text communities prefer to work on ways to theoretically expand the linguistic capabilities of the existing web, by wrapping largely English-only lexemes around existing, meaningful text. We have virtually no practical examples of such schemes working to any productive ends, and examples of them failing, not least among these the AI projects that the Semantic Web too nearly resembles.[10]

Today there is no more iconic exemplar of the web than Google's main search engine. Google relies on what has become a clear and repeated success strategy in computing: by putting huge numbers of multiple, parallel, redundant, and essentially "dumb" processors together, one can churn huge amounts of raw data in relatively little time, and retrieve essentially any connected aspects of that data in response to queries. This is *all* done with raw-text searching, even when the data resources may have structured elements, largely because there is as yet no full mechanism for querying a host's structured data (this is untrue, for example, in many business environments). To Google, and to philosophers, and to linguists, digital text is just text, even if it is XML. XML is just more text. It does not necessarily make it "easier" to find aspects of a text because they are "pointed out" via XML markup; it can make the searching task harder, especially when it is human beings and not machines who are the ultimate users of the search results. To the degree that Google has implemented sophisticated search algorithms that rank closeness of various search terms to each other, hidden markup may impede Google's own ability to search the text in question, or force it to maintain separate plain-text repositories of marked-up text.

Google's power, simplicity, and success and its utility for us relies in part on the assumption that much web data will be largely unmarked—except, ideally, for library card-like metadata that is already incorporated into web applications. This makes it difficult to see how searching might be *better* if text were widely marked up, especially if plain-text versions of texts are not offered in addition to richly marked versions. And unless a scheme is developed to decide which aspects of texts to richly mark in a way that does not simply repeat lexemes already occurring in the text itself, a scheme that itself seems improbable on conceptual grounds, it will be hard to see what additional lexical value the markup can add to the text in question. So instead XML is used as a series of minimal guidelines for metadata specification and formatting, which is fine enough, but in this way not a significant improvement over consistently applied HTML, and much harder for the researcher to understand. It is also used as a de facto way of standardizing web content. If the goal was simply to standardize web formatting of important documents we could have talked about that as an open political question, but it has not been considered.

I see nothing in particular in the W3C proposals suggesting that raw XML should become an authoring tool, and I do not see anything in Oxygen or other XML tools to suggest that they are meant to be used as primary document processors. (When XML or database content management is appropriate, for example in blogs, the XML is kept in the background and used to create a user-focused interface for content production, as in all modern blogging tools.) I see no reason to expect that the coming generations of digital humanists will prefer to write raw XML when writing connected prose; I know few who do. It is hard to imagine how connected prose would benefit from extensive XML markup; it is easy to see how a minimal sort of structuring markup might be useful for standardized institutional storage, but while this is a typical use of XML it is not necessarily in philosophical harmony with the rest of the web. Perhaps as importantly, corpora of language—both textual and spoken—are now a routine part of linguistic practice, and these corpora are not usually richly marked with semantic terms, for reasons already discussed. When such semantic tagging is used, it is usually done for further application processing and for research purposes—which has not yet produced powerful means of accessing otherwise-hidden aspects of the semantics in question.[11]

Digital text, for the most part, is just text, and for the most part text is just language. Language, a fundamental human practice, does not have a good history of conforming to overarching categorization schemes. It seems not merely reasonable but likely that the best-known humanistic worldviews would resist applications of schemes like the Semantic Web to ordinary textual data, and in particular to focus attention on what humanists have always put first: our responsibility to each other as human beings, and our profound interest in and respect for human creations, including both computers and language. While such a view is compatible with the perspective that embedded markup is itself potentially harmful (as no less a thinker than Ted Nelson has suggested, 1997; also see Smith 2001), it at least leads to what practice itself has shown the OHCO theorists: where semantic markup is concerned, less is more. Where the humanities are concerned, the linguistic imperatives offered by computers and the web seem less promisingly those of markup-based machine communication than the communicative opportunities computers may open for human beings who need them—and no less the avenues of linguistic communication whose existence computers help put into jeopardy.[12]

Monolingualism of the World Wide Web

Another tempting but inaccurate analogy between programming languages and natural languages can be found along the axis of *linguistic diversity*. It is no accident, and no less remarkable, that insofar as something akin to natural language "runs" computers, that language would have to be identified with contemporary standard written English. Contemporary standard written English is remarkably effective at projecting itself as typical of "the way language works"; it is also remarkably atypical, both from an historical perspective and in a synchronic perspective, that is, as one out of the world's 6,000 or so languages. Of the approximately 120 writing systems in active use, only a handful can be said to have developed English-style alphabetic orthography "internally"—that is, much prior to the imposition of direct colonial administration by European countries (Coulmas 1989, 1996; Skutnabb-Kangas 2000; also see Derrida 1976, 1979, 1996a; Golumbia 1999; Ong 1977, 1982). Some societies have found themselves compelled to re-write their languages so as to either comport with Western standards or, simply, to become Romanized or quasi-English (Skutnabb-Kangas 2000). Few have been standardized to anything like the Greco-Roman degree (in other words, most non-Western writing systems include many "left over" characters, alternate forms, competing systems, and so on); each of them presents unique difficulties for computers, such that native speakers of any of the world's non-European major languages experience a routine degree of difficulty in using these languages in the computational environment.[13]

Few English-only speakers realize the implications of the fact that almost all programming languages consist entirely of English words and phrases, and that most operating systems are structured around *command-line interfaces* that take English writing, and specifically imperative statements, as their input (Lawler 1999). The extraordinary success of software engineers in India, Russia, Japan, and Hong Kong (among other places) maps onto the metropolises created and maintained by world empires, and correlates no less with the spread of English-style education and enforced English language and orthography (Skutnabb-Kangas 2000). It seems no accident that computers rely on the availability of standardized text and that the availability of persons who are fluent in computer engineering emerge from cultures where English-style standardization is produced and often enforced. This has not resulted in the wide availability of native-language resources, even in the widely distributed alternate orthographies, most especially at the software development level. One might say that, despite the ability of computers to produce *documents* in Hindi or Japanese, computers and networks themselves speak and operate in only a fragmentary, math- and logic-oriented chunk of English.

This is visible most readily on the Internet. In at least three, connected ways, the web looks like an instrument of multilingualism, but on closer examination seems largely to be organized around Westernized, English-based categories and language concepts. First, the HTML for most web documents, the markup which surrounds the document's content (along with JavaScript and several other noncompiled script languages), is fundamentally in English, so that it is necessary to understand the English meaning of certain words and abbreviations in order to read a document's source (and in a critical sense, to interpret the document). Second, web servers and web software are themselves usually confined solely to English, necessitating (among other things) English-based CGI (Common Gateway Interface) programs and directories, meaning that the URLs of most web documents are largely in English (in fact, it is only recently that it has been proposed that browsers allow any non-Roman characters in URLs, despite which few web servers actually take advantage of this capability). Related to this is the fact that the entire operating system world is run by English products and with English directory structures, such that most web-based categorization tools (like Yahoo!) are organized around profoundly Western-style categories and category systems—often, the exactly equivalent English titles, viewable as the HTML link for any categories on any non-English Yahoo! website, including most of the pages that have Roman character representations and those that do not.

From the perspective of world linguistic history, programming and scripting languages represent not a diversity of approaches so much as a remarkable extension of an already highly standardized phenomenon: English. This might seem a strong claim, were it not exactly in line with one of the most remarkable features of contemporary world culture, namely, the global replacement of local languages with English and, to an important but lesser degree, other standardized languages (Illich 1980; Nettle and Romaine 2000). We have been taught to think of the computer revolution as a fundamental extension of human thinking power, but in a significant way mass computerization may be more accurately thought of as a vehicle for the accelerated spread of a dominant standard written language. (Computer-based writing may only be less successful, that is to say, than are mass media such as television and pop music as media for spreading prestige English as a spoken tongue.)

At the same time, one of the things computers have also done is to have helped expose and call into question the spread of English and other standardized languages, just as this spread has taken on new power exactly through the spread of computers and the bureaucratic systems of control they bring with them (Illich 1980; Phillipson 1992; Skutnabb-Kangas 2000; Spivak 1999; Warschauer 2002, 2003). The problem with this spread, which must always be presented as instrumental, and is therefore always profoundly ideological, is that it arises in suspicious proximity to the other phenomena of cultural domination toward which recent critical work has made us especially sensitive. I am thinking here of the strong tendency in the West (although not at all unique to us) to dismiss alternative forms of subjectivity, sexuality, racial identity, gender, kinship, family structure, and so on, in favor of a relatively singular model or small set of models. Of course some of this is due to the cultural oppression that goes along with every empire; what in particular seems to be at issue the world over is a loss of cultural diversity and a coordinate loss of linguistic diversity, and the coordination between these two is complex.

By "cultural diversity" here I mean something broader than what is sometimes understood by the phrase—not merely styles of dress or manners but the principles and guides by which the whole of social structure is elaborated, and within the matrix of which identity is crafted. Today we radically underestimate the power of these forces, despite their clear implication in the production of modern society, itself far more uncharacteristic than typical in the tens of thousands of years of human history (Mander 1992). This has become so much the case that we have encased in terms like *globality* and *modernity* the apparently inevitable spread of written English and other European languages (Spivak 1999). We have convinced ourselves that, because the people on the ground seem to want to learn these languages, then they must *only* constitute tools to attain economic status, rather than a deep part of one cultural position that has historically spread as much through explicit imposition as through mutual agreement.

Mass standardization and geographically wide linguistic and cultural uniformity are not necessities. In world linguistic history, there have been any number of periods of deep, longstanding linguistic interchange between high numbers of linguistically diverse groups, where high levels of structural diversity correlate with low cultural diversity over small geographic areas, but higher cultural diversity over larger areas (Dixon 1997; Nettle 1999; Nettle and Romaine 2000; Nichols 1992; Sapir 1921). In other words, there are areas where high linguistic diversity over a wide geographic area correlates with a high level of linguistic and cultural adaptation to local geographic conditions, and a great deal of linguistic variation and change over relatively short periods of time. There even seems to be anecdotal evidence promoting the usefulness of the kind of ecological management exercised by humans in such geographic areas, coupled with any number of attitudes toward technological progress that are quite different from ours (Abram 1996; Nettle and Romaine 2000).

There is simply no doubt that computers and languages are closely tied together, for reasons that are as much ideological as they are intellectual or philosophical. It is hard to understand how human beings could take advantage of computer power without linguistic interfaces of some sort;

many anti-computer prejudices hang on in the memories of those who had to interact with computers solely through languages composed almost entirely of mathematical equations (so-called assembly languages, machine languages, and so on) and (to human readers) meaningless symbolic abstractions (as in the physical substrate of punch cards and computer tape). At the same time, these linguistic interfaces exact a significant price in performance and, to a lesser extent, reliability, such that the great bulk of computer programming in the contemporary world—programming for devices that are embedded in larger machines like automobiles, airplanes, manufacturing equipment, and medical devices—is still performed in quasi-mathematical languages by a narrow band of experts.[14] In an interesting sense, these computers and languages are more language-neutral than are the great bulk of "proper" computers with which the general public is familiar, but their pervasiveness gives the lie to the view that our computing infrastructure is the only one possible; rather, the "English-only" characteristic of modern computers is clearly a layer that mainly serves social, and therefore ideological, functions.

There is no doubt that the widespread access to computers, and so distributed access to information that is updated frequently, is part of what has made linguists and social critics aware of the situation of so-called Endangered Languages. Computer users for whom the large majority languages are not their mother tongue are acutely aware that computers demand language sacrifice as a price of entry; this is not merely true, as might be expected, of speakers of minority and endangered languages, but even of non-Indo-European majority languages that do have computerized orthographies (like Japanese, Mandarin Chinese, and Korean); it can be no accident that English is rapidly becoming a shared lingua franca across the Indian subcontinent just as computers are spreading, nor is it accidental that Indian writing systems, despite their widespread availability, are much less widely used on computers than one might expect. Like Hollywood films and U.S. television, the computer exerts a powerful attractive pull toward English that is perceived by many non-English-speakers as "modern opportunity." To succeed in the world, to be something, to be somebody, one must abandon the old-hat, traditionalist models of thinking associated with "home languages," and move into the modern, technological language of the metropolis, which just means English. In this way computers serve one of the most disturbing and the least-considered powers of globalization: the economic power to tell people that their way of doing things is worth less than culture empowered with modern technology, that their ways of life are stagnant and uninteresting, and that to "make something of themselves" they must "get on board" with modernity, represented by the computer and the significant education computing requires, often (due to children being the ones who feel this pull most strongly) to the real disparagement of whatever they choose to leave behind.

While it may be a coincidence that something like half of the world's 6,000 languages are said to be "dying out" just as the computer spreads across the world, and this is exactly the frame in which the two events are presented in the literature even by sympathetic writers (see Crystal 2004), it is conceivable that these trends are in fact two sides of a single coin. Networked computing has helped to inform people of the eradication of minority languages, but often in a frame that suggests these languages are already "lost," and in any case so "backwards" and nontechnological that they are of little use to the modern age. Wikipedia is dedicated to presenting its content in every possible language, but like Unicode it is limited in practice to those languages that have already been "reduced" to written orthographies, and the significant lack of emphasis on making the web operate via sound helps to enforce the focus of these projects almost exclusively on majority practices. The lack of modernization and standardization found in some nonmajority practices often produces a kind of exhaustion in computer scientists; if Southern Indian languages cannot be fixed down to a small number of scripts, why bother with them at all? If the letter forms change so often when writing that one can scarcely determine a fixed set of forms to encode, computationalist ideologies suggest, maybe it would be better to just leave them off the computer altogether.

There are few more obviously disturbing applications of such thinking than in the One Laptop Per Child (OLPC) project spearheaded by Nicholas Negroponte. This project, which promises to give many of the world's disadvantaged children inexpensive laptops which they can use freely for any kind of education, has much to recommend it and yet on cultural grounds seems highly disturbing. There could be almost no more efficient means of eradicating the remaining non-Western cultures of the world than to give children seductive, easy-to-use tools that simply do not speak their languages. The fact that this problem is so rarely discussed in the literature on Negroponte's project shows the degree to which computers already have encoded into them a profound linguistic ideology, and the fact that few researchers if any are working on ways to solve this problem before "giving computers to everyone" shows exactly the values that propel much of the computer revolution. Like the Semantic Web, the fact that such resources are profoundly majoritarian is considered entirely secondary to the power they give to people who have so little and to the power such projects create. Of course disadvantaged people deserve such access, and of course the access to computer power will help them economically. The question is whether we should be focusing much more of our intellectual energy on making the computer infrastructure into an environment that is not majoritarian, rather than spending so much of our capacity on computerizing English, translating other languages into English, getting computers to speak, or, via projects like the Semantic Web, getting them to "understand" language for us.

PART THREE

CULTURAL
COMPUTATIONALISM

CHAPTER SIX

Computation, Globalization, and Cultural Striation

IN THE LATE 1960S and early 1970s, Marxist economists outlined a theory that was received with a certain amount of surprise, one that has been largely pushed aside today. The thesis was that despite the appearance of competition, most contemporary global economic power was held by a few, massive, concentrated centers—in short, monopolies. In critiques of Joseph Schumpeter (1942), orthodox pure "free market" capitalist economy, and also of more moderate, statist Keynesian economics, the writers Harry Braverman (1974) and Paul Baran and Paul Sweezy (Baran and Sweezy 1966; Sweezy 1972) suggested that capitalism exerts a continuous pressure, even in apparently democratic societies, toward monopolistic and oligarchical organization, and that the concentration of profit among a small group of institutions makes the systems that operate under the name capitalism nevertheless obey both macro-level laws of competition and at the same time laws of power politics, again demonstrating the resemblance of the modern corporation to the apparently pre-modern institution of the principality. Without a socialist revolution, which like many orthodox Marxists these theorists at times argued was inevitable, Braverman, Baran, and Sweezy specifically worried that a strong antidemocratic impulse in the most powerful corporations was starting to gain traction in the United States and worldwide, even as our culture told us that democracy was emerging everywhere.

Among the most powerful tools for what I will call oligarchical capitalism is the use of large-scale pricing power to manipulate human behavior and the actions of the working class so as to deprive them of real political choice and power, in the name of apparently laudable goals like efficiency, personalization, individual desire and need. While the discourses of these goals are also advertised as part of the computer revolution, when looked at from a perspective inside oligarchical capitalism they can be seen, like the work of Customer Relationship Management (CRM) and Enterprise Resource Planning (ERP) and other software regimes, to be variables that can be directly manipulated at the service of corporate interests. It is no accident that the changing nature of the machine is one of the tropes we see repeatedly in the works of the monopoly capital theorists, just as today the "transition to a service economy" is one of the unexamined truisms of contemporary culture. Despite the obvious differences between what we characteristically understand as physical labor and what we understand as service or informational labor, I am again arguing that this difference may in fact be far less salient to politics at both a personal and community level than the degree to which members of a given institution in fact participate in the management of the organization or are instead subject to strong, hierarchical rule.

Cultural Striation

Among the most widely used of computer technologies with impact not just on business *per se* but perhaps an even more clear and also covert impact on public life and culture are technologies whose explicit purpose is to striate the contents of public cultural existence, which in virtue of their creation as private, proprietary, and sometimes patented technologies puts them almost entirely beyond the oversight (and often even the knowledge) of the public. Financial, legal, and health care information often exceeds the mere recordkeeping functions of which the public is aware; software applications in these industries enable so-called data mining and other forms of analysis that allow the creation of what can only be understood as new knowledge, which is completely inaccessible to the general public. Yet this information is used exactly and explicitly for the control of public behavior, for the manipulation of populations and individuals as well as for the small-scale provision or denial of services. It is well known that so-called managed care insurance companies or HMOs engage in the denial of medical service to individuals precisely so as to maximize profits, even in cases of life-threatening illness. What is less-well-understood is the degree to which computer models have been used to dictate such policies, so that even the inevitable litigation that follows a pattern of service denial is precalculated in the system, and certain classes of individuals and conditions are specifically targeted for denial, not for policy or medical reasons but because they have been statistically identified as the best candidates for profitable service prevention.

Such models are often proprietary and as such inaccessible for examination by the public and academic researchers; the emergence of this circumstance from the historical protection of business secrets is understandable, but this history seems not to have anticipated the degree to which such policies could infiltrate almost every aspect of human life and, in part because of the closed nature of many computer systems, be almost wholly inaccessible for outside examination. Such a problem is only now being recognized in the provision of electronic election services by Diebold, itself a company with a long history in the development of closed, proprietary computational systems. Today, businesses in every industry make use of such systems of predictive analysis, data mining, and customer behavior emulation, all of which raise profound questions about democratic control of government, and the relationship of oligarchical capitalism to the regulatory functions of the State.

Among the few spheres in which such tools are visible for public view, if not control, or oversight, is the use of tools of highly precise statistical striation used throughout the advertising and sales industries under vague terms like "target marketing." In our age of the rhetoric of multiculturalism, postcolonialism, and identity politics, the overcoded racialist and gendered politics of such systems are strikingly overt, as is the ubiquity of such systems in contemporary circulations of capital.[1] In the trade this practice is called "geodemography," a term coined by Jonathan Robbin, "a sociologist who [during 1963–83] developed a computer-powered marketing technique" (Burnham 1983, 90), largely to predict the behavior of voters in political campaigns. The best-known current provider of such services is a U.S. company called Claritas, founded by Robbin himself, and today owned by the same Nielsen corporation that conducts surveys on media usage. Claritas and its forerunners have used computers to develop a suite of marketing applications which striate the consuming population into statistical aggregates that allow pinpointed marketing, financing, advertising, and so forth. In the popular media these efforts are sometimes referenced in terms of TV shows that "reach the crucial 19-to-34 male consumer," and so forth, but this characterization deliberately undersells the culturalist and racialist presumptions of contemporary computer-based marketing systems.

Typical among the product Claritas produces is one called Claritas PRIZM, which "divides the U.S. consumer into 14 different groups and 66 different segments" (Claritas 2007). The 14 different groups include Group U1, "Urban Uptown":

The five segments in Urban Uptown are home to the nation's wealthiest urban consumers. Members of this social group tend to be affluent to middle class, college educated and ethnically diverse, with above-average concentrations of Asian and Hispanic Americans. Although this group is diverse in terms of housing styles and family sizes, residents share an upscale urban perspective that's reflected in their marketplace choices. Urban Uptown consumers tend to frequent the arts, shop at exclusive retailers, drive luxury imports, travel abroad and spend heavily on computer and wireless technology. (Ibid.)

"Urban Uptown" can be viewed in contrast to Group U3, "Urban Cores":

Urban Cores segments are characterized by relatively modest incomes, educations and rental apartments, but affordable housing is part of the allure for the group's young singles and aging retirees. One of the least affluent social groups, U3 has a high concentration of Hispanics and African-Americans, and surveys indicate a fondness for both ethnic and mainstream media and products. Among the group's preferences: TV news and daytime programming, Spanish and black radio, telephone services and pagers, cheap fast food and high-end department stores. (Ibid.)

Each Group is further striated into what Claritas calls "segments." For example, "Urban Uptown" includes five segments (each of which includes a representative graphic icon), among them "04, Young Digerati" and "07, Money and Brains":

04. Young Digerati—Young Digerati are the nation's tech–savvy singles and couples living in fashionable neighborhoods on the urban fringe. Affluent, highly educated and ethnically mixed, Young Digerati communities are typically filled with trendy apartments and condos, fitness clubs and clothing boutiques, casual restaurants and all types of bars—from juice to coffee to microbrew.

07. Money and Brains—The residents of Money & Brains seem to have it all: high incomes, advanced degrees and sophisticated tastes to match their credentials. Many of these citydwellers—predominantly white with a high concentration of Asian Americans—are married couples with few children who live in fashionable homes on small, manicured lots. (Ibid.)

Similarly, "Urban Cores" includes five segments, among them "59. Urban Elders" and "65. Big City Blues":

59. Urban Elders—For Urban Elders—a segment located in the downtown neighborhoods of such metros as New York, Chicago, Las Vegas and Miami— life is often an economic struggle. These communities have high concentrations of Hispanics and African-Americans, and tend to be downscale, with singles living in older apartment rentals.

65. Big City Blues—With a population that's 50 percent Latino, Big City Blues has the highest concentration of Hispanic Americans in the nation. But

it's also the multi-ethnic address for downscale Asian and African-American households occupying older inner-city apartments. Concentrated in a handful of major metros, these young singles and single-parent families face enormous challenges: low incomes, uncertain jobs and modest educations. More than 40 percent haven't finished high school. (Ibid.)

While marketing methods like the ones employed by Claritas existed before the widespread use of computers, the close tie between computerization and this kind of heavily striated and statistical method could not be clearer: they are what Lisa Nakamura calls "cybertypes," which work to preserve taxonomies of racial difference (Nakamura 2002, 29; also see Nakamura 2007)—perhaps they are even elaborated with a particularly striated, hierarchical quality in cyberspace. Mass computerization is what enables such methods to be easily distributed and what allows the underlying data to be collected and analyzed.

The methods and categories employed by Claritas PRIZM exemplify the computationalist view of culture. Despite neoliberal claims to equal-access democracy and to the cultural power of multiculturalism and antiracist discourse, the PRIZM categories could not be more explicitly racialist. Perhaps more powerfully than the identitarian discourse often attacked by neoliberal mouthpieces, PRIZM sees individuals only and exactly in how they fit into racial, ethnic, and economic groups; Claritas customers purchase the PRIZM products exactly to target their messages (which may be commercial, charitable, or even political) to PRIZM groups and segments, and typically cannot see further down into the database to the individual level. Instead, PRIZM segments are specifically tied to various kinds of commercial and political behavior, and its customers choose to adjust their behavior according to the statistical predictions implied or offered by this and other Claritas software packages.

Explicitly racialized practices like so-called mortgage redlining have been at least partially eliminated by litigation and regulation, but such governmental practices presume corporations operate via exclusively racist operations: that a bank decides to charge higher mortgage loan rates to black people, for example. Governmental oversight has not found a way to manage—if legislators are even aware of them—the complex and highly striated groupings created by packages like PRIZM, despite the fact that they are in some ways at least as culturally disturbing as straightforward racist policies. Because a segment like "Big City Blues" includes not just "the highest concentration of Hispanic Americans in the nation" but also "downscale Asian and African-American households occupying older inner-city apartments," it is not even clear how EEOC-type legislation could be crafted so as to regulate its operation, unless it simply and overtly targets exactly the practices in which Claritas and other similar companies engage.

Yet the commercial services, financial conditions, and even political circumstances of any individual's life in the United States (and, increasingly, worldwide) are in many ways determined by services like the one Claritas advertises in PRIZM. Membership in a given Claritas segment is largely (though not exclusively) determined through postal zip code; if one belongs to a given segment in aggregate, there is of course no way to adjust one's membership in the group, nor could there be. Few Americans are even aware of the PRIZM segments or their power over so much of their lives, much less the other systems that are not even advertised to the public—in fact it is a testimony to the business-internal existence of such powerful computational tools as PRIZM that even a portion of it is exposed to the public via advertising, considering how overt its implementation of bias toward various races, genders, nationalities, and ages. PRIZM is just a tool to striate the U.S. population at a level of sophistication beyond that which most human beings can conceptualize without computational assistance, and in this sense both its existence and its effects can be and have been essentially hidden in plain sight; like the complex operations of airline ticket pricing software, it has grown so effective that its functions can be exposed through their effects with little fear of public reprisal.

As a type of product heavily used throughout many global institutions, PRIZM represents the kind of oligarchical power computers help to instance, concentrating power and pushing it upwards while reducing large masses of smooth data into tractably hierarchical, striated layers. These reductive striations become in some important way more real than the underlying data they represent, even if, as in the PRIZM case, what is represented is precisely people's everyday social behavior. Like the financial models propagated by banks and companies like Fair, Isaac, these representations can be said to have more commercial and even political salience than do individuals or explicit political groups, since individuals and even most groups have little access to them. To be sure, political parties in particular take great advantage of such tools, and there can be little doubt that they have been effectively used so as to predict and statistically manipulate political behavior, especially voting behavior, in ways that would seem quite foreign to the average citizen. Since both parties theoretically have equal access to at least some of these tools, one can argue that they are somewhat equally distributed—but at the same time the lack of awareness of the general public about such tools and their use in politics and public institutions suggests that they continue, today, to be used primarily for the enrichment of the power elite (Mills 1956).

Computationalist World History

Despite the obscurity of the processes used by companies like Claritas and software packages like ERP and CRM, to some extent their operation, since it is characteristic of so much computation, is readily visible to and even widely used by members of the public. In fact, within a wide variety of computer games, one can see a process exactly isomorphic to such software applications, in which quantified resources are maximized so that the player can win the game. The most direct example of such games are the so-called Real-Time Strategy (RTS) games, in which players build kingdoms by supervising the growth of basic resources such as food, stone, wood, and so on. By using "villagers" or "drones" to maximize the collection of such resources, the player attempts to outwit the similar efforts of his or her opponents. Such games reveal exactly the oligarchical-monopolist, Statist, even fascist politics at issue throughout the computerized world, its reductionist conception of social process and politics, the intertwined nature of economics and politics within the computer world, and its particular conception of how culture relates to the rest of the social world.

Playing an RTS game such as *Warcraft, Starcraft, Civilization, Alpha Centauri, Age of Empires, Empire Earth,* or any of a number of others, one experiences the precise systemic quality that is exploited for inefficiency in ERP software and its particular implementations (see Chapter 7). One simply sets the "difficulty level"—or degree of economic efficiency—to the degree demanded by the rest of the business system. This is of course a profit level determined by the various constituents of a company, most especially its financial determinants including its accountants and accounting software. Of course the values of some elements of the ERP formalization are bounded within limits set by the real world; presumably a car company is better off if it tracks the precise number of cars it is actually producing, windshields available, and so on—presumably. But it is clear that the values of these variables are set not by absolute, objective reality but by human beings whose ability to meet the demands of quantification are limited; companies today seem to be failing in no small part due to the ability of human beings to deceive themselves about the objectivity of the values ascribed to these abstractions. Though ERP runs on the logic of the game, winning at running a business is not the same as winning a game. Maximizing human social satisfaction is a goal we hardly understand, and it is not something we talk about often; in RTS terms, a "satisfied system" becomes static and uninteresting very quickly. This would seem to be somewhat the opposite of how we would like society to be arranged; we would seem to want our society to be as satisfied as possible, with as little conflict as possible between members (on a brief analysis).

Much of the time, such games are played against computer or so-called Artificial Intelligence opponents, avatars of the player represented by the computer, often representing possible real-world strategies. To a neutral observer, the play of an AI player and a human player are virtually indistinguishable (that is, if one watches the screen of a computer game, rather than the actions of the human player). What we call AI has among its greatest claims to successes within the closed domain of computer games, inside of which AI opponents might even be said at times to pass a kind of Turing Test (or perhaps more appropriately, human beings are able to emulate the behavior of computers to a strong but not perfect degree of approximation). Of course this is mainly true depending on the difficulty level at which the game is set. Because the world-system of an RTS game is fully quantified, succeeding in it is ultimately purely a function of numbers. By setting the difficulty level high enough, one can guarantee that the computer will win: it is simply possible to apply more computing power to a simulation than a human being can possibly muster.

One does not, at any rate, win an RTS game by maximizing efficiency; one wins the game, just as much, through the armies and destructive weaponry that seem unavoidably attached to almost every RTS model, which often represent explicit iterations of historical and science-fiction conquest narratives. Much of the game architecture was developed with either an "adventure" model (in which the hero gathers resources in order to fight successively more powerful opponents), or a so-called "civilization" model, in which either abstract (often space-based) civilizations, or actual historical civilizations from world history, fight with each other using successively more powerful weapons. In *Civilization* or *Age of Empires*, the user takes the role of an historical "conqueror" such as Napoleon, Cortés, or even, in one version, Montezuma; the increasingly elaborate and technologically sophisticated wars one produces lack precisely the unique contingency of history itself. Users play these games over and over, "addictively," playing one side and now the other, pitting two Aztec kingdoms against each other, displacing the unconscious of history itself onto the unconsciously driven will to power of winning the game through acquisition and violent, oppositional destruction. Somehow the rationality of software representation leads not to the world of choice but to the inevitability of *re-*

alpolitik. Instead of a paradise of informatic exchange, the world of computer representation is a bitter and political one of greedy acquisitiveness, callous defeat, and ever-more-glorious realizations of the will-to-power. It seems inevitable that the result of such pursuits is most commonly boredom. Like a sybaritic emperor, the unconscious desires served by such an approach are never satisfied, and can never find enough of the resources and excitement they need. The game thus "covertly" satisfies the unconscious, but offers only traumatic repetition as satisfaction, more consumption as the solution to the problem of being human.

Among the most paradigmatic of RTS games is Microsoft's *Age of Empires,* which has been issued so far in three major iterations. In *Age of Empires,* as in similar games, a player begins by choosing which race/-civilization/nation to play. While some games allow a certain amount of customization to such details, in *Age of Empires* these choices are programmatically constrained. One chooses a nation or race based in part on the graphical appeal of the animations used to represent the group, but also practically because each group gives the player certain characteristics (benefits and drawbacks) that are programmatically tied to the initial choice. While such choices are the precise domain of discussion in nearly all fields of humanities and education today, within the computerized world they are presented with a certainty that few thinkers of any stripe would today endorse. Again, population thinking within the striated computer world trumps individual variation.

In the full version of *Age of Empires II* (including its *Conquerors* expansion), for example, the player chooses from one of 18 "game civilizations," including such textbook standard groups as Britons, Huns, Vikings, Japanese, Koreans, Chinese, Aztecs, and Mayans. Of course for the sake of efficient gameplay such civilizations are restricted to ones that established geographically large scale empires, and also present most nation-states as internally consistent; while there are both Mongols and Chinese in the game, there is no question of representing the Mongolian minority that exists in the non-Mongolian part of China, or of politically problematic minorities such as Tibetans and Uyghurs, or of the other non-Han Chinese minorities (e.g., Li, Yi, Miao). There is no real ability to depict intergroup interactions, hybridization, or blending; the existence of racialized and national groupings is presented as a kind of natural fact that cannot be questioned or changed in the course of gameplay, as if this were also true of the global history the game will display: as if from the beginning of history until the present day there simply were groups with names like "Briton," "Hun," and "Byzantine" whose coming-into-being was outside of the history that, in historical fact, produced them.

The main reason for players to choose an ethnicity or nation in the course of the game is to realize certain benefits and drawbacks that affect gameplay as a whole. For example:

- Britons
  - Foot archer civilization
  - Shepherds work 25% faster
  - Town Center costs 50% less wood
  - Foot Archers gain + 1 range in Castle Age and an additional + 1 in the Imperial Age (for + 2 total)
  - Team Bonus—Archery units produced 20% faster
- Koreans
  - Tower and naval civilization
  - Villagers + 2 Line of Sight
  - Stone miners work 20% faster
  - Tower upgrades free (Bombard Tower requires Chemistry)
  - Towers range + 1 in Castle Age, +1 in Imperial Age (for + 2 total)
  - Siege units have + 1 range
- Aztecs
  - Infantry and monk civilization
  - Start with Eagle Warrior, not Scout Cavalry
  - Villagers carry + 5
  - All military units created 15% faster
  - Monks + 5 HP for each Monastery technology
  - Team Bonus—Relics + 33% gold
- Mayans
  - Archer civilization
  - Starts with one additional villager and Eagle Warrior (not Scout Cavalry) but less 50 food
  - Resources last 20% longer
  - Archery Range units cost −10% Feudal Age, −20% Castle Age, −30% Imperial Age
  - Team Bonus: Walls cost −50%

Much like the segmentation employed by Claritas PRIZM, these categorizations reduce the complexities of social life to measurable quantities; even further, they employ capability-based labels that define civilizations in terms of particular technologies and characteristics, so that, for example, the Britons can be characterized as a "foot archer civilization." These labels are tendencies, regardless of the degree to which they may or may not apply to historical entities—nations that never developed sea power, for example, will nevertheless develop sea vessels and weapons in at least some editions of *Age of Empires* and similar games.

The whole idea of applying modifiers and bonuses to each civilization hangs on the notion that there is one central history of cultural development that is at least in part common to each nationality and race. In the *Age of Empires* model, at least, this is strictly true: each nation starts in the "Dark Ages," when it has access only to materials made of wood and something like smelted iron, so that it can use swords; then advances to the "Castle Age," when it can use gold and stone to create masonry buildings and learns technologies like gunpowder; and then to the "Imperial Age," when it gains putatively cultural attributes like religion (Monasteries) and higher learning (Universities). The appearance of such buildings, like the animations for citizens, varies just a bit from civilization to civilization, but the underlying progressive history remains identical for each civilization, giving the impression that this progressivist idea of history is universal and was experienced in history by each civilization. As such, *Age of Empires* and similar RTS games do not merely argue but demonstrate that human history is unified, progressive, and linear, and that in particular the development of technology stands as the ultimate end of civilization. Culture *per se* is seen to be no more or less than decoration—a kind of costume, much as culture is seen in the neoliberal versions of museumized cultures the world over that have failed to fully integrate into the noncultural, central (and typically Western) view of technologically developed humanity.

In the most typical game played in *Age of Empires,* there are exactly two ways to win. Since every culture is by definition militaristic, committed to developing a similar kind of army and navy, one can choose to defeat each other nation and thereby achieve military victory (alliances are possible, but are downplayed significantly in this game). One can also win by virtue of overwhelming economic development: by setting the difficulty level of the game low enough (or by playing against human opponents of low-enough skill) that one can generate more economic resources than any other player, thereby creating and sustaining military power beyond the capability of any other player.

In addition to military conflict, the main gameplay of *Age of Empires* and other similar RTS games is twofold: the accumulation of resources and the development of city-states. In *Age of Empires II* resources come in four types: food, wood, stone, and gold. Each civilization may create dozens of basic citizens, which other than being gendered are otherwise indistinguishable, and similar but for clothing details across each civilization. These citizens (unlike in some more complex games like *Civilization*) never protest about the repetitive nature of their work; they simply devote themselves without rest to the collection of resources or to the erection and repair of buildings. The player's actions are limited to directing the citizens to a resource-gathering or building task; unless interrupted by military skirmish, the citizens simply carry out the task perpetually until the game ends. While gathering of wood, gold, and stone is limited to a single function, food can be accumulated through hunting (of sheep and deer conveniently located at random points on the world map), fishing, and both marine and terrestrial farming. Again, these activities are completely identical no matter the civilization one is playing, and food products are not really identified at a detailed enough level to identify what food is being produced nor how it is being consumed.

Instead, all the basic resources produced by a city are used by the player in the service of creating ever-more elaborate buildings and ever-more sophisticated soldiers; the bulk of the program's "technology tree" (the sequence of available upgrades for various devices, implements, and characters in the game) is devoted to military technology. While some attention is paid to the racially identified attributes for a given civilization—so that a civilization specializing in siege weapons will have more elaborate siege devices and more technology upgrades available—the general rule of thumb is that every basic unit and every basic technology is available to every civilization, and that each civilization passes through exactly the same phases of development as it advances in the game. Development ends with the Imperial Age, a triumphal goal toward which every civilization aims.

While its developers would surely claim that such features are a consequence of gameplay necessities and the use of the tools available at hand, there can be little doubt that a game like *Age of Empires II* instances a computationalist perspective on world history. According to this view, history is a competition for resources among vying, bounded, objectified groups; human beings are all driving toward the same accomplishments, even if our racial and national backgrounds tend to pull us with some force in certain directions; everyone would like to rise to advanced levels of technological accomplishment, which can be labeled with a term like "Imperial"; every society, if given the opportunity, would choose to become an empire. In this view there is no hybridization in Homi Bhabha's sense; there is no talking back to power; other civilizations are simply eliminated as their settlements are replaced with those of the winning side.

More than this: the pursuit of historical change is the pursuit of striated power, realized as both an individual "leveling-up" and a societal achievement of historical epoch, themselves licensed by the accumulation of adequate resources, which are always channeled back into an even more intensive will-to-power. There is no question of corruption or self-interest;

the State simply is the user, in a position of mastery that is not a difference of degree but of kind. The user is a godlike presence, controlling almost everything in the game but wholly opaque with regard the game narrative, such as it is. Despite being the most important single presence in the game, the godlike-princelike user does not engage in any of the activities of his or her characters, but instead revels in the total activity of all his or her minions. A true Hobbesian Prince, the user of *Age of Empires* allows his subjects no interiority whatsoever, and has no sympathy for their blood sacrifices or their endless toil; the only sympathy is for the affairs of state, the accumulation of wealth and of property, and the growth of his or her power.

Age of Empires II was one of the first mainstream games to include not just some apparently non-Western empires (Korea, China, Japan) but also indigenous cultures that, whatever their internal imperial ambitions, come down to us today as the subjects rather than the architects of colonization. In a 2006 expansion to *Age of Empires III*, called *The War Chiefs,* players can choose from three indigenous civilizations: Aztec, Iroquois, or Lakota. These figures are depicted with careful attention to detail and admiration, as if to say that if only their war technology had been a little better, perhaps we would today be living in an expanded Iroquois Confederacy instead of the United States—with a kind of condescension appropriate to history's winners. The three indigenous groups are advertised as follows:

The Sioux
With the discovery of gold in their sacred Black Hills, the Sioux had sporadic conflicts with the new immigrants, leading to the Indian Wars and eventually the Battle of the Little Big Horn. The Sioux Nation consists of three geographically distinct divisions of peoples who speak a Siouan language: the Lakota, Dakota, and Nakota. In the language of the Sioux, the names Lakota, Dakota, and Nakota mean "friends."

The Sioux were famed for breeding and training horses. Military advantages of the in-game Sioux civilization are primarily cavalry based. The Sioux strike hard and fast.

The Iroquois
The Haudenosaunee, or Iroquois, formed a League of Five Nations long before Europeans arrived in North America (a sixth Nation joined later). The Iroquois Confederacy had a constitution with rules for the selection of war chiefs, guidelines for council meetings, and even suggestions for proper oratory at funerals. Benjamin Franklin expressed great respect for the Iroquois Confederacy. During the American Revolution some tribes sided with the British, while others sided with the colonists, effectively dismantling the once-powerful Confederacy.

Equipped with artillery and siege weaponry, the in-game Iroquois civilization can mount a powerful but slow-moving assault.

The Aztecs

At their height, the Aztec represented the most powerful civilization in Mesoamerica. The Aztec constructed great cities, most notably Tenochtitlan on the site of modern-day Mexico City. Described by some early Spanish as grander than most European cities, Tenochtitlan's advanced infrastructure included temples, markets, and canals. In Aztec society, membership in the *calpulli* established each individual's religious and secular schooling, as well as warfare training. The men of a calpulli served together in battle and on numerous public works projects. The in-game Aztec civilization is based around a strong infantry consisting of several units, including elite infantry.

Such descriptions continue to reinforce the computational view of history and progress. Civilizations are described exclusively in terms of economics (especially resource accumulation), military technique, and contribution to modern Statecraft. Cultural characteristics are reduced almost exclusively to military attributes, which in turn reduce to the attribute characteristics realized inside of the game; the user is implicitly located above all such characteristics, a technological Prince of whom all the world's peoples are unaware and yet to whom they are all subject.

There is more than a passing similarity between race and civilization as it is realized in RTS games like *Age of Empires* and the Claritas segmentations: they are both faces of the computationalist view of culture, in which race and the State are not at all obliterated but instead essential attributes of the person at a group level which no individual can transcend. The only way to move out of a Claritas segment is to change where one lives, presumably by also changing economic situation as well; but there is little (if any) way to change the internal characteristics of the striated segments. There is no way to change what it means to be a Sioux or Briton or Korean in *Age of Empires,* other than by winning or losing the game; there is no means to alter the fundamental capitalist basis of economy or the fundamental nature of the State or the individual's relationship to it—despite the fact that in, for example, both Lakota and Iroquois societies in historical reality, it seems arguable that something like a relatively more nomadic and thereby less rigidly emplaced State were in strong evidence.

In *Age of Empires* the entire world is reconceptualized as fully capitalist and Statist from the outset, as if capital accumulation and Western-style technology are inevitable goals toward which all cultures have always been striving. "Under" each civilization is something like bare human life without culture, as if culture and humanity can be separated, and there can be little doubt that this bare humanity corresponds in some important way to the existence of the godlike Player who manipulates the game behind the scenes. Only to him or her are attributes changeable, learnable, flexible; the world he or she views is one of complete striation, a story already told and waiting for some kind of inevitable end. Those who don't get on board with the story simply are not worth representing at all, and even if we pay tacit obeisance to those cultures that were, in fact, the subjects of empire and colonization, it is only in so far as to explain why, in the crudest economic and racialist terms, they do not sit where "we" do today, in the abstract and godlike position of the subject (rather than object) of History.

Writing of an RTS-based world history game that has substantially more cultural flexibility than *Age of Empires*, the *Civilization* series developed by Sid Meier, Alex Galloway suggests that "the more one begins to think that *Civilization* is about a certain ideologically interpretation of history (neoconservative, reactionary, or what have you), or even that it creates a computer-generated 'history effect,' the more one realizes that it is about the absence of history of altogether, or rather, the transcoding of history into specific mathematical models" (Galloway 2006, 102–3). " 'History' in *Civilization* is precisely the opposite of history," Galloway writes, "not because the game fetishizes the imperial perspective, but because the diachronic details of lived life are replaced by the synchronic homogeneity of code pure and simple. It is a new sort of fetish altogether. (To be entirely clear: mine is an argument about informatic control, not about ideology: a politically progressive *'People's Civilization'* game, a la Howard Zinn, would beg the same critique)" (ibid., 103). Despite the fact that Galloway sees some of the inherent ideological commitments in the RTS genre, this view gives in to exactly the neoliberal/progressivist/neoconservative view that technology can stand outside of history and that computational processes are themselves synchronic, abstract, and deserving of new analytic methods and frames to be understood—exactly what I am arguing here is untrue. Surely a *"People's Civilization"* computer game might in fact deserve critique along the lines of informatic control; but it is to place computers and ourselves outside of history not to see that there is an historical reason why the successful and popular RTS games are not of the Zinn variety. Computation and striated analyses; essentialist understandings of race, gender, and nation; and politics that emphasize mastery and control do not merely walk hand-in-hand: they are aspects of the same conceptual force in our history.

Also writing of the *Civilization* genre, McKenzie Wark speaks of a "double development, which at one at the same time deepens and proliferates lines of the possible and the actual," which can be called America. It is what is both desired and feared under the rubric of that name, which no longer marks a particular topic but stands for the very capacity to mark and manage space itself, as topology. When playing *Civilization III*, it doesn't matter if the civilization you choose to play is Babylon or China, Russia or Zululand, France or India. Whoever wins is America, in that the logic of the game itself is America. America unbound. (Wark 2007, 75)

Wark comes closer than Galloway to seeing the inherent logics and politics of RTS games and the history they embody, but the proper name America is arguably both too specific and too general to capture what is at issue in the culture of computation. It is too specific because America is not pure computation and not the exclusive progenitor of computational views; at best computationalism can lay claim to a segment of American imperial thinking and history (something like the Federalist perspective associated with Alexander Hamilton); in this sense computationalism, like the conceptual authoritarianism of which it is but a contemporary avatar, has a deeper connection to and association with the development of everything we call the West (and, as RTS games suggest, everything that we call Empire in our world) than the name America would suggest. It is too general because, of course, computationalism is today distributed across varied geographies, nations, and groups, and finds not only advocates but dissenters in all of those societies. Races, nations, and genders are both striated and dismissed as decoration in RTS games in the name of a putative technologically driven urhumanity to which not just America, but other political groups lay claim. In some sense, at least, the impact of computationalism on the world is much less like the historical development of America, and much more like the worldwide reemergence of principality like domains of imperial control today associated with medieval and pre-modern political forms (Hardt and Negri 2000, 2004). A more apt name might be "neoliberalism."

Empires and Computation

Today the world is unevenly covered many times over by entities we routinely refer to as multinational corporations, just as much as and in some ways more completely than it is covered by State-based governments. The emergence of the multinational corporation is itself both a recent development and a return to formations that had been effectively brought under democratic control only with the most intense and directed efforts of both voters and workers. Despite the extreme claims of computational advocates to a general democratization of all forms of information and political control—which on some readings must be identified with something like the means of production for an information age—it is much less noted that the resurgence of neoliberal economics and politics has created a vast array of entities with extra-State political power and control, no longer subject to either the internal (labor union) or external (governmental) oversight that had been the hallmark of liberal political economy.

While at one level it may be harmless enough to imagine that the tremendous power placed at the hands of many individuals offers a democratization of culture, at another level such claims smack of something between naïveté and outright, condescending colonial thought—just, in fact, the intellectual regime we tell ourselves we have surpassed in this nominally postcolonial age. Among the most influential accounts of such cultural transformation is the *New York Times* columnist Thomas Friedman's (2005) *The World Is Flat: A Brief History of the Twenty-First Century*. Exactly as its presumptuous subtitle implies, Friedman's book outlines a series of cultural-economic changes whose shape can only be dimly glimpsed today, a messianic vision in which the "essential impact of all the technological changes coming together today" is that "people can plug, play, compete, connect, and collaborate with more equal power than ever before" (x). While the overt topic of Friedman's book is social change, its substance is almost exclusively technological, and it evinces everywhere a profound technological determinism, simply arguing that inevitable technological changes lead inextricably to social changes of a radical and egalitarian sort. Friedman suggests that what he calls "Globalization 1.0 and 2.0 were driven primarily by European and American individuals and businesses. . . . Because it is flattening and shrinking the world, Globalization 3.0 is going to be more and more driven not only by individuals but also by a much more diverse—non-Western, non-White—group of individuals. Individuals from every corner of the flat world are being empowered" (11).

The trope of empowered individuals, as if they are unconnected from the political and economic and cultural institutions in which they are embedded, is one of the most familiar of our recent times, and we see again and again that this trope does not indicate just how those who already have relatively less power will have any more political influence than they do now, when those with the most power already also have their power increased. Looking simply at computer technology, it seems arguable that this kind of information-technology-based power boost follows a kind of logarithmic curve: while the relatively disempowered are certainly enfranchised by getting on the Internet and getting access to a relatively basic computer, the powerful are themselves radically reinforced via high-speed Internet access; multiple desktop, laptop, and miniature computing devices; computational systems in their automobiles and home entertainment systems, etc. Nobody would, in fact, doubt that the very rich and powerful are among those who take the most advantage of new technologies. How does a 50 percent boost to someone in the bottom rung of society increase his or her power or influence when the top 10 percent is simultaneously experiencing a three- or fourfold magnification of their own power and influence? How much influence and power are there in our world?

Not only does Friedman's analysis simplify what he calls Globalization 1.0 (the colonial project from 1492 until about 1800) and Globalization 2.0 (approximately 1800 to 2000) in terms of the cooperation of ruling elites the world over with powerful interests, but his conception of the radical change underwritten in our current age relies specifically on quasi-magical transformations engendered by computer technology whose mere presence—in some cases, despite its obvious uses and affordances—through some mysterious mechanism makes our world much more equal than it is. Friedman's argument hinges on what he calls "ten forces that flattened the world" (51), all of which are innovations in Information Technology, and few of which transcend majoritarianism, concentration, and segmentation, and Friedman's rhetoric suggests there is no need to explain how his "forces" lead to the radical democratic organization suggested by the apparent meaning of the world being "flat" (and despite the strange and perhaps unintended suggestion that our world is subject to exactly the same rule of empire as was that of Columbus, whatever the operative geometric world pictures may have been in 1492).

Thus the first three of Friedman's "forces" is the introduction of the personal PC with Microsoft Windows; the second is the global connectivity that is approximately coterminous with the rise of the world wide web, but for Friedman also entails the 1995 commercialization of the Internet and Netscape going public; and the third is the introduction of what he rightly calls "work flow software," again almost exclusively a corporate innovation. Sounding virtually like a software advertisement, Friedman writes:

> Boeing wanted it so that its airplane factories in America could constantly re-supply different airline customers with parts, through its computer ordering systems, no matter what country those orders came from, and so its designers could work on planes using airplane engineers from Russia to India to Japan. Doctors wanted it so that an X-ray taken in Bangor could be read in a hospital in Bangalore, without the doctor in Maine ever having to wonder what computers that Indian hospital had. And Mom and Dad wanted it so that their e-banking software, e-brokerage software, office e-mail, and spreadsheet software all would work off their home laptop and be able to interface with their office desktop or BlackBerry handheld device. And once everyone's applications started to connect to everyone else's applications, work could not only

flow like never before, but it could be chopped up, disaggregated, and sent to the four corners of the world as never before. (83)

This is supposed to be an account of the world changing away from corporate power, but in practice it isn't even necessary for Friedman to demonstrate that corporations are getting less powerful; our current rhetoric, perhaps following U.S. popular and judicial usage, suggests that powerful corporations just are powerful individuals. While Friedman's apparently middle-class "Mom and Dad" certainly benefit from the availability and convenience of computerized tools, the main benefits Friedman describes empower centralized corporations to distribute their own work widely, and in some sense even more fully subordinating their workers to management.

Surprisingly, though, despite the ways in which Friedman's first three benefits replicate colonial logic and largely benefit large corporations, the rest of his ten "forces" are even more explicitly focused on corporations. In fact, they are largely devoted to exactly the kinds of business-process tools discussed in Chapter 7: ERP, CRM, and other supply-chain management software. Friedman champions open source software, especially Linux, but primarily because IBM realized that it could profit from the distributed community that had created it (which is itself largely made up of corporate employees working without compensation in their free time); arguably, we still talk about Linux precisely because of its utility to profit-making corporations. Yes, Linux was created through distributed means, but how the outsourcing of work to essentially donated labor contributes to economic or cultural flatness remains a mystery. Then Friedman champions the "withering global competition" (149) enabled by WTO-backed treaties and IT-fueled communication via what he calls "offshoring"; the supply-chain management techniques used by Wal-Mart: "as consumers, we love supply chains, because they deliver us all sorts of goods—from tennis shoes to laptop computers—at lower and lower prices and tailored more and more precisely to just what we want" (155), despite the fact that "as workers, we are sometimes ambivalent or hostile to these supply chains, because they expose us to higher and higher pressures to compete, and force our companies to cut costs, and also, at times, cut wages and benefits" (ibid.).

Here it is plain to see the rhetoric of IT-based transformation giving way to the most traditional, neoliberal, high capitalist claims: what has been flattened via IT is not at all individual access to culture, economics, or political power, but rather the "playing field" for capitalist actors. Thus the flat world of Friedman's title gives way to the familiar ideal of a completely free market, constantly changed by Schumpeterian "destructive transformation" which workers must simply endure; there is no question of worker rights, labor organization, or in fact any of the social values that, for at least much of the first half of the twentieth century, characterized the reformist capitalism in the United States and Europe. What is flattened in Friedman's program is not human interaction at all: it is the marketplace, and with it, labor. Just as Braverman suggests in *Labor and Monopoly Capital* (1974), technology may make an individual worker more powerful, but it simultaneously gives capital and the corporate manager even more power, both for the generation of capital and over the workforce itself: "it is of course this 'master,' standing behind the machine, who dominates, pumps dry, the living labor power; it is not the productive strength of machinery that weakens the human race, but the manner in which it is employed in capitalist social relations" (Braverman 1974, 158).

In a series of incisive and often scathing reviews of the claims for technology and their relation to political power, a number of U.S. technology historians (see especially Adas 2006, and Headrick 1981, 1988; also see Wright 2005) have begun to trace out how the notion of technological progressivism has been especially critical for U.S. identity and how it has promoted this progressivism as a necessary correlative of democratic politics over the globe. Along the way, other approaches to understanding and measuring the worth and value of cultures have been summarily dismissed, usually via the power of attraction rather than explicit critique. Promoting simply the manifest capabilities of modern technology, the avatars of U.S. imperialism implicitly disparage less technologically progressivist ideologies, with the powers of fascination and economic leverage to support them. Thus those groups in East and South Asian societies that also become fascinated with technology often implicitly (and often explicitly) begin to endorse exactly the same progressivist ideology, putting something that looks like "America" to much of the world at the top of a technological heap.

Yet in our current climate one wonders more and more if it is America, or the United States, or any specific nationality that has placed itself at the zenith of technology, or whether, viewed more subtly, a different kind of power has emerged to some degree of its own making. Rapid change in communication technologies and transportation, in particular, have made the geographic reality of nation-states far less meaningful than they once were. Changes in U.S. and worldwide corporate law, along with these technological changes, have allowed the so-called multinational corporation to be much more than it ever was. Even in the days of the State colonial companies, geographic reach was often accompanied by communicative lag, thus allowing time for Bhabha-style colonial ambivalence to develop in colonial outposts, at least to a limited extent.

Today's corporations no longer need to wait for information to percolate in from the remotest outposts; information is not merely solicited but actively collected from every point on the Earth. Where once much of the Earth was largely "smooth" terrain to which lines of segmentation might be intermittently applied, today all of the Earth's land mass, and a great part of its waters, are constantly surveilled by electronic monitoring, all of which inherently places locations on a single, global grid. The grid is so unquestioned and so available now that even mass applications are made available for individuals (see especially Google Earth), though without the analytic and surveillance tools to which corporations and governments have access. There would seem to be no position at all from which to question whether it is desirable or even ethical to persistently map every square inch of global terrain and make it available for electronic processing; since the benefits of such a scheme are so apparently obvious, only cranks or luddites might stand in opposition to them.

Alternate conceptions of culture and politics, which have at times receded so far into the background as to be nearly invisible, might cause one to wonder about such assumptions. Does technology really drive human development? Are we unable to choose what technology will do or should do, and instead must follow technological leads wherever they take us— with "what can be done, shall be done" as the whole of the law? Clearly that is the law of today's culture, from biotechnology to computer technology and even to industrial development, and the efforts of citizenry not directly involved in any given industry to monitor, control, or contain such efforts is met with extreme levels of political and media resistance; the opposition to the nearly unanimous scientific consensus about global warming suggests that our technological progress may make us more, not less, susceptible to deliberate ideological control.

Government, deliberately denuded in part through a series of ideological control measures applied over decades by corporate interests, today exists as much to license and pave the political way for corporate action as it does to constrain that action. And since it has been deliberately depowered, there is no longer a central authoritarian or even oligarchical ruler to worry about this loss of power. Instead, that power has been transferred to the corporations themselves, which appear as a series of globally overlapping quasi-totalitarian entities engaged in a "cold" but nevertheless endless war over resources. The entities fighting this war are nearly indistinguishable; as multinational corporations merge and acquire, divest and split, any sense of a "core business" often vanishes, so that all that is truly left of actual business practices is what is commonly today and perhaps rightly called a *brand,* and which might as well be understood as a national flag or heraldic shield. This sign to which employees are expected to give every aspect of their lives but for their actual blood is one that brooks no disloyalty whatsoever, and under which the employee loses nearly all of the rights governmental theorists like the founders of the American state thought critical to the well-being of any citizenry.

In 2003, one of the former editors of the *Harvard Business Review* published in that journal an essay called "IT Doesn't Matter" (Carr 2003; also see Carr 2004). The article caused a small explosion in the business community, in no small part because Carr was putting forward some obvious truisms that, from an economic-historical perspective, simply must be true: as new tools become more and more widely distributed, their effects become less distinctive and less capable of creating corporate advantage, rather than more so. "You gain an edge over rivals," Carr writes, "only by having something or doing something that they can't have or do. By now, the core functions of IT—data storage, data processing, and data transport—have become available and affordable to all. Information technology's power and presence have begun to transform it from a potentially strategic resource into what economists call a commodity input, a cost of doing business that must be paid by all but provides distinction to none" (Carr 2004, 7). Putting the matter rightly into historical perspective, Carr observes that "as was true with railroads and electricity and highways, it is only by becoming a shared and standardized infrastructure that IT will be able to deliver its greatest economic and social benefits" (ibid., 11).

While Carr's observations seem eminently grounded in history and logical analysis, they were roundly dismissed by business advocates, particularly those in the IT fields. Less noticed, though, is what Carr has observed about the role IT is coming to play in the contemporary corporation and in contemporary social life, which is namely that it is becoming ubiquitous for institutions of a certain size—not merely ubiquitous but unavoidable, a "cost of doing business." But where the other technologies Carr mentions—railroads, electricity, highways—were either built or owned by governments or recognized fairly quickly as the potential loci for oligarchical control, today such an argument is rarely if ever applied to IT, despite the fact that IT is arguably just as much if not much more invasive, much more personal, much more striating, and much more subject to authoritarian misuse than these earlier technologies. Carr's article and subsequent book have been roundly denounced by corporate computationalists, among them Bill Gates, arguably not merely because Carr notes the immediate falsehoods surrounding computers in particular but also because he begins to outline precisely the historical and ideological contexts that computers demand:

Because it marks a break with the past, the arrival of any new infrastructural technology opens the future to speculation. It creates an intellectual clearing in which the imagination is free to play, unconstrained by old rules and experiences. Futurists spin elaborate scenarios of approaching paradises (or, less commonly, infernos), and every new vision of the future serves as a foundation for wider conjecture. . . . Soon, the entire public becomes caught up in the excitement, sharing an intoxicating communal dream of renewal.

Although information technology is a far less revolutionary technology than electricity, it has nevertheless spurred a particularly extreme version of this phenomenon, which culminated in the millennial fervor of the 1990s, when visions of digital utopias became commonplace. With an almost religious zeal, the metaphysicians of the Internet promised to free us from the burdens and constraints of our physical selves and release us into a new and purified world of cyberspace. (Ibid., 138–9)

Despite our clarity about this historical pattern, it is striking how difficult it has been to resist as it emerges again—despite the fact that we know in some important way that such promises will always accompany significant technologies and that they must be false, we seem surprisingly recalcitrant to incorporating that historical understanding into our contemporary moment. No doubt this is in part due to a kind of social hope, a recognition that we face deep and significant problems in our world that demand resolution.

While it is clear that a certain strand of utopian enthusiasm inherent in every technological development—perhaps, as Wark might argue, one closely tied to particularly American ideologies of novelty and renewal (see, e.g., Adas 1989, 2006; Marx 1964; Noble 1977)—there is also a profoundly specific character of the IT revolution that we are especially reluctant to face head-on, despite the fact that our most trenchant social critics have tried continually to bring it to the fore. Computation is not a neutral technology; it is a means for expanding top-down, hierarchical power, for concentrating rather than distributing. The main argument for computers as a means of distributing power is that they increase the capabilities of individual users; but in order for this argument to reach the end its advocates claim, this expansion of individual power would have to somehow cease when it reached the levels of power elites and oligarchical institutions. Yet this is clearly not what has happened; instead it is specifically power elites and oligarchies who have access to the most powerful computers and the newest tools; to ignore this situation simply because those of us relatively low on social hierarchies also receive benefits is to miss the forest for the trees.

Among the only discourses of critical thought about computers today has to do with surveillance; we are repeatedly warned, and rightly so, that computational tools "increase surveillance" in society and increase the sense in which average citizens typically feel (and, in fact, are) watched. This worry is correct in so far as it goes, but it still neutralizes computation by viewing it as an instrument that carries with it certain mechanically produced effects: it remains a kind of technological determinism. The problem we still avoid in these discussions is not technological but social and political: there are powers at work in society that want to watch the mass of the citizenry, and that seek to control social movements via such surveillance. If we had no worries about this political power we would worry much less about the means available to it; if we knew that we could in fact supervise our own government via democratic control, it seems clear we would worry far less about the clandestine surveillance and political manipulation secretive organizations like the CIA have undertaken even before the wide spread of computers. Because computation does empower individuals of all stripes, including those of us who are already extremely powerful, we cannot hope that this sheer expansion of power will somehow liberate us from deep cultural-political problems; because computation sits so easily with traditional formations of imperialist control and authoritarianism, a more immediately plausible assumption would be that the powerful are made even more powerful via computational means than are the relatively powerless, even as everyone's cultural power expands.

Perhaps every bit as disturbing as these considerations is the question of just what power is being inflated as computation grows more and more widespread. Among the oddest but most telling of the cultural changes accompanying the computer revolution is the one that emerges out of the late 1960s social movements, in which a significant segment of youthful intelligentsia embraced the computer as a revolutionary technology that might transform the world along some of the same lines suggested by the counterculture in general (see Turner 2006 for an especially pointed history). In retrospect we can see that this has to be one of the most successful instances of co-optation in the history of social movements; for despite their appearance of transformative power, it is the ability of the computer to expand the feeling and fact of mastery that is most compelling about it. Much like their extended experiments with the profoundly capitalist medium of rock music and profoundly self-gratifying mind-altering substances—visible especially as the supposedly cognitively liberating psychedelic substances gave way to destructive and strongly isolating substances like alcohol, cocaine, and heroin—the counterculture was unable to escape the capitalist and hierarchical strand of dominant American culture it thought itself to be resisting. In the end, this revolution became about exactly the individualistic power it said it was resisting, in no small part via the embracing of a technology that wears its individualist expansionism on its sleeve.

We live in a society that has scarcely begun to learn how to situate itself historically—how to understand the world in which we have arrived and the processes that brought us to where we are now. Looking at the advent of television, railroads, electricity, light, and no less fundamental technologies like the wheel, printing, fire, gunpowder, we can see that they always entail as many problems as they solve, and that their ability to change some (but by no means all) fundamental features of human social life often effects ruinous changes on parts of the human world that in retrospect we may wish not to have lost. It is remarkable that in the act of selling ourselves a story about the revolutionary and progressive nature of technological change via the computer, we ignore the real effects the computer has on the world, and the way in which technology does not and cannot lead to the cultural and political change many of us hope can be created in our world. Just as we have begun to recognize that we may have been wrong for hundreds of years about the "backwardness" of the world's thousands of cultures and languages, especially with regard to their cultural and political sophistication, we have developed a technology that threatens, via a power that is predominantly cultural, to finish the project of eradication that we now say we reject under the name of colonialism. Just as we have begun to learn who the Inca, Aztec, and Maya really were and are, we are writing into life a story about them that says their cultures failed for good reason—because they failed to develop the technologies that characterize cultural evolution and that we use to justify our own mastery over the social and natural worlds (see Bowers 2000, 76–107, on the close ties between computationalism and social Darwinism). Even as we know this control cannot be complete and may in fact be engendering its own (and our own) destruction, the "old story" has emerged with an unexpected power: exactly the power of computation.

We want to imagine computers as deterritorializing our world, as establishing rhizomatic, "flat," nonhierarchical connections between people at every level—but doing so requires that we not examine the extent to which such connections existed prior to the advent of computers, even if that means ignoring the development of technologies like the telephone that clearly did allow exactly such rhizomatic networks to develop. What computers add to the telephonic connection, often enough overwriting exactly telephonic technology, is striation and control: the reestablishment of hierarchy in spaces that had so far not been subject to detailed, striated, precise control. Of course in some individual cases these forces may be resisted, but we must not allow these instances of resistance to obscure the tendencies created by our computation, in our world: and here, contrary to received opinion, it is the nature of our computers to territorialize, to striate, and to make available for State control and processing that which had previously escaped notice or direct control. In this sense the computer works to bring under particular regimes of cultural knowledge those aspects of culture that may have previously existed outside of official oversight; perhaps more disturbingly, these striation and territorializing effects have the consequence of establishing profoundly hierarchized, oligarchical institutions in which individuals are seen not as equal participants but as cogs in larger political machines, as objects available for the manipulation of those with real power. In this sense the rhetoric of revolution that surrounds computers today can be seen as a striking displacement for the real effects of consolidation and concentration that computers in fact enable, and that suggest the transformation of institutions that function via democratic participation, and especially that value the unexpected contributions of minorities, into profoundly majoritarian, unified, authoritarian structures, and that offer the renewal of colonial oversight just as we tell ourselves that the era of colonialism has passed.

CHAPTER SEVEN

Computationalism, Striation, and Cultural Authority

MASS COMPUTERIZATION is part of a complex world-historical politics in which reciprocal desires to see the world as computable and to see computer technology as an ultimate achievement of modernity walk hand-in-hand. It is no accident that globalization includes a massive migration of rural minorities toward cosmopolitan centers, and it is no accident that this migration is most typically accompanied by an explicit embrace of computer technology—which is said, it is critical to remember, to be a great supporter of distributed knowledge and productivity—and a loss of (and often concomitant disparaging of) minority languages and cultures. Such metropolitan migrants are among the most forceful in suggesting that this movement needs to be seen not as a loss, but rather as the rightful attainment of modern opportunity that can only be realized in majority language and technologies.

It cannot and should not be a goal of critical and political reading to deny anyone the right to change their life, to seek economic opportunity, to learn new languages and cultures. Yet at the same it cannot be the job of criticism simply to allow the surface articulations of such movements to stand of and for themselves, if and when there are also underlying political and historical forces at work. To the contrary, only by detailing exactly the nature of these forces do we hold out any hope of managing them. Our received histories of transitions that are accepted as transparent in the public ideology—the Early Modern transition to print culture, for example, or the colonial annexation of much of the world not already part of major empires—have been shown with a certain amount of conclusiveness to be both more contingent and more politically shaped than we are (or can be) taught in school. Yet when it comes to our own cultural frame, we are often content to accept the presentist extension of exactly this ideological picture.

From both internal and external perspectives, computers demonstrate their overweening commitment to striation as a grounding cultural principle. Despite the insistence of neoliberal writers on the libratory potential of computers, the computer investment in striation is worn quite plainly on its sleeve, perhaps hidden in plain sight. While we must often look to not-yet-developed paradigms and marginal practices for signs of what looks like a return of nomadicity or smoothness, striation is everywhere in computers, at levels from the smallest to the largest. The process of what Armand Mattelart calls "networking the world" (2000) is itself a massive and underappreciated act of striation. After all, in principle, the world was always networked, by any number of analog means; it was then further networked by analog electronic technologies such as land phones, the telegraph, radio, and so on. Today one can scarcely avoid proclamations that the world is being networked as if it never had been before, as if global communication is now possible and had always before been impossible; as if we had always previously been perfectly isolated individuals and computer technology now allows us, finally, to speak with each other.

Of course this is highly odd, since nothing of the sort is true, even if computer technology does enable an acceleration of worldwide communication. Yet perhaps even more than communication itself, what computerized networking entails is the pinpoint location of each object and individual in a worldwide grid. The cellphone, a vanguard technology of computerization although not always recognized as such, relies on digital technologies such as packet-switching to transfer partial messages from point-to-point. We are told that cellphones free us to move anywhere we wish, like nomads, no longer tethered to a central location; no doubt there is some truth to this. But at the same time the cellphone itself, precisely demarcated via a numeric identity akin to the Internet's IP number, becomes an inescapable marker of personal location, so much so that with much more frequency than land-line phones, it is routine for cellphone users to be asked why, at any hour of the day or night, they failed to answer their phone—as if the responsibility for such communications lies with the recipient and not with the maker of the call. If I call you I *expect* (rather than *hope*) that you will answer. What excuse is there, after all, to be "away from" a device that is always in one's company?

In this example, a previously smooth space—the space from which one felt free not to answer the phone, to be away from the phone, perhaps even to use the inevitable periods of unavailability as a means to use space and time for one's own ends—now becomes striated, and in this sense *visible only as its striation becomes visible*. This is an important characteristic of striation, in that we do not simply have "smooth" or "free" spaces that we resist letting be incorporated into striation—rather, we typically rely on the smoothness of space (and time) not even recognized as such for important parts of culture and personal practice. This smoothness, as with the "lack of a toothache" in Buddhism, becomes apparent only when it is removed. For some of us, striation comes on without recognition at all—thus we have had for years cellphone advertisements that present as a virtue the ability for these devices to keep one in constant contact with one's employer, as if this were an obvious virtue for all persons rather than for employers. It is beside the point that some employees enjoy this relatively unmediated contact with their jobs—except at the highest level, this sort of contact is largely uncompensated and, over time, extremely stressful for the individual worker.

Spreadsheets, Projects, and Material Striation

Among the exemplary tools of computational striation is one that has long been considered among the personal computer's most important applications, namely, the spreadsheet. Conceptually, a spreadsheet is somewhere between a word processor, which is generally capable of creating ordered tables of information, and a true database, which can perform extensive computations on stored data. In practice, the majority of word processors and other text-processing applications, including ones for the web, rely heavily on a table model that is not unlike the basic table at the heart of spreadsheets; database applications consist of tables and relations between them. As such, it is slightly inaccurate to think of these three main, everyday computer applications as entirely different in kind; it might be more accurate to think of them, along with other applications that are currently part of the Microsoft Office suite, as similar bundles of capabilities in which different aspects are brought to the foreground. This is one reason why it was crucial to Microsoft to own the entire suite of what are now Office applications, in that the potential always exists for one way of looking at the capabilities to swamp the others unexpectedly.

Spreadsheets are a chief example of computational thinking and of striation because they existed before computers proper; they became nearly ubiquitous with the rise of business and personal computing and eventually came to redefine significant aspects of business and personal conduct; they also take extensive advantage of real computational resources. Spreadsheets are one of the chief computational applications to walk hand-in-hand with scientific management (see Liu 2004 for a thorough discussion of this connection) and to remake the world in a computerized image, while passing largely unnoticed in the public eye. Today nearly all corporate bodies are organized in large part according to the logic of spreadsheets, including educational institutions and other nonprofit entities. Along with databases and project management software, spreadsheets make possible and encourage the capitalization of almost all resources, far beyond the ordered capitalization of physical labor that Taylor studied so carefully.

In theory, a spreadsheet is nothing but a table: a simple, ordered document composed of rows and columns. The canonical spreadsheet application is one familiar to any corporate employee and most investors: the balance sheet. Balance sheets existed long before computers, but it is a fundamental mistake to see them as a mere accounting artifact of interest only to financial professionals inside of companies. No doubt there was some truth to such an understanding before the widespread use of computers, when the terminology and perhaps more importantly the data underlying balance sheets was inaccessible to all but finance professionals and perhaps the president and CEO of a company. In those days, the data for balance sheets could be collected only with great effort, close to the SEC filing deadline, and of use only in the highest-level decision making.

Balance sheets (and other financial tools like income statements, annual reports, etc.) and the computer were more than made for each other: they are computational devices that existed long before computers became physical objects. With the advent of computers, the thinking behind balance sheets could be widely expanded and implemented at every level of corporations and other organizations, rather than existing as esoteric tools for only the initiated. Today, to be the manager of a segment of any size within a modern corporation means essentially, at least in part, to manage a spreadsheet. This spreadsheet is not merely an abstraction used for reporting purposes; it is a literal device that is connected, usually by direct networking, into the master spreadsheets used by financial employees to assemble the organization's official balance sheet. While the information in the manager-level spreadsheet might, in general, be kept hidden from subordinates, it is in some ways more real than the persons employed by the company. It frequently includes information of vital importance to the employees, for example productivity rates, employee costs, costs vs. revenue generation, and so on, and yet is in general considered part of "management information" to which only manager-level employees are entitled access.

When managers meet for regular supervisory duties with their managers, it is the spreadsheet reality and not the everyday physical activity of employees that is the most "real" object of discussion. Here hierarchy and striation are clearly visible: whatever the corporation may say with regard to labor law and other constraints about who is "management" and who is a "worker," it is when spreadsheets become the focus of discussion that it becomes clear who is part of the management and ownership of a corporation and who works for it. This is among the brightest lines in contemporary corporate life, and raises profound questions, not under direct consideration here, about the nature of the contemporary corporation and its political and economic power in our social lives. Often, the managers and owners of a company, who may themselves constitute less than 1 percent of the total number of employees of a given company, see the reality portrayed by and manipulated via spreadsheets as the "actual" reality of the company, and the rest of the corporate activities as a kind of epiphenomena connected to the spreadsheet reality only via metaphoric and metonymic processes. As such, these extensions are much more ephemeral and expendable than most employees themselves may understand, and as such they may be widely globally distributed: not just because the work of a company via networks like computers can be shipped out all over the world, but because actual work is now a kind of extension of the company's central mission, which is exclusively visible via the company's spreadsheet reality.

The spreadsheet reality is profoundly striated: it is arguably just the application of striation to what had previously been comparatively smooth operations and spaces. The spreadsheet encourages everyone in management to think of the parts of a company as "resources" that can be understood as "assets" or "liabilities"; each human being is more liability than asset, regardless of rhetoric about "human assets" or "human resources." One of the most interesting characteristics of spreadsheets is their division not just of space but of time into measurable and comparable units. The common quarterly balance sheet is always presented in terms not just of the current quarter of operations but of the prior quarter, and this information is of critical importance to investors and analysts who follow each particular company. What has happened to revenues, costs, inventory over the recent quarters? Are they increasing or decreasing? Companies almost always want to be in a position where revenues, sales, and assets are increasing, costs are not increasing unless justified by new products or services that will result in even greater revenues, etc. From this view the human activity of employees—which in some cases can represent the bulk of the active hours for years—appear as little more than distant decimal places in calculations rarely present on the "summary" or "master" financial statements.

While spreadsheet thinking encourages a typically computational focus on a Platonic, numeric reality that in some ways supersedes experiential reality, it is not at all the only computational means used by contemporary organizations to striate and structure the everyday world. Within corporations and other large organizations, among the most significant means for managing human beings and their actions is a device loosely known as Project-Management Software and that is most famously represented by an application available as part of the "professional" versions of Microsoft Office, namely, Microsoft Project. Microsoft Project is similar to a spreadsheet program, and in fact its functions can be and are performed with spreadsheets, but it has been adapted to the specific needs of "project management," which can generally be understood as a euphemism for "human activity management." While some activities can be and are tracked via project management software, its chief purpose is to follow and track the actions of individuals, who are represented as computable symbols in the application. These symbols also represent "dependencies" and other relational concepts, providing the project manager with a visual representation of any sort of large-scale institutional activity.

Any sort of activity can be represented in a project management document, and this software is frequently used as a kind of large-scale to-do list for employees, but its main purpose is to provide project managers with computational, hierarchical, and striated authority over the human beings contributing to a given project and to the company as a whole. The project might be as small as a simple software upgrade or as large as the creation of an entirely new product. The project manager in such situations often serves an interesting liminal position between management and employee, and the document he or she maintains is typically connected both to central corporate resources and to the spreadsheets that are management's main concern. The manager and project manager may have supportive and interested meetings with employees at various levels, but often their main concern is with the "project reality" and its relationship to the "spreadsheet reality," which is often enough their own main point of responsibility with regard to the company's structure.

No doubt, project structuring via heavily striated applications like Microsoft Project contributes to efficiency and can aid employees in tracking their tasks; there is little doubt that being certain of accomplishment can contribute to a sense of employee well-being and to the documentation of services rendered to the corporate entity. But the main point of project management software is to provide the benefits of striating smooth space to those at the top of the hierarchy, and in some cases to abstract out the capital and other resources from human collectivities only in so far as they contribute to the numerical spreadsheet reality on which management must focus. As such the facts of day-to-day life in the corporate entity become less and less the actual activities of human beings and more and more the facts (or actually symbols and figures) included in the project management document. At higher levels of management it is quite possible to fulfill corporate requirements well only by interacting with spreadsheets and project documents; what is only required in addition is to mask, via the human performance of lower-level managers, the degree to which this computational reality supersedes social experience.

In *The Laws of Cool* (2004), Alan Liu draws attention to the ways that Frederick Taylor's system of "scientific management" was applied first to blue-collar physical works, especially in Henry Ford's production plants (91–5), and then "migrated to the white-collar environment" (96) through fields like industrial psychology and employee testing, ultimately producing the famous "organization man" (Whyte 1957) of the 1950s whom Liu rightly associates with the first wave of comprehensive computerization in the form of industrial mainframes. In this environment, Liu writes, "there arose a . . . universe of information-for-information that manifested itself not just as more information but as a mental construct of that information: an 'overview,' 'visible' rending, 'voice,' or 'reflection.' This construct was secondary and figurative relative to the 'real' work at hand . . . But secondary and figurative overlapped with primary and real" (108). "The definitive feature of the mainframe era," Liu writes, "was precisely that it insisted that IT conform to organizational patterns optimized for the earlier automation paradigm." Citing James Beniger, Liu suggests that "computerization in the mainframe era was the logical extrapolation of the apparatuses of 'generalized control' that originally fostered the great bureaucratic organizations of industrial society" (112).[1] Liu's goal is to account for the "culture of cool" surrounding computers that clearly did develop as early as the 1970s and which in modified form continues to this day. While it is no doubt accurate to see a change in the methods and implementation of computation as a society-wide technology in the various decades since the 1950s, it is nevertheless clear that the kinds of organizational control and global surveillance that were so obvious in personnel management then may have been pushed out of the spotlight, but have also continued to be developed unabated. Those structures of control are no less effective for appearing less personalized and rigid on the surface than they did in the

1950s: to the contrary, I am arguing that they are more effective and perhaps more insidious precisely because they appear to be more individualized today (see Zuboff 1988 for a few hints along similar lines).

An organization fueled by the use of Microsoft Project and other similar tools is not necessarily the one best positioned for corporate success. Rather, the widespread use of Microsoft project reveals a thoroughgoing belief in computationalism, showing how deep the belief in chess-style striation can filter down to the level of nearly every employee of the contemporary organization. Perhaps it is somewhat familiar how software tools now enable doctors, lawyers, and other professionals to precisely track how each minute of each day is spent and to whom the time can be billed, and at what rate. Subjectively, such precise oversight of every moment of every day seems likely to produce high levels of stress and paranoia, and threatens to take over the relatively "smooth" space of the apparently "self-scheduling" mid-level office employee with a thorough striation according to which each moment of time must be accurately documented, perhaps even via automated logging tools. Subjectively, again, the response of most employees to the sight of their time so precisely scheduled, tied to project income and expense, "rolled-up" into global pictures of corporate finance and resource management, can only be understood as profoundly dehumanizing in just the way that the most stringent Fordist management of physical labor is. But the effects of global surveillance via Fordist shop management (as distinguished from the theoretically more-benign intent of Taylor's original plans) were in part countered by organized labor and its collective revolution against such rigid supervisory regimes. Today's computerized methods of employee tracking and surveillance are both more effective and less visible, and have so far seemed less tractable to organized resistance, despite the apparent computational knowledge and interest of the people whose work is so closely monitored and controlled.

In this sense, it is a triumph of what Liu calls the "culture of cool" that computational employees can accept, and in some cases help to implement, the tools and methods that can contribute to extremely high-stress work environments, severe productivity demands, and real-time, invasive surveillance of work activities (and personal activities conducted at or during work-time). It should be no surprise that as tools become more sophisticated and as organized labor is increasingly disempowered through a variety of methods—including the prevalent view in white-collar firms that all employees are salaried "management" and therefore not subject to hourly and weekly work limits—that the effective methods developed by Ford in particular should return to the workplace. What is perhaps surprising is that many workers would come to accept, implement, defend, and support the methods that are used to restrict, manage, and in some cases automate and outsource their own employment.

Tools for Authority

One area of computing that has so far remained outside of critical attention is the proliferation of engineering protocols which are used by corporations for the implementation of large-scale systems (large both quantitatively and geographically). The most well-known of these are called "Enterprise Resource Planning" (ERP) and "Customer Relationship Management" (CRM), though these are only two examples of a widespread approach in business computing. Some of the best-known software manufacturers in the history of commercial computing, including SAP, BAAN, Microsoft, Oracle, PeopleSoft, Computer Associates, and others, have derived much of their income from these protocols. They have been explicitly developed and implemented for the purpose of defining and controlling the system of social actions and actors; they constitute a sizable fraction of the work taken up by the thousands of engineering students produced by today's institutions of higher education. They are the "skills" that computer scientists and engineers develop to "use" in the world at large, and they are always construed and described as such. They are "tools," supposedly free of ideological weight, and so far largely free from critical scrutiny. Like other such phenomena, on reflection they turn out to be among the most precise and deliberate structures of political definition and control, and they remain so far largely outside of the purview of cultural interpretation and understanding.

ERP is one name for a system of strategies in business computing that began to be explicitly articulated in the 1980s, though their roots extend back further than that. A perspective from inside industry shows the clear connections of ERP-style technologies not to information processing as much as to trends that we now identify as forming the so-called Industrial Revolution itself:

> Instead of being responsible for and capable of building an entire product from start to finish, the Industrial Revolution spawned the division of work into specific defined tasks. The division of tasks (division of labor) led to greater efficiency, productivity, and output—the ultimate aim of the Industrial Revolution. This, in turn, led to specialization in different areas, such as machine operators, assemblers, supervisors, industrial engineers, and so on. Whether this specialization led to the discipline of inventory and materials control is not clear, but we can assume that certain people were allocated the

task of purchasing material for the business, and others were employed to sell the finished product. . . . This logic of breaking down the responsibility for production between different functional areas is evident in ERP systems, even though their objective is to integrate all operations and support more efficient sharing of data about business processes. (O'Gorman 2004, 26)

Computing does not merely enable accountants to keep better records of monetary transactions; it provides whole new levels and kinds of power and control over money. This power and control, as businesses almost immediately realized, could be extended to every aspect of running a business; today, ERP vendors see

"backoffice" functions (such as operations, logistics, finance, and human resources) and "nontransaction-based systems" or "front-office" functions (such as sales, marketing, and customer service), as integral components of ERP systems. These inclusions result from the emergence of Supply Chain Optimization (SCO), or Supply-Chain Management (SCM) and Customer Relationship Management (CRM) strategies and systems . . . This "beyond the corporate walls integration" [is sometimes referred to] as extreme integration. (Sammon and Adam 2004, 7)

"Enterprise Resource Planning" sounds vague until one realizes that "Enterprise" means just "organization," especially "big organization," and "resource" refers to every constituent of the organization, whatever its real-world label (a pattern that is reflective of Object-Oriented programming approaches more generally; see Golumbia 2001); ERP thus refers to software designed to allow business executives and IT managers to subject every aspect of their organization to computerized control.

By computerized control we are referring not to simple recording and tracking, but just as much to development of control and planning structures that would not be available to the business without the kind of large-scale planning and allocation made possible by computers. The kinds of constituents that can be identified by computers are to greater and lesser degrees formalized; they are "business models," abstractions from the real world that allow the computer to manage them as representations; and the strategies suggested by computation are those that the computer finds it especially direct to provide. ERP business process analyses look for so-called "inefficiencies" in the system, finding places, for example, where a resource is sitting idle when it could be doing work. We know that "profit" will never fail to be included as the primary value toward which the system is skewed. In some systems of discourse, cultural studies has uncovered what seem to be covert marks of orientations toward capital; in ERP systems these orientations are explicit.

The inefficiencies exploited by technologies like ERP are almost strictly economic inefficiencies. Economic in this sense refers to the entire process of software representation: from modeling the real world as a series of economically valued objects, to assigning putative quantitative values to phenomena that, in the real world, seem not to have direct quantitative equivalents (this despite the fact that some features of the environment can be "construed" as consisting in quantifiable elements like food inputs). The world represented within the ERP infrastructure departs from our world precisely in that the unconscious, irrational, and largely interactive nature of social and personal life is replaced with explicit, conscious inputs. The maximization of these conscious inputs represents the maximization of efficient output—maximizing profit, or winning the game. (ERP is as much ideology as it is actual software, and the literature of ERP is replete with vendors selling their customers elaborate ERP packages that are ultimately rejected by the customer; see Sammon and Adam 2004.)

Most of the time, in the "real world," one does not win at business in quite this way. In fact it is fairly hard to say just how one "wins" at business, or just what "winning" at business is. Is it owning the business, selling for a profit, becoming rich? Working for many years and retiring? Is the business run in the interests of the managers, the Board of Directors, the shareholders, the workers, the customers? In many cases, it seems the ERP approach actually does attempt to answer these questions, by offering up enticing and increasingly abstract values for apparently quantifiable problems. Human values that are hard to quantify are, often as not, simply ignored. The movement of "shell corporations," "tax shelters," "A/R and A/P," "subsidiaries," can all be manipulated, but "human happiness" and "social well-being" must be actively imposed by human managers. "Sustainable business model," "reasonable growth," "nondestructive interaction with the environment"—all seem as well to be values that a business can pursue, but which are not likely to be default settings for enterprise software.

In recent models of enterprise-wide software, control and monitoring mechanisms move beyond the representable "resources" and toward a more loosely defined object known as the customer. The best-known post-ERP software paradigm is Customer Relationship Management (CRM), which is a marketing term for a suite of contact, maintenance, and knowledge software modules. This integrated suite of applications, which range from simple contact management functions (the names, addresses, phone numbers, etc., of customers) to highly focused personalization features, is designed "to gain efficiencies in direct mail campaigns and to communicate more effectively and relevantly with" consumers. The software helps companies to "develop dialogues" with consumers "based on their needs, encourage more loyalty and retention, and generate more financial success" (CPM Marketing Group 2001). "An important hallmark of a CRM system," the same press release for widely-used software goes, is its ability to track an organization's outbound and inbound contacts with its customers in a closed-loop feedback system . . . These communication records are matched against individuals and households within the database to access activities, behaviors, and service utilization, and to calculate ROI" (ibid.).

This is not the storage and maintenance of bare information, but the interpretation and subsequent management of information to maximize "return on investment (ROI)." By ROI we mean, simply, profit (despite some accounting mechanisms designed to make it seem slightly otherwise). We are looking to minimize our own resources while maximizing the appearance of providing resources to the consumer. Using CRM, we can "value data and its ability to predict future behavior"; "leverage value-based services to support targeting, cross-selling/up-selling other financial products" (whatever "vertical" we happen to be operating within), and develop additional ways to "track and measure results to calculate ROI" (Gauthier 2001). Thus the entirety of the company–customer encounter is finally reduced to its quantitative equivalents, the human being reduced to virtually nothing but actor reading knowledge-based scripts. One can imagine being unable to determine whether one's interlocutor is a live human being, or a set of taped phrases taped from a live encounter—an odd if dramatic example of an apparently spontaneous Turing machine. What motivates such a machine, perhaps more purely than it can motivate a human being, is plain on the surface: "the data used to manage your customer relationships are always clean and up-to-date. . . . The result is a marketing system that boosts short-term marketing return and helps build customer relationships that improve long-term profitability" (Fair, Isaac n.d.).

> Profitable customer management begins with knowing your customers. Yet few companies have the cross-channel knowledge required for consistent, personalized customer management and marketing decisions. With MarketSmart, information is collected at all your push and pull touchpoints—including email, direct mail, stores, inbound and outbound telemarketing, Web sites and kiosks. As a result, you now can have a complete picture of each customer's behavior and preferences—a picture that will help drive profitability across all of your channels and product lines.
>
> MarketSmart integrates powerful decisioning tools that help you create, test and execute strategies across your business. By combing Fair, Isaac's gold-standard analytics with best-of-breed software tools, MarketSmart offers you unparalleled decisioning power. It also gives you the ability to analyze marketing results and integrate strategies across channels. Imagine knowing which

elements of a multi-channel marketing campaign are effective and which aren't. Or automatically triggering personalized Web pages and offers based on a visitor's clickstream and purchase history. Or how about matching the right action to the right credit account at just the right time. You can with MarketSmart. (Fair, Isaac n.d.)

The corporate author of this product description, Fair, Isaac, is the country's leading vendor of credit-scoring software and credit scores, an explicit formalization of the customer relationship built on just such mechanisms, setting the quantitative lives of most consumers beyond their apparent intentional control. The development of elaborated systems of social control such as personal and small business credit scoring represent the sacrifice of knowledge and control to quantitative formalizations. Who has given their consent to this control, and under what circumstances and with what understanding has this consent been given?

Nowhere are the effects of CRM more paradigmatically evident than in health care, especially in so-called managed care. The inefficiencies exploited by managed health care are precisely based on the use of ERP and CRM simulations and management systems. Today, nearly everyone in the United States knows at least something of what it is like to have one's health managed by one or more of these systems—systems that respond not to comprehensible human processes but to abstract gaming simulations, where responses to our behavior are dictated not by precisely inefficient— unformalized—human systems, but by gaming conjectures spinning several "moves" ahead of us in a game—one structurally very similar to an RTS game—we are often not aware we are playing. The response may be, take this medicine instead of that, which may in no way reflect the likelihood of the medicine to treat our problem, but rather may be an opening gambit against our requesting proper treatment for whatever underlying (possibly environmental) condition that need be addressed. Unless one is prepared to treat the health care system as an "AI opponent" in the "game," one is likely not going to receive maximal care for one's state of bodily health, but rather a set number of resources dictated by the "AI opponent."

There is no doubt that adding CRM to health care represents an extension of insurance. We all understand—don't we—that insurance is the addition of statistical profit tables to pools of investment, advance payment for risk that either pays off handsomely or, sometimes, goes against the house. When a number of Illinois area hospitals implemented CRM systems, the "closed-loop feedback system" of communication enabled a range of "target campaign management solutions for each provider" (CPM Marketing Group 2001). "The campaigns focused on education and awareness, wellness, disease management and intervention in clinical areas such as cardiology, women's services, orthopedics, neurology, pediatrics and senior services. To attain program goals, [the hospitals] used the CRM database and software to segment the audience for each campaign, to ensure messages reached the right individuals" (CPM Marketing Group 2001).The whole infrastructure presses on what is beyond awareness, instead of true dialogue with a human doctor we trust, who understands the range of our health issues and can present us integrated information. Even if such a tool would be useful to a doctor, does advice that is predicated on "exploiting inefficiencies" by "segmenting markets" with the goal of "maximizing ROI"—does this advice really fall into the realm of "informed consent"?

CRM makes it possible for health care providers to focus on "bottom line benefits" by affecting the consumer's "propensity to use External Service Providers" (Gauthier 2001). It helps the organization to exploit already existing strategies involved "acquir[ing] and retain[ing] profitable customers." In the best cases, of course, "patient-centric relationships are possible within an integrated systems, people, and process environment," but in practice these multivariate goals are subordinated to ROI. In one case study, a "physical therapy practice uses CRM to accelerate orthopedic surgeon approval for continued care, and therapist productivity. A large physical therapy practice wanted to increase quality and consistency of clinical documentation to increase therapist capacity, referrals." The solution involved "predefined fields and drop-down menus to simplify process, accuracy," allowing "quicker approvals for orthopedic surgeons on modalities, progress and follow-on treatments; increased patient referrals" and "increased patient/therapist time, increasing practice revenues while maintaining quality treatment" (Gauthier 2001). In a second case study, a "large hospital seeks to target market customers for elective LASIK eye surgery/vision correction in highly competitive, non-differentiated market." Here CRM "data mining software that uses legacy system patient data to identify high-propensity characteristics that will help predict future services behavior" allows "more efficient marketing campaigns and greater return on investment" (Gauthier 2001).

In a third and most telling case study presented by this CRM consultant, "a pharmaceutical company uses CRM to promote and create a community around its leading drug to build brand value and customer loyalty." Here, an "Internet Community" is created "with focus on 'trusted advisor' role to insulate the brand from competing drugs"; this is because "customer relationship and retention represent primary lever of profitability," because (despite the fact that) "educated patients depend on value of information, not just medication" (Gauthier 2001). So despite the fact that the information provided by the CRM system may be wrong—in other words, the competing product may in fact be more appropriate for any given individual's condition—the CRM system is structured to maintain "retention." But "targeted marketing campaigns" satisfy the "educated" consumer's need for "information," which must be of high value, nevertheless false, or at least tailored to obviate those factors that might make a competitive product better.

Understood as both a business model and a specific kind of software application, CRM is most often implicated in the kinds of business practices that are typically understood by the term *globalization*. CRM helps to implement a hard-and-fast division between the sovereign intelligence that runs organizations and the various intelligences that work for them. A small coterie of management typically has access to the setting of parameters in CRM software, while more employees use the software or help to maintain it. As such, CRM software (and its affiliates) has contributed to the Hobbesian picture of a corporation as run by a small, even oligarchical, group of princely leaders and a large, undifferentiated group of workers (whom labor laws have typically not yet recognized in this fashion). These workers, although they may be asked to contribute "creatively" to many aspects of the corporation's life, are nevertheless systematically barred access to the true management decisions that are implemented in software, and, due to software in particular, have much less input into how and why business decisions are made.

Thus modern corporations of all sorts have taken on a peculiar character that derives in no small part from the changes made possible by the computer. It has become virtually impossible for individual customers to interact with "the corporation," in the sense that managers are now tasked solely with the operation of business rules below the level of true business operation. Corporations use the statistical knowledge generated by CRM and other applications to manage how their customers interact with them, so that, for example, it may prove highly profitable to simply deny customers, via networked knowledge of incoming telephone numbers, any access to customer service representatives at all, even if such access is contractually or legally necessary. The costs required to fight litigation in these areas would be far outweighed by actually providing the service in question. While the rhetoric of CRM often focuses on "meeting customer needs," the tools themselves are constructed so as to manage human behavior often against the customer's own interest and in favor of statistically-developed corporate goals that are implemented at a much higher level of abstraction than the individual:

CRM analytics can perform predictive modeling of customer behavior, customer segmentation grouping, profitability analysis, what-if scenarios, and campaign management, as well as personalization and event monitoring. These functions take advantage of a customer's interactions with a business in real-time.

CRM is a highly iterative process. When data from any source is harvested and fed back into the system, it improves the personalization capability of the very next customer transaction or e-mail campaign.

More traditional marketing processes such as direct marketing often see months of lag time between a campaign's execution and the review of its metrics. With each loop of the cycle, Internet-based CRM analytics are updating, tweaking, and improving delivery of personalized, relevant sales opportunities, all in real-time. The analytics also help build a more finely tuned relationship between a business and its customers.

In addition to the personalization that benefits a customer's purchasing decision, CRM analytics will soon provide useful data that can benefit enterprisewide processes. CRM analytics will also be integrated more frequently into the general operational workflow of noncustomer systems, including financial systems and manufacturing, to provide a more singular view of customer-centric data than do the traditionally segmented departmental views offered by legacy CRM.

When all of this data can be interpreted to a variety of enterprise systems, transactional decision making and enterprise planning—from cross-selling opportunities to supply-chain and just-in-time inventory control—will be enriched.

Although several vendors are providing ad hoc, niche CRM capabilities, only a handful have emerged with the driving analytics necessary to benefit enterprisewide decision making in a meaningful way.

Data mining and analytics are not without risk. The predictability of human nature is never a sure thing, so modeling real-world transactions carries a certain degree of error which can greatly affect the quality of the data that influences decisions. CRM analytics, being more about the process than the technology, demand a degree of human interpretation for the data to yield the most beneficial results. The CRM tools merely fortify one's abilities.

Although automation can go a long way toward streamlining internal processes, technology also quickly depersonalizes the customer's experience. CRM analytics offer insight and personalization that can go a long way toward improving that experience and building customer loyalty. (Sharp 2003, 55)

Such decisions emerge with special force when seen through the lens of computerized statistical reasoning.

Thus nearly all interaction with contemporary corporations is mediated precisely and specifically by computerization, both internally and externally. When customers are told that "all lines are busy due to high caller volume," it is more than possible that one's account has simply been judged incapable of generating sufficient profit to the corporation to license personal interaction. Much of the work that is outsourced via CRM (and its sister applications) is precisely of this sort, and much of the reason that customer service centers in particular can be outsourced to majority-language-speaking cosmopolitan centers, like those in India and South America, is because these centers do not, in fact, provide what is traditionally understood by the term "customer service." Their goal is largely not to resolve customer problems, but instead to manage problematic human requests via computerized scripts that have been precisely engineered to limit the amount of time each customer spends on the phone and so to maximize the number of calls each worker can process. The main job of an outsourced customer service worker in these environments is not to deviate from the script. Often, these workers have virtually no power to affect any aspect of the customer's account at all; they are simply provided with computerized scripts for managing client emotion, at a precisely calculated ratio that costs the company less than the litigation that would follow the provision of no obvious customer service whatsoever.

Internal and External Striation

Arguably, many large corporations today actually do not conduct the services they advertise and which they claim to provide in advertising and official documentation. Among the most telling scandals in the late 20th-century business culture involved the telecommunications companies that emerged in the wake of the court-ordered breakup of the AT&T monopoly. Since AT&T had largely built and retained the contracts to maintain the physical infrastructure for U.S. telephone service, companies had to be created to split up AT&T's monopoly power while essentially adding little physical capability to the phone system. The companies that emerged, especially MCI, Worldcom, and Sprint, were huge corporate entities created through the legal machinations of institutional investors, but exactly what the nature of their businesses were was never firmly established. In under two decades all of these companies were exposed as something close to out-and-out criminal conspiracies, ones in which computerized services via CRM and CRM-like technologies played critical roles (Jeter 2003, Malick 2003).

In each case, these companies were operated by small groups of owners with large financial stakes in the underlying investment transactions that created the companies, and with a significant interest in the fate of the various stock issues attached to the companies. But these oligarchical rulers were virtually unconnected to the thousands of employees and customers who believed that the companies existed to conduct their core businesses, providing telecommunications services. Rather, the companies employed essentially enough personnel to provide the bare minimum of services and to give customers the impression that attention was being paid to their problems, yet these systems of customer support were separated by hard layers from the management coterie. Of course this is no difference in kind from the operation of some corporations in the past; it is a difference in degree. Computerization does not offer a wholly new way of doing business; it offers new speed and intensities with which to accomplish the goals that have always been there.

A similar scenario, also tied profoundly to computerization, played out in the collapse of Enron Corporation in 2001. Originally a traditional utilities company, Enron became a favorite of Wall Street investment banks due to its use of computer technology, especially networking and data collection, to exaggerate the market characteristics of the relatively staid power exchanges. Everything about Enron's success was predicated on the transformational powers of digital technology, so much so that Enron eventually began to trade in network bandwidth as well as more traditional power commodities. Yet after the company's bankruptcy and the criminal prosecution of its principal managers, especially CEO Kenneth Lay and CFO Andrew Fastow, it emerged that in fact many of Enron's claims were false, and involved accounting tricks that ranged from old-fashioned to sophisticated, but all of which were essentially understandable as fraud and theft. The outside shell of Enron offered huge new efficiencies brought about through a variety of supply-chain management technologies; but inside the company, Enron was a profoundly competitive, masculinist, oligarchical structure in which power and the pursuit of power reigned supreme. Computers were vital to this structure, perhaps more for their ideological functioning than their abilities to manage information. In recounting a skit performed at one of Enron's annual meetings, the corporate biographer Mimi Swartz recounts the use of a Wizard of Oz frame to describe Enron's own employees learning how its critical RAC (Risk-Adjusting Committee) technology worked. In the skit, a trio of Enron employees go looking for the technology in Oz:

> Once in Oz, the group looked for the Wizard of RAC, but all they found was a large black box that screeched "Go away" and "Too busy" and "Put it in writing." Finally, someone stripped away the front of the box to reveal Rod-

ney Faldyn, [mining unit deal manager Jere] Overdyke's head accountant, dressed in a scarlet satin pimp suit.

"I'm Andy Fastow," he said, "the Wizard of RAC."

"Where are the computers?" Dorothy and her team asked. "We thought RAC used computer models."

"Naw, dude," the pimp said. "I make all the funding decisions around here." He told Overdyke, the scarecrow, he didn't need a brain to do deals at Enron. Sutton, the Tin Man, didn't need a heart, either; Fastow said he had gotten by just fine without one. And the earnings-stealing Lion was offered a job in his funding department—"You're my kind of guy," the Fastow character told him. (Swartz and Watkins 2003, 123)

Both the utility and the ideology of computers are fully on display in the Enron story (Eichenwald 2005; Swartz and Watkins 2003). There can be little doubt that the Enron story is at least to some degree representative of exactly what is at stake in the digital transformation of society—promises of benefits to consumer that ultimately benefit most those at the top, and benefits which themselves prove evanescent on close scrutiny.

We are often told that we live today in a "service economy" that has supplanted the "manufacturing economy" of earlier phases of capitalism, while acknowledging that the form of globalization known as "outsourcing" now manages manufacturing activities in place of U.S. factories. It is hard to see principled distinctions in any of these cases. It is hard to see what is different about being employed in a so-called developing economy for a global corporation in a manufacturing facility making silicon chips (often a highly skilled job requiring an advanced degree) or sitting in a cubicle practicing carefully coached colloquial U.S. English and following a script designed to prevent a customer from using up too much of the company's time. Both represent a significant separation of capital and responsibility from the human being operating in the name of the corporation; both create profit via the exploitation of unequally distributed resources, the inequality of which is visible only to the sovereign who can see it. In both cases one can argue that such employment is better than no employment at all, but this typical neoliberal defense fails to explain why these are the only available alternatives. By establishing a powerful hierarchical order that is coded into machine applications and business rules, computers thus help to radically increase the stratification of the world's population, even as they work hand-in-hand with capitalist development to raise countries, in succession, up the "ladder" of economic development. Rather than anything like diversity or opportunity, computerization thus offers accelerated processes of capital extraction and exploitation that we like to pretend we have grown past—in large part because the oligarchical owners have in an important sense transcended everyday financial needs, while employees remain ever more caught in and by them.

There is no entity more characteristic of contemporary world capitalism and its global reach than Wal-Mart and its associates; there are arguably few stronger examples of oligarchical capitalism itself, nor of the resemblance of the contemporary corporation to Early Modern principalities—nor, for that matter, of the importance of dynastic succession in what we tell ourselves is an opportunity-based meritocracy. What is less well known is the degree to which Wal-Mart is both exemplary of and the actual source of some of the processes of the computerization of the modern institution, especially the corporation. While Wal-Mart's reliance on computerization—its evangelistic fervor for the implementation and development of computer schemes for business process management of many types—is poorly known, perhaps even less well known is the close tie between these processes and the more overt practices of antidemocratic globalization and exploitation for which Wal-Mart has deservedly received a fair amount of negative press.

Wal-Mart goes to great pains to hide business practices that its critics have alleged discriminate against various minority groups, including women, and that take advantage of monopoly power to effectively put other corporations out of business, while turning the responsibility for these developments onto the consumer's demand for lower prices, as if consumers have much choice in whether or not to buy a product for a lower price, or whether we live in a system not created by consumers that dictates this preference as a matter of principle (see, e.g., Brunn 2006; Lichtenstein 2006). But it goes to far less trouble to mask its computational activities, since these are often understood as marks of accomplishment, and Wal-Mart can presume that few critics will read through the technical and business language to follow the discourse of oligarchical control that is, for all intents and purposes, openly exposed there. Wal-Mart prides itself on developing computer systems that are used today by many corporations, even if it usually takes advantage of these systems in proprietary systems that are used only metaphorically by others, or in systems resembling the ones created by Wal-Mart, perhaps patented by it, and then emulated by software companies and others.

In its corporate information division, also known as "investor relations," Wal-Mart has historically always provided extensive information about its computer systems, while carefully guarding its patents and trade secrets. Even in its general information releases, Wal-Mart typically offers sentiments such as:

Technology plays an important role in helping Wal-Mart stay customer focused. Wal-Mart invented the practice of sharing sales data via computer with major suppliers, such as Procter & Gamble. Every time a box of Tide is rung up at the cash register, Wal-Mart's data warehouse takes note and knows when it is time to alert P&G to replenish a particular store. (Wal-Mart 2007)

In typical computationalist fashion, this language explicitly gestures at benefits for individual consumers while eliding altogether the main reason for which Wal-Mart uses computer systems, which is to maximize profit by minimizing a variety of previously smooth spaces in the supply chain— here, the space devoted to warehousing excess product or left empty due to selling faster than predicted. Wal-Mart's implementation of a variety of ERP software packages for supply-chain management creates pressure in several nodes in the economic system. Now Wal-Mart's suppliers must either themselves implement supply-chain management systems, or risk the same warehousing issues that used to be the provenance of Wal-Mart itself; in turn, other companies are pressured both externally and internally to comply with Wal-Mart's system, which in the most usual case involves implementation of similar computer systems.

Wal-Mart has historically been explicit that its development and use of sophisticated computer systems is a central reason for its decades of success in world markets. Despite the reputation for computers as an outsourced, globally distributed enterprise, in fact when computing is central to the operation of an institution, the institution is often careful to keep control of this practice very close to its centers of power:

As with 95% of Wal-Mart's IT projects, the Information Systems Division will manage the work from programming to process reengineering, relying very little on commercial software and not at all on outsourcing. . . . Yet Wal-Mart spends below the average on IT for retailers—less than 1% of worldwide revenue, which reached $256.3 billion in 2003. "The strength of this division is, we are doers and do things faster than lightning," says [Wal-Mart Chief Information Officer Linda] Dillman, the owner of a Mercedes SLK 320 convertible that gives her the opportunity to drive in the fast lane in her private life, too. "We can implement things faster than anyone could with a third party. We run the entire world out of the facilities in this area at a cost that no one can touch," she says. "We'd be nuts to outsource." . . .

Wal-Mart's reputation for designing applications and working with new technology acts as a powerful recruiting tool, drawing 95% of new IT employees to its Bentonville, Ark., headquarters from outside the state. And many of those who come to work for Wal-Mart's Information Systems Division stay for a long time. The executives in charge of key operations, including the company's data warehouse, its human-resources systems, and its international systems, each count a decade or more of experience with Wal-Mart. (Sullivan 2004)

Most of Wal-Mart's software applications are concerned with striation and surveillance of various sorts—with the control and authority that are the hallmarks of computationalism everywhere. One of Wal-Mart's most famous innovations was the development of a centralized satellite surveillance system for its delivery systems, so that, for example, it could pinpoint the geographic location of any truck on its way to or from a Wal-Mart distribution center as well as to a limited extent the product being delivered.

In recent years Wal-Mart has been at the forefront not just of ERP and supply-chain management software, but of a relatively new technology, Radio Frequency Identification Device (RFID) and the associated Electronic Product Code (EPC) system. Like the intensively computational bar codes before it, RFID identifies products via alphanumeric tagging. Where bar codes identify items by the class to which they belong (or what philosophers would call *type identification*)—every box of shredded wheat, for example, has the same bar code printed on it, allowing cashiers to retrieve the price for the item from a central computer—RFID specifies tokens of items. Each cereal box now includes a unique RFID chip, allowing the central authority to track precisely when and where it is processed, delivered, and sold.

Of course there are manifest benefits to such a system; the benefits are not at issue in the present discussion and RFID would not even be considered if it did not offer benefits to both Wal-Mart and its customers. Like similar technologies in the past, RFID and EPC have raised a certain amount of consumer and democratic concern, such that Wal-Mart in particular has been compelled in the name of public relations to contribute to a global effort called EPCGlobal (http://www.epcglobalna.org/) whose job is to promote public awareness of the uses of RFID and EPC and their benefits for consumers. Rather than demonstrating democratic control over this technology, though, the existence of EPCGlobal points more generally to the obvious privacy and surveillance issues raised by technologies like RFID that suggest the provision of worldwide, pinpoint surveillance to centralized authorities. The ethical standards promulgated by EPCGlobal are themselves far less worrying than are the inevitable more secretive applications of similar technologies that are sure to follow on the heels of RFID. Such technologies radically reformulate critical tenets on which concepts like personal privacy and private space, let alone public space, are themselves constituted in a democratic society, and while their explicit use by law enforcement and the government may at least at times be raised for policy discussion by lawmakers (though perhaps less often than some might wish), their widespread proliferation by multinational corporations is far less subject to democratic investigation and control, and at the same time perhaps more pervasive and constitutive of the contemporary lifeworld than are the surveillance technologies used by government.

PART FOUR

COMPUTATIONALIST
POLITICS

CHAPTER EIGHT

Computationalism and Political Individualism

As we have noted one of the most persistent refrains in computational discourse is that "computers empower users." The obvious transparency of this fact typically short-circuits additional reflection; since in our society it is accepted as an unalloyed good to grow the power of individuals, it must follow that the computational empowerment of users is also a good thing. Looking more closely, it is clear that an individual is a complex and multifarious construction, and it is not immediately obvious which aspects of the individual are bolstered by engagement with the computer; if we resist the overall characterization that the individual should in all circumstances have his or her power expanded, it is also not obvious that expanding individualism is beneficial for society *tout court*.

To begin with, the notion of the "user" posited by the empowerment thesis takes for granted that this user is the one at the heart of modern liberal individualism (one might even say *neoliberal* individualism). From a poststructuralist perspective, the idea that individuals in this sense are the exclusive or even the main carriers of cultural force must, at least, be called into question. Such an observation extends not merely to the examination of discourse as a cultural force outside of particular human beings, which has been the main effort of our analysis so far; it also helps to spread our focus our from discrete individuals as the beneficiaries of computational power to the various cultural forms that also benefit from computational power. This is not to deny the particular relationships between individuals and computers—there is much to say about this relation, too, that seems elided in the bare phrase "computers empower users"—but to emphasize that we simply do not know yet even to look beyond the liberal subject for the empowering effects of computerization, and that there is something self-serving to simply presume that the liberal human subject—the subject of democratic politics—is the user most fully enabled by widespread computational power.

It is clear, for example, that not merely individual human beings but also institutions are empowered by computerization; many of the most pernicious effects of computerization (surveillance, as in Bogard 1996; control, as outlined in particular detail in Beniger 1986) stem exactly from this form of empowerment. To the degree that human beings exist in part in social tension with institutions, the fact that both are empowered by computerization must give some pause. Since on some accounts a major contemporary social problem is the disproportionate power wielded by institutions vis-à-vis individuals, in what sense does increasing the power of both help to solve this problem? Since we are considering an abstract notion of social power here it makes little sense to think of measuring the degree to which various institutions and human beings are empowered via computerization; yet in recent times it is by no means clear that the ratio of institutional to individual power has changed much, or tilted much toward human beings. Our computers are built to enable exactly the kinds of bureaucratic and administrative functions that are by and large the provenance of institutions; it should be no surprise that these functions in particular are enabled by computers.

Here it is crucial to remember that the personal computer—sometimes taken to be the object of the putative computer revolution—followed both chronologically and conceptually on the heels of institutional computers, and did little (if anything) to displace this overarching computer paradigm. Today, the main part of each person's computing time is no doubt spent in the office, where he or she may be surprised to find the degree to which every aspect of his or her work—supposedly freed and empowered by the computer—is also monitored and analyzed in a way that previous labor could not have been. While the individual worker certainly does feel empowered at his or her terminal—she or he may have literally displaced functions that would have required two or three human beings in the past—much of that power is directed upward, centralized, concentrated on the institution's function in the most literal way. This is empowerment in a sense, but it is not the kind of emancipation we are often led to expect.

Individualism

With regard to individual human beings in particular, it is arguable that the empowering effects of computers tend in the direction of what the Canadian political theorist C. B. Macpherson (1962) so accurately analyzed as "possessive individualism." By this phrase Macpherson meant not merely the acquisition of goods and capital that are the hallmark of the contemporary world, but a deeper sense that our individualism is something that each of us owns in a commerical sense and that this ownership is what makes us a kind of master of our own selves. Such an inwardly focused conception of self makes it more difficult than it might otherwise be to look outward toward the community and toward cooperation; it walks hand-in-hand with the "every man for himself" vision of individualistic (neoliberal) capitalism today said to be the heritage of Thomas Hobbes and (probably wrongly) Adam Smith. On this view the individual is solely the product of his or her own enterprise, regardless of social or economic circumstance; the individual is similarly justified in pursuing self-interest at almost any (or, according to some libertarian thinkers, any) cost.

Arguably, the strong sense of mastery experienced by users as they sit at the computer terminal—the sense that the computer is a kind of quasi-cognitive entity that obeys the human user's orders to a high degree of precision—walks hand-in-hand with an exaggerated sense of individual importance. Many of the hallmark functions of computerization are performed in the name of a kind of communitarianism, such that we focus on their putative social functions, while we downplay the nearly coterminous inflation of the individual—which is to say, in another sense, "user empowerment"—that are strongly in evidence. Among the most obvious effect of this sort is the individual desire to create resources regardless of the social need for them, and the subsequent justification for such resources even when they have been created almost without regard for their role in the larger society; here the chief phenomena are the "personal home pages" so characteristic of the early phase of the web, and the blogs, Facebook, and MySpace pages so evident at present. Especially in the case of blogs, it is clear that the real inspiration flows not from a social need but from the individual desire to be seen. Many blogs read as if the user sees him- or herself at the center of the world, with his or her posited audience hanging on every action the blogger takes—almost as if the blogger was a different order of human being from the blog's readers.

In the business world there is a pattern that seems to capture this paradoxical and disturbing aspect of contemporary computing neatly. Organizations of whatever size—from large investment banks to small shops (though it is especially true of the former)—approach contractors with a similar and strange goal. "Have the customer (or internal user) come to my website," they say, "and *stay there*." The so-called "competition for eyeballs" on the web often enough turns into an individualistic desire to dominate the (imagined) user's attention in a way that is quite contrary to even the actual patterns of use of the web, but entities rarely if ever want to hear this. "Do *you* use a single website for even a part of your business practice?" is a question the successful contractor learns not to ask. One is acutely aware of trying to satisfy the organizational ego, even of what should be the most self-sustaining institutions, through a fictional effort to make the client think that users will be satisfied never to leave their domain; even, in the example of an investment bank, that their internal users will be content to use only a prescribed set of financial resources when that practice would be detrimental to the user's assigned job function. The computer seems easily to inspire dreams of individual domination and mastery, of a self so big that no other selves would be necessary, of a kind of possession of resources that could and would eclipse that of any other entity. In some circumstances the folly of such desires is the last thing anyone can point out; better to add fuel to the impossible dream, even though they have already seen the downfall of many institutions that buried their niche excellence in a welter of generic "me-too" features duplicated on a hundred other websites. Rather than the community participation some evangelists advertise, computers and the web seem to bring out an especially strict and fierce individualistic competition, as if the web is on the verge of an extreme concentration from which only a few super-individuals will emerge. Arguably, the discourse of communitarianism exists in no small part as a compensation for the extravagant individualism we know is visible everywhere on computers.

Individualism meshes tightly with computationalism about the mind, language, and society. The connections here are ideological, and their existence helps to demonstrate the functions of the computational ideologies for our society. Emphasis on the mechanical, algorithmic, and exact functions of cognition and language closely parallels the view that what is remarkable about these phenomena is their instantiation in the individual, almost to the complete exclusion of their social realizations. To Chomsky and other high rationalists, language is primarily a tool for cognition and its communicative functions are secondary; this helps to explain how and why the Chomskyan perspective on language should become so powerful just as computers become ubiquitous. This contrasts, of course, with any number of traditions in both linguistics and philosophy according to which, at the least, we can't distinguish very well between cognitive and communicative function, or on other views (including some plausible accounts of evolutionary development) communication is primary.

Views based on the power of computation are therefore likely to privilege the individual, often viewed in isolation, over more distributed social functions. In the philosophy of mind, the functionalist view that the mind is a kind of computer (discussed in Chapter 3) abuts a view that Tyler Burge (1979, 1986) and Hilary Putnam, among others, have labeled "individualism" in a philosophical sense.[1] To literary scholars familiar with the work of Lacan and others the controversy over individualism may seem surprising, because it hinges on the philosophical view that the system of language is effectively contained entirely in the brains of individuals—where Althusser, Lacan, and other poststructuralists would insist that language is something like a system into which the individual as such is introjected, and is therefore not even understandable as a purely individualistic object. As such what is remarkable about this part of the history of philosophy is the strength with which individualism could emerge again (as it has before), such that there could be a controversy about the question whether words receive their meanings wholly from each brain, or in part from their social function. In philosophy and in linguistics, and in society in a larger sense, computationalism and exclusive individualism rise together; I am suggesting that they are two halves of a single coin, a picture of human social life that privileges physical mechanism and especially its precise and controllable instantiations over all the inexact, fuzzy, analog features of the world that, while difficult to control and even at times to name, are nevertheless among the most vital facets of human life.

Mastery

Psychologically, the signal experience of working with computers for the power elite is that of *mastery*. This is part of what distinguishes the experience of the ruling classes from others, and arguably it is what has helped to create the impression that computers might help to dissolve political hierarchies. Proficient computer users experience profound feelings of mastery much of the time, and it seems clear to me that a great deal of our contemporary enmeshment with computers hinges precisely on this experience of mastery. This is one of the most critical insights of Sherry Turkle's groundbreaking *Second Self* (1984), a study that depends on direct psychological interviews with computer users. Turkle rightly directs our attention not merely to adult computer users but to the ways in which computers become integrated into development; "the child's passage from what I call a 'metaphysical' to a 'mastery' stage is made transparent through the child's relationship with the computer when interest shifts sharply from philosophizing to 'winning'" (320). "The computer . . . and the possibilities it offers for working with issues of control and mastery, actually enters into both cognitive and emotional development. It offers a medium for growth and, in certain cases, a place for 'getting stuck'" (ibid.).

Arguing that "three modes of relation to computing" are "metaphysics, mastery, and identification" (ibid., 321), Turkle rightly notes that "for many people, one or another of them becomes predominant." Among engineers, it seems to me that the experience of mastery is the most prominent mode of relation, with identification as a secondary but important mode. The programmer experiences mastery in a subject-object relationship with the computer, spending enough time in this relationship that it becomes in essence his or her decisive psychological orientation. Before the computer, the programmer feels, I am the absolute master; the computer does exactly what I tell it, when I tell it, and how I tell it. There is a tremendous—one might say excessive and revealing—pleasure in seeing these orders carried out successfully; there is also often a similarly revealing and overdetermined frustration when the master's orders do not seem to be followed.

Of course most of the actual members of the power elite are not "power users" of computers in this sense. But for some of these individuals, the mastery relation is the one between themselves and the rest of the social world; they often (in a relatively Hobbesian mode) experience much of the world hierarchically, made up of a few "superior" individuals like themselves and many laborers whose needs and desires are of only of passing interest. For the power elite, the laboring body of the corporation is itself a kind of computer (and in many ways a literal computer) over which he or she exerts nearly the same pleasurable mastery the programmer experiences in front of the computer. In this sense, and this conclusion can be only speculative, there is a structural identification between programmer and power elite that largely serves the elite's ends. Sitting at his or her desk, the programmer imagines him or herself a master in much the same way the boss is a master; no matter that the programmer is master over a single inanimate machine, where the boss has mastery over a complex network of social actors and other resources. "I am like the boss," the worker can say to him/herself. "I am a boss; it's good to be a boss; someday I want to be just like the boss and exercise masterful power just the same way he/she does."

In this way the power elite can solicit the endorsement of the working classes without ever intending to share power at all (as Mills 1956 makes clear); power is shared through the provision of a device, the computer, that provides a kind of illusion of social power in its structural proffering of relational power. Because the machine is inanimate, it helps justify the ways in which capital must treat human resources as existing on a different plane from the capitalists themselves. Furthermore, when individuals get "stuck on" this experience of mastery—especially when they sublimate their human-relational (in Freudian terms, affective and sexual) needs onto the computer, its inability to fully respond can fuel self-reinforcing "neurotic" development. There is no mystery here; the inability of programmers to "relate to" romantic partners is a famous aspect of our contemporary life-world. I am arguing that there is something deeper going on here than mere "nerdiness" or social withdrawal. The computer is, in some sense, sexually satisfying to the adolescent who already feels estranged from human social relations; the fact of its ultimately unsatisfactory nature powers the engineer's exaltation of the computer as the human itself: in a familiar psychoanalytic operation, the engineer introjects the inadequate hated/loved object, both blaming it for its failure and identifying with it in a profound way. Experiencing mastery over the computer, the individual also comes to see him/herself as a computer, in part so as to exercise computational mastery over others in the social world: "you are all just machines anyway," his/her unconscious says, "why don't you all bend to my will?" The thought is accompanied with its opposite: "I am a machine and can't provide what other humans want; my only recourse is to submit more and more to the abstract, absolute master I see elsewhere in the world."

There are curious and unacknowledged correspondences between the use of the computer and Freud's specific concept of mastery as described in his early writings, particular in the *Three Essays on the Theory of Sexuality* (1905), where mastery is referred to as both an apparatus and then as a drive *(trieb)*. Mastery proceeds from the infant's physical endowment; it is particularly associated with the use of the hand, which in turn becomes associated with masturbation: "the preference for the hand which is shown by boys is already evidence of the important contribution which the instinct for mastery is destined to make to masculine sexual activity" (Freud 1905, 188). Mastery in this sense is linked to sadism and cruelty, "independently of the sexual activities that are attached to erotogenic zones" (193), and also to the "instinct for knowledge, [which] corresponds on the one hand to a sublimated manner of obtaining mastery, while on the other hand it makes use of the energy of scopophilia" (194). Intensely engaged in the use of both hand and voyeuristic vision, the computer programmer is thought to be outside of sexuality, but arguably there is an intense and sadistic economy of sublimation and identification at play even as sexuality appears not to be invoked (Žižek 1997 touches on related issues).

It is this pattern of relation that forms what is perhaps the psychological core of my argument. Much of the rhetoric advancing the computer as a solution to our social problems joins together the inherent technological progressivism of our form of capitalism with the desire to be the master. The computer gave me mastery, the advocate says; it is all the mastery I could attain; it should be all the mastery anyone else can attain; put them, too, in this relation to the machine. That this ideology conforms to the needs of the power elite and of the circulation of capital does not occur to the advocate, or seems tremendously secondary to that experience of mastery; I was empowered by computers (and badly); this is the only experience of empowerment that should be available. Arguably, this is the reason that so much contemporary writing about our social problems turns on the computer's utility; rather than emerging from genuine intellectual consideration of real computers (though this is certainly sometimes the origin of such sentiments), the intuition emerges from a desire not to master, but to put the whole world in the position of the master's opposite: the slave.

Here, again, and somewhat speculatively, the question emerges of the particular utility of computerization for the U.S.-style worldwide cultural hegemony called globalization. There is the strong American insistence on the newness of the machine; this has been characteristic of U.S. ideologies, especially technocratic ones, from the country's inception, though in earlier times it was easier to see their emergence as a response to the deep histories which characterized European and Asian powers. The United States had to insist that newness was as important and potentially as world-saving as were the historical traditions of the other major powers; arguably this continues as a primary aspect of the major U.S. ideologies. But the computer adds another element: it adds what appears to be a legitimate replication of the master–slave relationship out of which the United States was built and which now haunts it as not merely a psychological specter but as the specter of its relation to capital. We needed laborers who we could understand as subhuman in order to perform the work that was necessary to us as social rulers; the work was as necessary as was our psychological falsehood: that we did not need it, that it was beneath us, so far beneath us that entities who were hardly human could be entrusted to do it. Far from it: the labor was absolutely critical to building our empire.

In many ways, the computer is a more perfect slave than another human being could ever be; it also provides a template for seeing ourselves as slaves in a way that plantation owners never could have imagined. To be sure, the computer is not a human being; there is nothing ethically wrong with "enslaving" it (if that concept even makes sense). But perhaps there is something wrong with us as human beings treating any object outside ourselves as a perfect slave, even if that object is absolutely without the resources to resist or even to comprehend its enslavement. Surely this unconscious weight is part of what conditions the repeated "robot" narrative we tell in SF narratives, where despite the complete lack of any programmatic means to understand its subjugation, the robot nevertheless does come to comprehend it, and rises in vengeance against cruel authority. The lacunae in the preponderance of these stories is the notion that the robot might be right to resist enslavement, or that we humans might have been wrong to have created such slaves in the first place because the slavery relation—the relation of absolute mastery—is ethically compromised to begin with. From an anti-authoritarian perspective, it is wrong to put absolute masters at the head of our institutions of all sorts, and it is only slightly less wrong for those of us in the working classes to aspire to, and identify with, absolute mastery.

The trope of mastery provides one of the most powerful connections between the various spheres in which I am arguing that computationalism today is especially influential. Through the process of identification, including the desire to see oneself in the machine and also to be aligned with political and institutional leaders, the contemporary academy has endorsed a variety of efforts to find within the brain a computer that could be mastered: a syntactic engine outside of "us" that nevertheless our "wills" and "beliefs" could master. This pattern is found both in the early program of philosophical functionalism, in which it was presumed that there must be a computer of some sort that was either the whole of or a significant part of the human mind (Chapter 3); in the desire to find in human language a syntactic "engine" that operates without regard to meaning, a project that has split linguistics itself as a discipline and that is still found in the generative grammar and computational linguistics projects (Chapter 4); in the installation of elaborate software programs that provide the owners of capital with heavily processed, concentrated, and statistical views of the human activity in institutions (Chapters 6 and 7); and no less in the persistent assumption, evident in so many different spheres in our culture, that somehow mass computerization will lead to a more democratic, more open society—when so much about computerization clearly angles toward authority and centralized power.

Rationalism

A main part of my argument, which on some accounts would seem not even to require demonstration, is that there are strong historical and conceptual ties between computationalism and rationalism, and that these associations have consequences throughout computers and computational rhetoric. Furthermore, computationalism entails not merely rationalism *per se*, but a particular species of rationalism with clear conceptual and historical weight, which we nevertheless seem all too ready to forget.

At its most basic, when we talk about rationalism we talk about the philosophical view that everything worth addressing in human cognitive life is at bottom a form of logical reasoning, and that cognition not characterizable in logical terms is simply failed cognition—bad logic, failed reasoning. While this view does not deny the presence of emotions and other nonlogical mental processes, these are generally understood to be secondary to logical reasoning; sometimes the view goes far enough to suggest that along with language, or even as a capability closely connected to language, rationalism is *the* distinctively human trait, the thing that we have and that animals (for the most part) lack. In this guise rationalism has a long and distinguished trajectory in the history of Western philosophy (especially, but not exclusively); one of Western philosophy's concerns from the beginning (which is to say, the pre-Socratics) has been to specify and understand the nature of reason in a rationalist sense.

It is relatively familiar to historians of computers and of philosophy that there is a significant overlap between those figures who are generally thought of as exemplary rationalists, and those thinkers whose works are said to prefigure the science underlying modern computers. Chief among these is of course Gottfried Wilhelm Leibniz (b. 1646, d. 1716), the German philosopher whose work in mathematics and logic is often taken as the starting point for histories of computing. In Leibniz rationalism begins to take on the more specifically mathematical and logical form that is of particular interest for computation; it also takes on the fascinating political and intellectual characters that continue to inform it to this day:

> Leibniz is from the great rationalist tradition. Imagine Leibniz, there is something frightening there. He is the philosopher of order, even more, of order and policing, in every sense of the word "policing." In the first sense of the word especially, that is, regulated organization of the city. He only thinks in terms of order. But very oddly in this taste for order and to establish this order, he yields to the most insane concept creation that we have ever witnessed in philosophy. (Deleuze 1980, 1)

Leibniz believes that thought operates via symbols and rules; symbols (generally words) and rules which will ideally be those understood in formal logic:

> the rules of *common logic*—which geometers use too—are not to be despised as criteria for the truth of assertions: for example, the rule that nothing is to be ac-

cepted as certain unless it is shown by careful testing or sound demonstration—
a sound demonstration being one that follows the form prescribed by logic. Not
that we always need arguments to be in syllogistic order as in the Aristotelian
philosophy departments . . . ; but the argument must somehow reach its conclusion on the strength of its form. Any *correct calculation* provides an example of
an argument conceived in proper logical form. Such an argument should not
omit any necessary premise, and all premises should have been previously
demonstrated—or else have been assumed as hypotheses, in which case the conclusion is also hypothetical. Someone who carefully observes these rules will
easily protect himself against deceptive ideas. (Leibniz 1684, 3)

Here rationalism takes on something more of the specific form that is so
vital to computationalism. Rationalism is not simply the operation of rea-
soned principles, with these defined in general (or, we might say, analog)
terms; rather, it is specifically the application of the rules of formal logic—
essentially, mathematical rules—to symbols whose meaning is, in an important sense, irrelevant to the question whether our reasoning is valid.
Reason is syntax: it is the accurate application of principles like *modus ponens* to any substance whatsoever.[2]

The resemblance of cognition, according to this perspective, to the digital and algorithmic operation of computers cannot be overstated. It is this
resemblance that launched both functionalism in analytic philosophy (Chapter 3) which went on to license the discipline called cognitive science, and
the host of computational approaches to language, including, most famously, Chomsky's program of generative grammar (Chapter 2). In these
programs, too, a strong distinction between syntax and semantics must be
maintained, and the most crucial operations of cognition are in important
ways independent of context and meaning: there is a kind of logical engine
in the brain—again, most easily understood as a computer—that processes
symbols into their right arrangement. Whether this facility is innate in
human beings or a learned facility—whether it is a description or an
evaluative proposition—has not yet been determined; we are simply here
identifying cognition with a logical, syntactic process, with rational calculation.

The inherent problem introduced by the rationalist perspective is that it
does not seem sufficient in and of itself to explain what is happening in human minds, without either positing some kind of meta-level authority
(which creates a kind of infinite regress, since this authority ultimately does
much of what we assume the brain does *in toto*), or depriving human beings of the reasoning powers in general. Derrida is one of the thinkers who
draws our attention most forcefully to this paradox, but it is a worry that
goes back at least as far as Kant: if cognition is just rational calculation,

and therefore decisions have outcomes determined by the right application of logical rules, what do we do about the conscious appearance that we are able to make choices and decisions? Unless our view is that *good* cognition is calculation—in which case we also need to provide an account of *bad* cognition, which becomes something other than calculation (thereby troubling our definition of cognition just as calculation)—then we appear to be little more than machines, whose conclusions are automatically generated from premises via the application of logical rules.

Computers certainly do operate via logical principles—via something like the syntactic rationalism at least one version of Leibniz appears to endorse. Computers always arrive at the conclusion logic demands; when they fail to do so they are not operating at all. Some find this a satisfactory analog of human cognition, but today many of the most sophisticated philosophical views have come to reject it. Cognition includes that part of our minds that appears to have something like free will with regard to thinking; though we are certainly capable of following logical rules like *modus ponens,* our thought also seems capable of going in many other directions, and even when we decide on an action that contradicts good logic, we nevertheless appear to be thinking even then.

As discussed in Chapter 3 above, Hilary Putnam in particular has subjected rationalism to a thoroughgoing (and on some accounts Kantian) critique, showing that at its best rationalism turns out to be either a normative theory or one that ultimately "hides" its problems in the form of that *ur-*mind who chooses whether or not to follow logical rules (and which to some of us might just appear to be the mind itself). Furthermore, and most crucially, rationalism is not simply a philosophical theory among many; it is an instrumentalist view, according to which the brain itself is a kind of tool that is posited for the use of some other entity—some "higher" authority—that is both analogous to the way human beings use computers and that has distinct, and hidden, religious connotations. Here Putnam and Kant help us to connect rationalism to that part of its doctrinal history we have not discussed yet at length: the philosophers most strongly associated with rationalism are the ones whose political (and even institutional-intellectual) views have most often been thought of as profoundly conservative, as favoring authoritarianism and as denying the notion that most of us are capable of thinking in the full human sense.

Most famously, of course, this appears to be the view of Hobbes, and it is no accident that Hobbes is both the figure who seems to have posited the role of computation in the polis earliest in Western thought, and who has become the patron saint of contemporary neoconservatism (via, for example, the works of Leo Strauss). Strauss himself, in one of the founding texts of neoconservatism, *Natural Right and History* (1953), helps to make clear that rationalism is not simply the commitment to a certain kind of reasoning: rather it builds on a conception of the place of such reason in the natural world. "The tradition which Hobbes opposed had assumed that man cannot reach the perfection of his nature except in and through civil society," writes Strauss, but to Hobbes, "the individual is in every respect prior to civil society" (184). Rationalism is a complex of views, disturbingly similar to those which underwrite modern computationalism. What is most striking is what rationalism of the Hobbesian variety says about political authority: the sovereign is a different order of being from those over whom he rules, and "command or will, and not deliberation or reasoning, is the core of sovereignty" (187). The path from rationalism-as-cognition to the absolute sovereign "is not meant to be more than the strict consequence from his premises" (190) that is, the premises of natural law. In addition to being perhaps the chief exponent of rationalism in the Western philosophical tradition, Hobbes is "generally recognized to be the classic exponent [of] the doctrine of sovereignty," according to which "the rights of sovereignty are assigned to the supreme power on the basis . . . of natural law"; "plenitude [of power] belongs to the ruling authority as of right" (191).

This doctrine, as Strauss's approving invocation of Hobbes shows, has played a curious and in some ways determinative role in 20th-century political and intellectual practice. In several recent books (esp. Amadae 2003, Edwards 1996, and McCumber 2001) researchers have shown the deliberate creation of rationalist doctrines in the mid-20th century by U.S. think tanks, particularly the RAND corporation, such that this thought appears to be the spontaneous work of university academics but actually forms part of a coordinated plan to shape U.S. democratic practice. Of course, using rationalism as a basis for democracy makes a great deal of sense on the surface; but the deeper connections between the concept of natural right and the need for an absolute sovereign must be played down to make the theory palatable. Nevertheless, their connection in contemporary U.S. thought is hard to mistake, and it is no accident that the U.S. political administration most informed by Straussian, neoconservative thought is also the one that insists on the absolute right of the sovereign to act outside of constitutional or congressional restraint. As Strauss puts it, "Hobbes's doctrine of sovereignty ascribes to the sovereign prince or to the sovereign people an unqualified right to disregard all legal and constitutional limitations according to their pleasure" (Strauss 1953, 192).

Amadae in particular shows how, as a bulwark against communism, (what we would today call) neoconservative economists and political theorists developed a theory of personal choice that exalted individualism, rationalism as cognition, and the ability of individuals to make decisions, especially economic decisions. Thus the history of communitarian thinking—that whole tradition that sees the individual not as necessarily prior to "civil society"—had to be downplayed. That most famous tenet of the U.S. version of Adam Smith, according to which we are all bound to pursue self-interest to its maximum, was of course for Hobbes and the neoconservatives a principle of natural law, and according to that same law the sovereign must have absolute power above any constitutional restriction. This tension between the power of the individual and that of the sovereign—even if, in some abstract sense, the sovereign is taken to "be" the people—is an inherent feature of the rationalist worldview, because it is precisely from the same "principles of nature" according to which rational calculation is natural, that emerges the absolute power of the sovereign.

In a somewhat paradoxical fashion, by restricting true cognition to rational calculation, rationalism can be said to diminish rather than exalt the role of cognition in human experience and judgment. There are at least two strong arguments that support this contention. The first is an argument found repeatedly in Derrida's writings (see especially Derrida 1990, 1992, 2005), according to which the problem in rationalist conceptions of thought is that they evacuate the notion of decision that is supposed to be their hallmark. If cognition just is the procedure by which we follow rules as logically precise as *modus ponens,* what happens to questions of ethical and political responsibility? Logical rules allow for no substantive ambiguity; either a proposition follows or it does not. If our decisions are established for us by logical procedures, who or what makes the decision to act ethically or unethically? Can we even say we are making any decisions at all (unless we posit, as suggested above, an *ur*-mind that rules over cognition but which begs the rationalist question altogether)? As Derrida puts it:

> Each time a responsibility (ethical or political) has to be taken, one must pass by way of antinomic injunctions, which have an aporetic form, by way of a sort of experience of the impossible; otherwise the application of a rule by a conscious subject identical to itself, objectively a case to the generality of a given law, manages on the contrary to *irresponsibilize,* or at least to miss the always unheard-of singularity of the decision that has to be made. (Derrida 1992, 359; emphasis in original)

This is precisely the singularity Hobbes and Strauss want to bypass; it is exactly the characteristic of the (partially hidden) view of absolute authority in rationalism that it can admit no place for human beings to be responsible for themselves.

The second objection to rationalism is connected to this one, but also has more direct connection to computerization. Hilary Putnam, in particular, makes this objection clear by refusing, in his later works especially, to philosophize about mind and language without also turning to social and ethical questions. Perspectives that isolate rationality from the rest of human experience instrumentalize reason: they make it a kind of (supposedly neutral) tool, for the use of an unspecified authority (found either inside the person or in the sovereign). On this view, Putnam says, "whatever our reason for being interested in them, all facts are ultimately instrumental" (Putnam 1981, 181). Logic, being the basis of science and scientific reason, places facts above values in terms of their physical reality, but also diminishes facts and reasoning about them to a "narrow conception of rationality" according to which it is "valued solely for the sake of applications"—that is, the uses to which it can be put, or its technological consequences.

Rationalism is often called an instrumentalist view of thought precisely because it entails the idea that thought itself (and perhaps the language in which it is most often expressed), is a tool, a *technē* or technology, an instrument that is ultimately "meant" for the use of some other authority. As Putnam writes, "the contemporary mind likes demonstrable success; and the contemporary mind is very uncomfortable with the very notions of judgment and wisdom" (1981, 179); hence instrumentalism is "powerfully appealing to the contemporary mind" and part of a general bias in favor of scientific and technological reasoning. It is thus no accident that proponents of rationalism are often proponents of technological progressivism, perhaps most classically in computer history in the figure of Leibniz himself, who continually worked to build machines that would in some way or another perform the actions of thought for human beings. Amadae (2003) points to the concomitant emphasis on rationality and technology in the rational choice theorists, not least as expressed in the writings of the RAND corporation, historically a major proponent of both in contemporary U.S. thought. As Amadae puts it, "the mathematical formalism structuring rational choice theory is impelled by the same academy-wide momentum propelling an increased emphasis on formal models as an indication of scientific standing" (158), also pointing to the influence of one of the founders of modern computing, John von Neumann, on rational choice doctrine (via his writings on game theory, von Neumann and Morgenstern 1944). Because cognition itself is formal, syntactic, and thereby instrumental, we are extending the human cognitive apparatus by building out our scientific and technological instruments; because this is the only sort of knowledge worth the name, and knowledge solves social problems, we need only build out our technology sufficiently to address any problems that emerge. The bifurcation between the rationalist tradition and anti-rationalism is evident in current debates about global warming, where leftists tend to want to insist on holistic solutions that include overt changes in social behavior, and those on the right tend to insist almost exclusively on technological solutions to the problem.

For at least one hundred years and probably much longer, modern societies have been built on the assumption that more rationality and more *technē* (and more capital) are precisely the solutions to the extremely serious problems that beset our world and our human societies, all of them characterizable through the real histories that these materialities constitute. Yet the evidence that this is not the right solution is everywhere. This is not to suggest that rationality is wrong or misguided or that we should eradicate it; it is to suggest that our societies function best when they are balanced between what we will call here rationalism and whatever lies outside of it. To some extent this is a perpetual tension in all societies, not just in ours or in so-called modern ones; what is distinctive about our society, historically, is its emphasis on rationalism and its terrific adeptness at ruling out any discourse that stands against rationalism. In other societies and places just the opposite might be true, in a way that our own rationalism moment makes difficult to see. In this way, one power of the computer and computational institutions is to make it increasingly hard to see that rationalism is just one mode of cognition, and not cognition itself. When we presume that the subject of politics just is the rational subject, stripped of her cognitive capacities outside and beyond rationality, we do not merely privilege one form of decision making above others: we work away at the fabric of the polis.

CHAPTER NINE

Computationalism and Political Authority

F OR MANY PROFESSIONALS today computers are a way of life. Within large universities, for example, both Computer Science and Electrical Engineering (which today is largely devoted to computer-related activities) are typically enormous schools, often dwarfing individual disciplines in the Arts and Sciences parts of the university. The value of this approach is said to be immediate employment after graduation, either in the computing industry or in one of many associated fields. Engagement with the computer dominates the entire educational experience for these students. Management practice today relies heavily on computer modeling of business systems; much of the software sold by major manufacturers like Siebel, Computer Associates, Oracle, and other major computer companies is devoted to Business Process Modeling (BPM), in which a variety of practices are reconfigured so as to be transportable across computing platforms or, more profitably, from the analog world to the digital world. (These transitions are what have led advocates for a long time to speak of the "paperless office," despite the apparent continued reliance on paper even for computational activities.) Even more strong, and less apparent on the surface, is the pervasive use of computer models in the sciences (for example, in modeling the molecules used in drug design) and in business itself, so that top business school graduates move to so-called "consulting firms." These firms often maintain large staffs of software designers in-house, or work closely with software or hardware companies (software companies like

IBM, Oracle, and Siebel are themselves largely comprised of consultants, making both types of organization surprisingly similar).

The job of these firms is to "re-engineer" corporate practices either from the analog world or from one digital platform to another. Each transaction that can be sold results in a profit for the consultant, which is the main goal of that party; each transaction is typically sold to the buyer as potentially profit-generating, usually through "efficiency." Sometimes this efficiency is easy to see and specify, sometimes it is openly speculative, and sometimes it is not clear at all. Regardless, the basic operation of much business in the world today, especially the business associated with the keyword "globalization," is conducted in the name of BPM and other solutions that are focused around providing management with *simulative control of business practice*. The general thrust of this work is to reduce social process to form, ideally to the CEO's preferred computational form, which often continues to be the spreadsheet.

In this sense, computational practice reflects social imbalance: more pointedly, it is *classed*. Despite the strong sense of "being cool" (Liu 2004), of being "the people who 'get it,' " and so forth, the educated elite who operate computers—whether they are programmers or accountants, administrators or assistants—are too close to the actual machine to get more than a glimpse of the abstract machine that the corporation embodies. The corporation is much more like Hobbes's Leviathan than we may want to admit: it is an automaton with many parts, most of which are small and interchangeable, but like a person it has something like a "brain," and that brain controls it and seeks, as Hobbes and capitalists alike would see it, only its own self-interest. What computer workers easily miss is that their role is not the same as those of the parts of the "brain," unless the corporation is explicitly structured in that manner. The true power relation to the computer involves the raw distillation of information to a point, the ability to get a bird's-eye view (or a God's-eye view), especially if one is in the bird's seat. The spreadsheet, with its emphasis on the pure reduction of social information via computational means into numeric data, especially percentage data—ratios, that is to say, the hallmark of rationality—provides the most direct view of "the facts of the matter" about a corporate entity.

Styles of Computational Authority

When so-called computer geeks rise to corporate ascendancy, despite some popular belief to the contrary, it is usually not through direct expertise in computer programming. This is true throughout the computer industry, but one of the most instructive stories is also one of the most central, because it is sometimes told exactly the other way. The success of Microsoft, we are told, is a "triumph of the nerds," where introverted and generally creative engineering types gain access to capital via "building the best products." While such idealistic vision might inform some computer industry narratives, Microsoft's story is explicitly quite different. Despite his reputation as a programmer, according to Bill Gates, "for the first three years, most of the other professionals at Microsoft focused solely on technical work, and [Gates] did most of the sales, finance, and marketing, as well as writing code" (Gates 1995, 41). The other key Microsoft employee, Steve Ballmer, was a math major at Harvard with Gates. Gates reflects that "Steve and I led very different lives, but we were both trying to pare down to the minimum course time needed to get top grades" (40). He tells one instructive story:

> [Steve] and I would pay very little attention to our classes and then furiously inhale the key books just before an exam. Once we took a tough graduate-level economics course together—Economics 2010. The professor allowed you to bet your whole grade on the final if you chose. So Steve and I focused on other areas all semester, and did absolutely nothing for the course until the week before the last exam. Then we studied like mad and ended up getting As. (40)

There is a reason Gates tells us this story and a reason that he is the person who drove the company that has accumulated the most capital-power in modern industry. The computer instantiates for Gates the principle by which he orders his world: find a loophole that one can systematically exploit, whether or not the "intended purpose" of the task at hand is served by the solution or not. In domains like education, the computer instances a principle that might be thought to be diametrically opposed to any strong program of education: rather than learning the matter at hand in a thorough way, computers often enough walk side-by-side with the pursuit of algorithmic techniques to "game" the system—to find any way to succeed other than straightforwardly doing the assigned work.

Gaming the system does not, of course, mean that one cannot also be effective at whatever skills are at issue; in fact, Gates himself was a tremendously talented student. The problem was that "at Harvard, he was one of the top math students. But he was not *the* best" (64). Gates clearly had to be not just one of the top figures but *the* top figure in whatever field he chose:

> "I met several people in the math department who were quite a bit better than I was at math," said Gates. "It changed my views about going into math. You can persevere in the field of math and make incredible breakthroughs, but it probably discouraged me. It made the odds much longer that I could do some

world-class thing. I had to really think about it: Hey, I'm going to sit in a room, staring at a wall for five years, and even if I come up with something, who knows. My mind was pretty much open . . . I really had not zeroed in on something" (quoted in Wallace and Erickson 1992, 64)

Clearly what was of main importance to Gates was to "do some world-class thing," a desire that might be most easily characterized as egotism and even narcissism—the desire to make the self as all-powerful as possible, to achieve sovereignty, especially over the rest of society. Despite its instrumental appearance, the computer is an especially effective model of power in our society, and especially provocative for those who see the possible applications of that model to the social sphere: to enact one's own will-to-power, in whatever form one obeys that impulse.

Gates, in his personal dominance of Microsoft, does not vary far from the hierarchical model of power we associate with traditionally white, male, authority figures in contemporary Western society. Though the company itself has gone through waves of more and less "progressive" management policies, over time the ruthless pursuit of monetary goals within the company, in other words for the accumulation of the specifically most useful form of contemporary social power, has emerged as the company's overriding singular goal. Ballmer, not originally especially interested in computers, quickly becomes the second-most important Microsoft employee, specifically surpassing the extremely talented computer scientists (Bob Wallace, Paul Allen, Nathan Myhrvold, etc.) who might have shared power. Instead, what Gates needed was exactly what he found in his "alter ego," Steve Ballmer. In no small part that must be due to Ballmer's ability to think "algorithmically"—to see multiple paths to manipulating the objects in a problem field, regardless of bounds that may have been imposed by external forces, just as he and Gates algorithmically "gamed" the Harvard system.

Perhaps even more openly than Gates's, Ballmer's personality exemplifies the techno-egotist subject that has its own power as virtually its only focus. Ballmer and Gates, despite being two, in their relation to Microsoft as a whole, perfectly instantiate the Leviathan principle. The company is an artificial animal, a body whose parts must work in concert for the accumulation of power and for no other goal. There is little other logic one can apply to Microsoft's corporate actions over time: as it has successively shut down entire fields of software applications development (from operating systems, to word processors, to spreadsheets, to presentation software, to packaged office software, and so on), even it cannot argue that its overtly prized "innovation" has thrived in these fields. Or if it has, it does so according to a monopolistic principle that is in explicit conflict with the competitive ethos the Western market espouses. Microsoft's message is that its power is so immense that it can itself innovate the computer industry as a whole. Its argument is that it has earned this power through success, but the inverse story seems even more likely: that its successful pursuit of power has driven its market dominance.

Microsoft's position as a fulcrum in the development not just of particular products but of our human computing power itself raises a number of subsequent questions. One thing Ballmer and Gates share is an extremely typical performance of gender (see Ullman 1997 on gender in the computing industry), even if each one plays a different type. Ballmer, in particular, resembles other successful business leaders, in the use of a charismatic and argumentative personal style. Contemporary CEOs often share some part of this style. It is a particular kind of relation to mastery, to wielding power, to the spreadsheet-view of the corporate entity itself. While women are found in this and similar roles with increasing frequency, this is still by far the exception rather than the rule, and female CEOs are often accused of "performing male." This is no accident, since for any number of reasons the computer as we understand it today is gendered in profound ways, and in every part of its development, manipulation, and history.

We like to tell ourselves that computing is a universal ability, perhaps *the* cardinal ability, by which thought itself is defined, despite the overwhelming social evidence that computing is quite biased toward males and toward the way maleness is performed in our society. On the rare occasions this subject is broached in public discourse, it is framed in terms of failure to attract women to engineering, or in culturally conservative terms as a failure on women's part to take up mathematical and technical fields. What is rarely considered at all is the possibility that the fields themselves are structured so as to be hostile to women (and to other minorities) not via direct attack but through the values that are actually promoted within technical culture.

We find it easy to divorce technology from the raced, gendered, politicized parts of our own world—to think of computers as "pure" technology in much the same way that mechanical rationality is supposed to be pure reason. But when we look closer we see something much more reflective of our world and its political history in this technology than we might think at first. The "strong AI" movements of the late 1960s and 1970s, for example, represent and even implement powerful gender ideologies (Adam 1998). In what turns out in retrospect to be a field of study devoted to a mistaken metaphor (see especially Dreyfus 1992), according to which the brain primarily computes like any other Turing machine, we see advocates unusually invested in the idea that they might be creating something like life—in resuscitating the *Frankenstein* story that may, in fact, be inapplicable to the world of computing itself.

Adam reminds us of the degree to which both Cyc and Soar, the two most fully articulated of the strong AI projects, were reliant on the particular rationalist models of human cognition found in any number of conservative intellectual traditions. Cyc (Lenat and Guha 1990) explicitly represents all knowledge as propositional and all knowledge as pure computation; despite its continued existence after more than a quarter of a century, the project still has few if any demonstrable results. Soar, a more sophisticated project run by the leading AI researcher Allen Newell (see Newell 1990), is still a symbolic system, but one that does not attempt to lay out "all available knowledge" in propositional form as does Cyc. Instead, Soar, which has also not produced significant results, "is heavily based on Newell and Simon's earlier psychological work (Newell and Simon 1972), which [is] limited in quantity and also confined to artificial logic-type problems" (Adam 1998, 124), and uses what Newell and Simon call "the physical system symbol hypothesis"— the intuition that thought is logical mechanism. Both of these projects, then, "conform to a rationalist point of view, where the rational is tacitly defined against a male norm" (127).

Despite its offer to encompass all of human cognitive activity, even in its most articulated forms the propositional model plainly fails to capture much that seems to be of vital importance to cognition: at least the thing we call know-how, and that is close to what Foucault calls *savoir*. There are things the computer knows how to do that we know how to do; we don't know what to make of the fact that both we humans and computers can in fact compute. The computer knows how to add numbers; so do we. We might even say that computer has *savoir* about addition. But it does not have *connaissance;* it does not know *that* it is adding, or even *that* it knows how to add. At the same time, a human being can have *savoir* about things that it seems inconceivable to teach to a computer. The problem with Cyc is not in its programming; it is a perfectly good model for capturing computational relationships. But "it is hard to see how Cyc . . . could represent the knowledge embodied in, for example, traditional midwifery. This is not only because Cyc would have no way of expressing gender-specific experiential knowledge, but also because it does not have a realistic way of learning its craft" (Adam 1998, 119). The midwife learns her craft by practice and observation and only occasionally through what looks like propositional communication; it seems arguable that aspects of her performance could not even be reliably reduced to propositions, even though they can be reliably shared with another human being.

The knowing subject posited by both Cyc and Soar is just that knowing subject posited by the most narrow and conservative of Western intellectual traditions. The apparently neutral presentation of this subject masks its cultural particularity; this is by no means to say that "computational reason" cannot be applied by those other than dominant Western male subjects. It is to say that the modern dominant conception of subjectivity is organized around a male or masculinist model, a model that is no less innocently positioned with regard to race and culture than it is to gender. The view that the knowing male subject exercises reason through propositional-logic style calculations is familiar in the West in a variety of guises. It is particularly relevant to the sovereign subject, the computer programmer, the technical or social engineer who sees in the computer model itself the means for accumulation and administration of power. The ruling elite, characteristically male, usually white, usually from the West (but often also from the East), applies and enforces computational practices precisely to concentrate power.

Culturally, then, it is imperative that the claims of computer "evangelists" about the technological direction of society be viewed within a clear historical frame. In the chronologically postcolonial time period, it is easy to forget what the world looked like until recently when colonialism went hand-in-hand with technological advance. It is also easy to ignore the history of communications technology and the degree to which these tools have been used for resource extraction and economic control of less-privileged peoples and areas (see especially Mattelart 2000, 2003). The fact that less-privileged people will often say they want access to these technologies, want to learn English, want to "become more Western," all must be taken (as they always are) not just as signs that the Western way has much to offer: it also shows that the Western way carries with it the (until recently, overt) denigration of other cultural styles just in virtue of their being different. Largely confined to the modern languages of metropolitan centers (see Crystal 2001; Golumbia 2003), computers and the World Wide Web make clear the cultural choice for minorities wherever they are encountered.

Postcolonial theory and gender studies, like other strands of recent cultural theory, draw our attention rightly to the overt cultural structures used in the past to support a distinctly hierarchical worldview. We used to say out loud that some cultures and peoples were just plain beneath those of us at the top. Now we say we have abandoned those beliefs in favor of a general humane egalitarianism—each of us is "capable" of "doing his best." But we rarely interrogate those beliefs about the present in terms of the present's own cultural technology. To some extent media that focus on cultural representation *per se*—for example movies and television—have been remade to reflect this cultural egalitarianism, even if some of us believe that core ideas about cultural superiority lurk relatively intact in some of these representations. But our culture produces new communication technologies at a rapid rate, and it is too easy to assume that these new technologies will follow our overt egalitarian dogma instead of a deeper story about hierarchy that has not yet been unseated. In that sense, one attitude that we do not see yet displayed but which is notable for its absence is the one that says of digital media: look what other media have done to imbalance the world already; what right have we to start new media when we have so poorly figured out what to do about the old ones?

Computers, new media, digital media in general do not seem to occupy the forefront of cultural thought. When people who think about culture carefully—whether their own or those of others—listen for those works that seem rich in human dimensions, they so far do not often reach for digital works. This is striking because other media have been useful for minority and experimental artists from early in their histories. Despite the fascinating achievements of digital artists and media producers, there are few works that we can point to as "breathtaking" or "overwhelming" in the way we do with examples of many other media. Of course computers play vital roles in the production of television programs, movies, and even the writing of books. This is the real "computer revolution," the ability to emulate (and also to administer) aspects of real-world cultural production. If anything, contemporary culture's worship of celebrities and promotion of "real-world" people to television stars demonstrates how much media rely on social engagement and simulation for their power. The computer's power is just not that sort of power—it is not a human power, but a power humans can and do use.

Computationalist Governance

Until recently, computation has never been seen as providing especially democratic power to the masses; rather it has always clearly been seen as belonging principally to the elite, to the top of the hierarchy, precisely through the translation of technological intermediaries, who have themselves at times been thought of, precisely and exactly, as computers (see Grier 2005, and also Liu 2004). On reflection it is hard to avoid the particular associations in philosophical and political history where computation finds advocates. Computation is particularly invoked prior to the invention of digital computers as a means for an imperial ruler to define, comprehend, and deploy the masses of labor and military power at his disposal. We associate computation with large-scale construction and agricultural planning processes, in that these often enough involved a great deal of repetitive calculation and, in effect, simulation.

In Western intellectual history at its most overt, mechanist views typically cluster on one side of political history to which we have usually attached the term *conservative*. In some historical epochs it is clear who tends to endorse such views and who tends to emphasize other aspects of human existence in whatever the theoretical realm. There are strong intellectual and social associations between Hobbes's theories and those of Machiavelli and Descartes, especially when seen from the state perspective. These philosophers and their views have often been invoked by conservative leaders at times of consolidation of power in iconic or imperial leaders, who will use such doctrines overtly as a policy base. This contrasts with ascendant liberal power and its philosophy, whose conceptual and political tendencies follow different lines altogether: Hume, Kant, Nietzsche, Heidegger, Dewey, James, etc. These are two profoundly different views of what the State itself means, what the citizen's engagement with the State is, and where State power itself arises. Resistance to the view that the mind is mechanical is often found in philosophers we associate with liberal or radical views—Locke, Hume, Nietzsche, Marx. These thinkers put both persons and social groups in the place of mechanical reason, and as we all admit, tend to emphasize social and relational duties rather than "natural right" (see Kreml 1984 for an apposite characterization of these tendencies and their intellectual histories).

Computing presents itself as just this sort of technical tool, a tool providing *savoir* more than it does *connaissance*. What it tells some users how to do is how to orient themselves in a sovereign position with regard to the world: first the computer, then the objects inside the computer programs, then the computer programs themselves. This presentation of the computer to the growing self offers challenges and opportunities. One clearly well-worn path it offers is to master the machine, by whatever route one chooses, and so to find oneself part of the (apparent) elite whose role is to contribute to the social-computational infrastructure. The relation these individuals have to the machine is unlike the relation they have to most people, and most other objects. The machine responds to their commands. The more he learns, the more he learns how much the machine can be made to respond to his commands. Generally, at some point, in fact, he learns the deep secret of computing: the computer never disobeys him. It always does precisely what he tells it. Sometimes he tells it to do things that ultimately frustrate him—he knows, for example, that the computer is quite capable of playing chess better than he can. But he remains in ultimate control of the settings of the chess program, and no doubt knows "cheats" that allow him to bypass good (legal) play on the part of the chess program.

This lesson of mastery-over-computer is widely learned in society, and exploited not just by engineers and computer scientists but by individuals who go on to a wide range of careers. Intuitively, it does not seem as if this is the best strategy to make one's way into the power elite, although no doubt this transition does happen (just as many women have this relation to the computer, despite the overwhelmingly male population of all the fields in which computational thinking is especially predominant). The better strategy is to take to heart the real core of the Hobbes-Machiavelli-Descartes message: in other words to practice the absolute egotism that their philosophies share with contemporary techno-capitalism. But this requires one to have access to true social and capitalist power, which only few of us have (or are willing to sacrifice other parts of life to achieve). We all know that this equation is constitutive of contemporary subjectivity: that we are literally constructed by the absence within ourselves of the egoism that makes true success possible. We all share in the rational knowledge of what is required of us, thanks to the abstract machine that is equivalent to thought.

For most of us, mastery over computers is part of a poor compromise with the rest of society and most critically with other people. We allow ourselves the fantasy that our relation to the world is like our relation to the computer, and that we can order things in the world just so precisely. But eventually, under whatever circumstance, we find that reality fails to compute. Things do not make sense, especially in the social world. Dr. McCoy, despite his apparent hysteria, is just as necessary for Kirk to make decisions as is Spock. Other human beings, like us, have wills, and do not always act as our own ideas of rationality would suggest. In fact, in the face of other people, our own ideas about what is rational come to seem self-interested, if we are willing to look that far. But we have to be willing to look. Nothing in the computer particularly encourages that looking-outward, while much about it suggests otherwise.

In this sense the computer's technological bluff is most critically a social bluff. The computer does not offer a real model of the relation between the self and other ordinary people. But it does model the way certain kinds of political and capitalist power can be wielded over society, and over other people to the degree that they fit into the model. It presents specific tools for understanding, ways of knowing (*savoir* again) that can be understood better in a metaphorical sense: one can hold power over society in much the same way a programmer or "power user" can hold power over a computer. It is no accident that the most powerful individuals tend to abstract this model far away from actual computers; CEOs and corporate presidents rarely emerge from the ranks of engineers, and exceptions like Andy Grove of Intel prove the rule. Some effective CEOs reject the computer model of sovereignty, but they in general must constantly fight the pressures of Wall Street whose nature is fully computational to the extreme. In this way, companies that try to foster either internal or external humane practices must constantly battle with computational understanding; and one suspects that some of the most successful companies find ways of using rather than fighting the computational imperative.

Some of our most sophisticated and thoughtful perspectives on computers hover around the question of the computer's modeling of mastery and its relation to political power (also see Butler 1997 and Foucalt 2000 on the relationship between political and personal power). Both Sherry Turkle (1984, 1995) and Joseph Weizenbaum (1976) seem rightly concerned about the computer's "holding power," but this formulation seems to share too much with other media, especially technological ones (television, radio, telephone). More importantly, these valuable critiques tend to focus on the admittedly disturbing circumstance when people, especially children, might be inclined toward an other-aware psychological structure, and have that development in part thwarted by the compelling nature of the computer itself. This is the parent's complaint: go outside and play with your friends instead of sitting in front of that (computer, television, radio, comic book, mystery novel, etc.). These complaints seem overwrought at times, but also right on target: it is necessary for a child's becoming-self to interact deeply, personally and bodily, with other children. It is not necessary to the becoming-self that a child use a computer, watch television, or even read books; it is necessary that she or he use language. It is certainly necessary to becoming a "contemporary person" that one use these media on a regular basis, but we can all see that they are not at all necessary for becoming a human being. We leave this as an ambivalent crux about modernity in our parental role, and it is critical to think carefully about it: to be vigilant.

The concern Turkle and Weizenbaum (and even as sophisticated a writer as Galloway 2004) do not seem to focus on what happens when the computer is the right instrument for the particular child—when the computer itself, or even more profoundly, the social metaphor the computer offers, are ready-to-hand for the child set to adopt them. These are children usually from elite backgrounds, with parents and teachers and mentors powerful enough to keep them from overindulging their egoistic pleasure in the human–computer relation, so that they become neither a "programmer" nor a "hacker." Both programmers and hackers are within the operation of the computational systems, and the privileged individual is made to see another possibility, namely that the extensive computational-social system is controlled by human beings and human groups. The computer model eclipses the computer itself. Society must be managed and is being managed. Our best model for managing it is in the computer, is the computer, and we manage it with computers and with computational understanding.

We are accustomed to recognizing in a general way that part of what makes the totalitarian political formations of the 1920s and 1930s so frightening is their use of the mass media that were then emerging throughout Europe and Asia. This includes not merely the broadcast media like films and radio, via which individuals have little power to talk back to their rulers, but even apparently interactive media like the telephone. Despite the obvious fact that the telephone can be used to convey any information whatsoever, with no structure at all imposed by the machinery, and thereby can clearly enable any sort of political activity and organization, it is clear that the telephone and telegraph aided totalitarian power in collecting and internally disseminating the information it needed to maintain strong centralized control.

At the bottom of most of the claims about instant communication and worldwide networking, computationalism presents a view of politics in which mass actors, either corporations acting in concern with the State or acting with the power traditionally associated with States, execute majoritarian decisions from a central perspective; whatever the diversity of the input story, the output is unified, hierarchized, striated, authoritative. This kind of unification haunts even those web projects that appear, to us today, to be especially disorganized, loose, and distributed, such as Wikipedia, Linux, and other open source software, social "tagging" and other features of the so-called Web 2.0 along with the rest of the Semantic Web, and even the open-text search strategies of Google. While appearing somewhat chaotic and unstructured, they are both tightly structured "underneath" and in formal conception, and also part of a profound progression toward ever more-centralized structures of authority. Thus even skeptical writers like Galloway (2004) and Chun (2006) would seem to have mistaken certain elements of distribution as characteristic of the whole system; what Galloway calls "decentralization" is less fundamental to the Internet than the tremendous process of centralization and absolute authority that is the base structure of computationalism, and that provides a highly authoritarian structure of power that truly drives the great majority of the worldwide digital revolution.

Computationalist Order

Along with its insistence on exact definition, the computer insists everywhere on hierarchy. Few objects and procedures can exist in computers without being placed into hierarchies of various kinds; no doubt this emerges from the logical basis of computing theory, but it also seems to exist in a kind of interactive reflex with the computational enforcement of digital precision. It is certainly possible to create computational objects that are largely nonhierarchical; but in practice this is the exception rather than the rule.

One of the most visible loci of computational hierarchy is in the contemporary software paradigm known as Object-Oriented Programming (OOP). Because the computer is so focused on "objective" reality—meaning the world of objects that can be precisely defined—it seemed a natural development for programmers to orient their tools exactly toward the manipulation of objects. Today, OOP is the dominant mode in programming, for reasons that have much more to do with engineering presumptions and ideologies than with computational efficiency (some OOP languages like Java have historically performed less well than other languages, but are preferred by engineers because of how closely they mirror the engineering idealization about how the world is put together). In this sense, OOP is an especially apt example of computationalist discourse: it emerges from presumptions about and facts about computers, but is fundamentally an intellectual object not required but inspired by real computers (see Smith 1996 for some account of the importance of objects to the philosophy of computing).

OOP languages ask the programmer to begin by defining the "objects" on which a given program is going to operate. These might be books in a library, paragraphs in a book, or monsters and heroes in a computer game. There is a tremendous neatness to this approach; one programmer can literally be assigned to programming the code that creates the monster, for example, while another can work altogether separately on the environment in which the monster exists. In truth, this approach is even more theoretically satisfying than it is practically satisfying; in practice, because it is hard even in idealized worlds (let alone in our material world) to cleanly demarcate environments and objects, it is often difficult to figure out what to program where, what to name an object and what to leave in an environment, and so on.

It is not simply the object/environment distinction that is so attractive to the computationalist mind-set; it is the hierarchies that OOP languages generally demand. In reality, a programmer does not create a single "object," like a "monster"; the programmer creates a class of objects—for example, "monsters"—and then fills it with any number of sub-classes, hierarchically related to the overarching class; these sub-classes are then filled with individual objects. In an abstracted example, an OOP scheme for a typical computer game might look something like this:

Class:	Monsters
Subclass 1:	Humanoid, Reptilian, Avian,
	Cyclopean, Alien
Subclass 2 (Humanoid):	Archer, Fighter, Sniper
Subclass 2 (Avian):	Bird, Pterodactyl, Bird-man
Object 1:	Monster > Avian > Bird

In a real program these classes and sub-classes would be much more extensive than in this example, but the basic principle is clear. Each object is defined hierarchically by where it fits into the larger scheme of objects; each object belongs in a class and does not belong in other classes; classes (but for some exceptional instances) do not overlap. This is much like the "classical" model of speciation to which Western science has been attracted for hundreds of years, but even in that case scientists are aware that it is an idealization: that the material world does not fit so neatly into the categories our scientific programs prefer.

In the world of computers, though, objects do fit into hierarchies neatly, even if it is conceptually clear that the fit is poor. In the abstract example just offered, it is easy to see that the sub-class "pterodactyl" might just as reasonably fit into "reptilian" as it does into "avian"; but in the programmatic reality of the computer this conceptual observation is unimportant. For the purposes of the program a pterodactyl just *is* an avian and is therefore not a reptile; it is easy to see how this could be conceptually satisfying in a way that the physical world is frustrating; even so hierarchical a concept as species itself turns out to be deeply problematic when examined closely (see, e.g., Hull 1986, among his many writings on the topic). The world's hierarchies do not achieve metaphysical "reality" even when they are socially as real as can be; questions like who has social power and who does not have it turn out to be extremely vexing on close analysis. Nothing of the sort is true in computational hierarchies. Everything either fits or does not fit. Because these facts are so apparent in the conceptualizations underlying OOP, computer scientists have proposed alternate models that are less objectifying, including "Aspect-Oriented Programming" or AOP (see, e.g., Filman, Elrad, Clarke, and Aksit 2004) and "Subject-Oriented Programming" or SOP (see, e.g., Harrison and Ossher 1993); it is in no small part because of the lack of fit of these conceptualizations with computationalism that they have found so little traction in computing practice. (Of the two, AOP continues to be explored as a necessary alternative paradigm for situations where the pure object hierarchy proves too restrictive; SOP never developed far beyond a way of critiquing the problematic assumptions behind OOP.)

One place where the computationalist emphasis on hierarchy can be seen with special clarity is with regard to language. Most programming and scripting languages are defined hierarchically (as are most systems of formal logic, which I argue in Chapter 2 are called "languages" via a highly tendentious metaphor); this is nowhere more true than of XML, the wildly popular markup language, which demands multiple hierarchies at every point. When XML met the world of (human) languages, engineers became extremely frustrated with the "failure" of human languages to be characterizable in hierarchical terms. As discussed at greater length in Chapter 5, engineers insisted that all texts—including oral "texts"—should be able to be defined exactly in a hierarchical fashion, which some engineers advanced as the "OHCO Thesis," that a text is an Ordered Hierarchy of Content Objects. The frustration of the engineers is palpable on almost every page of these writings (e.g., DeRose 1999; DeRose et al. 1990; Renear 1995, 2001; Sperberg-McQueen 2001): not only is there a demand that textual scholars *pretend* that texts and language just are arranged hierarchically, but there is also a looming undercurrent of frustration that languages and texts *aren't* hierarchical. Clearly the engineering presumption is that they are hierarchical, and this presumption emerges from engineers who are somewhat familiar with texts and language; one can only imagine the presumptions of engineers who do not work at all closely with texts.

Closely allied to the emphasis on hierarchy is an emphasis on categorization. Every in contemporary computing one sees a profound attention to categories—one might even call it a mania for classification. In the contemporary so-called "Web 2.0" and "social web," one of the main technologies is an XML-fueled insistence on "taxonomy," "folksonomy," and "ontology." These words cover an engineering presumption that we would be much better off if the data on the web was collected into hierarchically arranged categories—categories that are ultimately meant for machine processing more than for human processing. Currently, almost every major website has implemented one kind of tagging function or another—from the keyword tags on Amazon.com to the large-scale tagging function on sites like Digg .com. What seems so obvious about these sites but is rarely discussed in computing circles is that it is the categorization itself, and not its ultimate use, that is so fascinating to us; for every practical application of tagging (there are few of these in practice that help us use the web at all, and most of these are nothing more than ordered popularity lists), there are tens of examples of categorization for its own sake. Arguably, the mania for categorization is just that: a mania for putting things into categories, rather than any kind of demonstration that such categories are useful for anything. That there can be so much tagging on the web and so little consideration of what it is for is indicative of the general cultural orientation of the computational mind-set: put things into categories, arrange things hierarchically, define things neatly, and everything will work out in the end—even if we have no account at all of how the categorization actually gets us to the desired end.

Another critical form of computational authority can be thought of as an emphasis on *concentration*. In general, computers concentrate power. When we say they "empower users," we mean that users can do more with less—more from the inertial perspective of sitting in front of their screen—than they could do in earlier periods with other computational and quasi-computational resources. In earlier times, an accountant would have to use an analog computing device—an adding machine—to perform mathematical calculations to be recorded on a paper spreadsheet. Today the computational power built into software spreadsheets allows the accountant to perform more audits more quickly than before; to do more work at his or her desk than a single individual could perform in the past; and to model a variety of alternative scenarios in a way that was physically unfeasible. In this sense the accountant has much more power to view, change, and manage an institution's finances than he or she had in the past, or to do so with far fewer human resources and much tighter control over the computational resources that have replaced the human ones.

Similarly, the typical view of a computer operator in many institutions—for example, a machine operator running manufacturing robots, or the Information Technology department of corporations, universities, and other institutions—have a kind of centralized view of the rest of the institution that was never previously available. Sitting at a single monitoring station, the archetypical panoptical observer about whom Foucault (1975) talks at great length today has access to a far more comprehensive view of the institution he or she was monitoring, through both video and any number of computational tools that in some cases work with video.

In *Protocol* (2004), Alex Galloway points out all the ways in which the web is a decentralized network, from the worldwide distribution of personal computers to the Internet's reliance on distributed systems of identification and control—systems designed during the Cold War so as to make the computer network reliable even if a significant portion of the network were destroyed (e.g., by a nuclear device). This is both formally and practically true; it is surely one of the most striking and most salutary developments of the worldwide computing network that in some ways the Internet "includes a movement away from central bureaucracies and vertical hierarchies toward a broad network of autonomous social actors" (32–3). But this observation seems in part too presentist and too focused on the individual (and in this sense recreational) use of computers. It is presentist because it presumes that people in their social lives prior to the Internet did not exist as a "broad network of autonomous social actors," a claim that does not seem credible on its face; and its focus on the individual does not address how computers are used in large institutions like universities, corporations, and nonprofits. Despite the formal decentralization of the network protocol used in these organizations, their structure seems to me to remain highly centralized and hierarchical—in some ways, in fact, more controlled and centralized than they could ever have been without computerization. This is a bias toward the screen-present: because we can see (or imagine we can see) the physical network, we believe it is more real than the evanescent social "networks" on which it is built and which it partly supplants.

Rather than a centralized computing infrastructure (although many institutions continue to have these), computerization concentrates and focuses power upwards—it gives the managers and owners of companies far more consistent, more striated, and more controlling power than they have ever had before. Even if management is able to distribute its workforce widely in a geographic sense (via the kinds of global outsourcing discussed in Chapter 6), the managers and owners are only that much more aware of their direct connection to the relations of capital that form the substance of the corporation; in other words, it no longer matters if the workers are located near the managers because the managers are able to exercise all their power from their own location(s). The media today are replete with stories of employees fired for computer or phone activity in which they engaged, blithely unaware that every single activity of employees is fully surveilled by corporate managers. We can see such events as examples of surveillance, which they no doubt are; but they are just as much examples of the concentration of power enabled both by computer representations and by the existence of the computer network itself.

The term *concentration* figures in our history in an important way, as the word for the extermination camps used by the Germans in World War II. While there is certainly no direct connection between the concentration of computing power and a program of genocidal extermination, it is also the case that computing plays a critical role in the concept-structure of the camps, and in particular the reason we call them concentration camps at all. In the camps human beings were reduced to something less than the full status which we typically want to accord to each one of us; and what Foucault calls "population thinking," which certainly is associated with a widespread reliance on computational techniques, was dramatically in evidence in German practice. Furthermore, the Germans relied on early computers and computational methods provided by IBM and some of its predecessor companies to expedite their extermination program (see the controversial Black 2002); while there is no doubt that genocide, racial and otherwise, can be carried out in the absence of computers, it is nevertheless provocative that one of our history's most potent programs for genocide was also a locus for an intensification of computing power.

The discourse of a radical computer revolution is so widespread as to be largely unquestioned throughout society: something has changed so dramatically, this discourse suggests, that we simply don't know how fully any number of social and physical facts may be changed in its wake. Despite its ubiquity, however, this talk is remarkably loose about just what it is supposed to mean; while words like *revolution* and *age* suggest the most widespread kind of change, the components of this profound change are not always clear. Thus Manuel Castells, perhaps the chief sociological theorist of the new age:

> For most of human history, unlike biological evolution, networks were outperformed as tools of instrumentality by organizations able to muster resources around centrally defined goals, achieved through the implementation of tasks in rationalized, vertical chains of command and control. Networks were primarily the preserve of private life; centralized hierarchies were the fiefdoms of power and production. Now, however, the introduction of computer-based information and communication technologies, and particularly the Internet, enables networks to deploy the flexibility and adaptability, thus asserting their evolutionary nature. (Castells 2001, 2)

To some degree, at least, arguments like this one are perched on extremely tendentious assumptions both about our present and, perhaps even more so, about the past. "Centralized hierarchies were the fiefdoms of power and production": even if true, to what extent is it true? In the early modern era, when lords really did have fiefdoms, what licenses the proclamation that communication was "centralized" and not "networked"? Why and how can we assume that networks are not centralized, when our world is full of networks, both physical and abstract, that precisely *are* centralized? Some countries, even today, lack strongly centralized governmental structures (India, many South American countries), and some centralized governments do not exert full political control at their geographic limits; what licenses the view that communication in India is "centralized" while the Internet is "networked"? Are the variety of social collectivities in Africa centralized, and have they always been? In South America? In China?

This symptomatic discourse shows that, to begin with, revolution is not a useful concept when it comes to the analysis of technology and communication systems, despite its ubiquity. It simply is not clear what a communication revolution would be, or perhaps more accurately, it is not clear whether communication revolutions are in any way as dramatic as the political revolutions from which the terminology derives. If the advent of a markedly new technology is a revolution, then the 20th century saw at least half-a-dozen revolutions and probably many more, all of which had profound effects, yet none of which, I would suggest, radically changed the social and political fabric that must be the most central concern of human societies. Despite this, we seem irresistibly drawn to the view that something is changing utterly: we want to believe that we live today in something new called the "information age," as if past generations had not been involved deeply in the exchange, storage, preservation, and use of information: but what else were they engaged in? Yes, their systems of production were more heavily weighted toward physical objects than are ours: but this is an almost-imperceptible difference in quantity, not one that is truly qualitative, unless one simply discounts the production of books, recordings, photographs, and so forth in the times before ours. We have always lived in an information age; we have always relied on networks for communication; we have always used computational systems for the management of large-scale aggregations of human beings, material things, and whatever we want to call information; it is only by focusing almost exclusively on the tools we have in front of us that we can imagine the products we are using today are revolutionary.

This is not to suggest that we should not be entertaining the idea that computer technology represents a revolution: we should consider the idea seriously. But it seems to me we should also be considering the idea that these technologies are not revolutionary in the ordinary sense, and it is this kind of analysis that our society seems to frown upon and that is to some extent hard to locate in the massive amount of writing generated today about the world of the digital. If by revolution we mean either something like the political revolutions with which we are historically familiar (e.g., the French Revolution, the Russian Revolution, the American Revolution), it is not easy to see how the comparison holds between these events and the advent of digital technologies. Even if, closer to home, we imagine that the computer revolution is something like the "scientific revolutions" of which Thomas Kuhn spoke and which are also historically familiar in the sense of the "Copernican revolution" or even the discoveries of relativity or quantum mechanics, it is still not easy to see the qualities shared by these intellectual events and the rise of digital technologies. Where these events did, to some important extent at least, constitute something like epistemic breaks with earlier scientific paradigms, we have yet to see a convincingly original paradigm emerge from the world of the digital, and this is after we have seen digital technology grow and spread for something like 80 or more years. In the case of earlier scientific revolutions, theory preceded practice and it was the theory that was revolutionary; on this model the most revolutionary aspect of computing would be Turing's discovery of the "universal machine," and therefore the algorithmic means to carry out whole classes of computational activities; yet it would not be fair to say, as with quantum mechanics or relativity, that everyone working in these fields had to adjust their thinking to accommodate the new model Turing introduced. Instead, Turing can be said to have codified what was already well understood in theory and was even more clearly already implemented in practices throughout human society.

Thus, for the purposes of this analysis it seems critical to lay aside the idea that computers represent a truly revolutionary change in human society or instance an epistemic break with prior models of knowledge. Of course computers are new in some sense, and of course there are new computers and new digital technologies everywhere around us; but the mere presence of such technologies cannot of itself justify the view that we have entered a new age, unless we mean something different by that term than is usually understood. Our world still requires huge amounts of industrial production to function and has always relied on information transfer in the circulation of capital. As a heuristic, then, this study adopts the view that revolutionary change must be demonstrated before it should be taken as dogma; that we have not yet seen clear demonstrations of the fact of revolution in our society; and that it makes sense then to examine computers themselves and the discourses that support and surround them as if there has not been a revolution: not something dramatically new (even if there are of course many new things) but something like an increase in and increasing emphasis on something upon which society, and capitalist society in particular, has always relied.

Computers provide an unprecedented level of specification and control over every aspect of human society (and the rest of our environment). Where possible, computers simulate processes from the business world, from institutional administration, and from the environment; depending on the domain, these simulations may be used either to guide human behavior or to fully govern it. In other domains, where physical manipulation is needed or where true formalization is not possible, computers control the machines and processes that produce or govern almost every aspect of society. Segmentation itself implies formalization; "perfect" processes from the computational standpoint are those which can be entirely operated through simulation and/or automation (for example, digital television recorders; CAD/CAM software and the physical models they produce; CGI and full animation in films; nearly all accounting, investing, and banking processes). Perfectly segmented processes are found everywhere, perhaps even characteristic, of what we today understand as modernity, business, government. The most successful managers and businesses today appear to be the ones who maximize efficiency by understanding how to focus on striated objects and processes and to bypass smooth ones.

Conceptually there is a powerful tie between the theory and implementation of modern political authority and the figure of computation. In the single text that might be said to most clearly define the notion of political sovereignty in the West (one that also explicitly connects views of human understanding to political philosophy), *Leviathan* by Thomas Hobbes, computation figures in two precise and related ways. Both are quite well known in their own way, but they are generally not related as tropes in Hobbes's especially tropic writing. The first occurs famously on the first page of the Introduction to the volume:

> NATURE (the Art whereby God hath made and governes the World) is by the *Art* of man, as in many other things, so in this also imitated, that it can make an Artificiall Animal. For seeing life is but a motion of Limbs, the beginning whereof is in some principall part within; why may we not say, that all *Automata* (Engines that move themselves by springs and wheeles as doth a watch) have an artificiall life? For what is the *Heart,* but a *Spring;* and the *Nerves,* but so many *Strings;* and the *Joynts,* but so many *Wheeles,* giving motion to the whole Body, such as was intended by the Artificer? *Art* goes yet further, imitation that Rationall and most excellent worke of Nature, *Man.* For by Art is created that great LEVIATHAN called a COMMON-WEALTH, or STATE, (in latine CIVITAS) which is but an Artificiall Man; though of greater stature and strength than the Naturall, for whose protection and defence it was intended; and in which, the *Sovereignty* is an Artificiall *Soul,* as giving life and motion to the whole body.[1]

We dismiss this today largely as metaphor, wondering even what sort of automata Hobbes can have had in mind, since by his own example suggests that watches are alive. From the citizen's perspective, the view seems metaphorical to the point of absurdity; but from the sovereign perspective it seems quite rational—it seems to justify a line of antidemocratic action on the part of the sovereign individual. The sovereign is already inhabiting the

artificial soul of the people in his own being; the transubstantiation inform-
ing this exchange is fully licensed by God; the actions of the King are inherently in the interests of the parts of his body.

The parts of the body politic—in other words, individuals—the body that
before was a "body without organs," and that is now an artificial animal, to
be made up in the new automaton called the State, cannot themselves escape
computational state administration. Like pieces on a chess board, the activities of citizens are administered computationally, their own human powers
essentially irrelevant to the operation of the giant machine that is equivalent,
in a transubstantiative act, to the body and will of the King. But citizens cannot simply be ordered to submit, in the sense that this would deny the most
fundamental principle of "natural right" that Hobbes recognizes but whose
satisfaction the sovereign alone can realize. They must feel it is in not just
their interest but their nature to submit to the sovereign; they must have
within them a simulacrum of the mechanism that constitutes the Leviathan
itself. Thus in *Leviathan*, Chapter 5, Hobbes writes:

> When a man *Reasoneth*, hee does nothing else but conceive a summe totall,
> from *Addition* of parcels; or conceive a Remainder, from *Subtraction* of one
> summer from another: which (if it be done by Words,) is conceiving of the con-
> sequence of the names of all the parts, to the name of the whole; or from the
> names of the whole and one part, to the name of the other part. And though in
> some things, (as in numbers,) besides Adding and Subtracting, men name
> other operations, as Multiplying and Dividing; yet they are the same; for Mul-
> tiplication, is but Adding together of things equall; and Division, but Subtract-
> ing of one thing, as often as we can. . . . REASON, in this sense, is nothing but
> *Reckoning* (Adding and Subtracting) of the Consequences of generall names
> agreed upon, for the *marking* and *signifying* of our thoughts.[2]

While by no means its origin, this passage serves as an appropriate proxy for
the association in the West of the view that the mind just *is* a computer with
the pursuit of political absolutism. One name we give to this view, somewhat
contrary to its content but in accordance with its political lineage, is *Cartesian rationalism*, including its strong association with possessive individualism. A more descriptive name for the view might be *Hobbesian mechanism*.
These thinkers were lumped together at the time under the term *mechanists*
as opposed to *vitalists* (who thought living matter was different in kind from
mechanisms like watches), and it is the mechanists we associate especially
with the rest of possessive-individualist doctrine. A contemporary name for
this doctrine, I have been suggesting, is computationalism.

Contrary to the views of advocates and critics alike that the computer age
should be characterized by concepts like "decentralizing, globalizing, har-

monizing, and empowering" (Negroponte 1995, 229), it seems more plausible that the widespread striating effects of computerization walk hand-in-hand with other, familiar concepts from the histories of rationalism. Globalization, itself, is a kind of hedge word for what in other ages has been called, simply, imperialism, in the sense that a limited number of central authorities exercise high levels of political and economic control and influence over geographically distant terrains. Even at their most apparently radical, computer advocates rely to a striking degree on these concepts to justify their projections, falling back on an explicitly Leibnizian-Cartesian model of Enlightenment that can claim, at best, to be one strand of the form of thought that has underwritten social progress the world over. It is no accident that these core values, which have often been called into question in a variety of intellectual traditions, must be masked in a language of radical democracy and social consciousness. The computer, not least via its association with certain left-leaning social movements of the 1960s and 1970s (see Turner 2006 for an especially telling history of this association)—perhaps most easily exemplified by the rhetoric (but perhaps not the reality) of Apple computer—cloaks a deep, formal, and in some ways inherent commitment to high rationalism in the rhetoric of distribution and decentralization; but for every advance computerization offers along these axes, it offers even more benefits to exactly those forces that it does not advertise, perhaps most crucially because of the usefulness of computerization to exactly the kinds of centralized power that many thinkers have come to call into question.

Out of the preference for looking at the screen, rather than looking at the world, computer advocates suggest that authority is dissolving—that the world is becoming borderless, decentered, and governed by either everyone (in the best case) or by a strong majority (in the next-base case).[3] No doubt this is true of many computer applications and websites: no doubt Digg .com, YouTube, and Wikipedia do reflect the wants and needs of a heterogeneous population. But in the real world, at nearly the same time these democratized forms of media become wildly popular, few would argue that our actual political systems have become radically democratic. If they have changed at all in the late decades of the 20th century and the early ones of the 21st, the most discernible change has been a shift toward absolutist, authoritarian rule: and not merely a shift in this direction among the political classes, but a general tolerance for this sort of rule among the general population. Arguably, the Bush-Cheney political administration comes as close to fascism as the U.S. has ever come, in at least 100 years, precisely because of the close ties between the government, the military, and corporations that grow increasingly large and increasingly resemble governments. Within corporations rule is absolute, and the computer is everywhere an instrument for this absolute rule. There would be no way of proving such a thesis, but the contrarian idea in the margins of this book is one I hope can be considered more seriously as time goes on: in the absolutist bias inherent in their form, and most especially in the discourse surrounding and inspired by them, computers lead in and of themselves not (or, less drastically, not *only*) toward more democracy but toward authoritarian rule; the corollary, which must be true regardless, is that political change and political action need to proceed first of all from people and their direct impact on social relations, and only secondarily from representations on the computer screen.

Computers without Computationalism

T HE MAIN GOAL of this book has been to describe a set of ideological phenomena: the functions of the discourse of computationalism in contemporary social formations; the imbrication of that discourse in a politics that seems strikingly at odds with a discourse of liberation that has more and more come to characterize talk about computers; and the disconnect between the capabilities of physical computers and the ideology of computationalism that underwrites much of our own contemporary investment in being digital. Because human being as such is terrifically mutable—especially on an anti-essentialist, poststructuralist account like the one endorsed here—there is little doubt that the more we imagine ourselves to be like computers, the more computer-like we will become; conversely, the more we imagine computers can take over sociopolitical functions, the more we will give up our own influence over those phenomena—and the more they will pass into the domain of exactly the powerful agents (states, transnational corporations, and capital itself) that already dominate so much of social life.

I agree with the efforts of critics like Alex Galloway and McKenzie Wark and digital activists like Richard Stallman, Lawrence Lessig, Siva Vaidhyanathan, Eric Raymond, and Jimmy Wales, that those of us involved in the creation of computer resources need to keep agitating not merely for open source and free software, but also against the development of regimes of corporate ownership not merely of "intellectual property" but of what must be understood as simultaneously inventions and discoveries. I am not persuaded that inventions like the telephone were aided by patent control; although I would disagree that such inventions are "fundamental" discoveries like physical phenomena such as fire or the division of physical material into elements—discoveries that on any alternative account of human history we were likely to have made at some point. While it is no doubt inevitable that forms of long-distance communication would develop in any plausible human history, I am not persuaded that the exact forms of the telephone, telegraph, etc., are metaphysically necessary.

Computation hovers provocatively between invention and discovery. Perhaps some of the most extreme computer scientists (Ray Kurzweil, Stephen Wolfram, Claude Shannon, Konrad Zuse) believe that digital computation in particular is a fundamental part of the physical universe; certainly there is at least some interesting evidence to support this view. At the same time, it seems equally if not more plausible that a wide range of calculating, quasi-logical, and simulative mechanisms exist in the physical world, and that digital computation is simply one means of replicating some of these phenomena, perhaps the means that is most available to us for cultural reasons—in other words, we found digital computation because our society is already so oriented toward binarisms, hierarchy, and instrumental rationality. The idea of "analog computation," while usually taken to refer to complex machines built for specific (as opposed to general) computational purposes, may be not at all far-fetched; perhaps it is accurate to think of the human brain as an analog computer, a computer whose fundamental logical operations includes not on/off but instead a series of continuous gradients. Because we do not know how to answer these questions, we simply do not know whether digital computation is something we have invented out of whole cloth and that is wholly contingent on other facts of our social world, or whether we have discovered a process as fundamental to our physical makeup as is the oxidative process that can culminate in fire.

What is clear is that today, were a process as fundamental as fire to be discovered, there would be tremendous commercial pressure to keep it first in the domain of particular corporations; second, in the commercial and governmental realms; and third in the domain of technological bureaucracy. This is exactly the kind of expert containment that I am urging we resist, even if technocrats in particular dismiss such concerns as extraneous: they are wrong, because they have been socially conditioned to see their expertise as the only relevant perspective on the phenomena they study. When we turn to developments as important as the human genome and its concomitant technologies, stem cell therapy, and other biological research in particular, we have learned to understand that these technologies actually ignore nontechnical input to their great detriment. If they truly hold important promise for society, their potentials and consequences must be widely understood, debated, and even managed by the polis in general: including technologists, but not to the exclusion of laypeople.

Yet if computerization is as fundamental a development as many people claim, much of its most significant power remains closed behind the walls of technical expertise (a closure that Zittrain 2008 wisely observes becomes more rather than less widespread as the technology develops) and profit-oriented intellectual property restrictions. I am suggesting that this emerges because of the particular character of computerization—because of its close association with computationalism. Again and again this association promises more than it can deliver. It suggests that everything is ultimately computational, and that by increasing computational power we will eventually attain some kind of unprecedented mastery over everything important to human society. In this way even the recent left-liberal championing of computational power, while not altogether misguided—the close involvement of the left with the development of computer technology is nothing less than essential for any political future I can envision—still seems conditioned on a computationalism about which one might imagine caution on the political left. One can easily imagine technical experts themselves becoming much more self-critical than many of them appear to be today— both more critical of the very idea of closed computer architectures to which few nontechnicians have access, and even more strongly, critical of their own supposed mastery and importance. One hallmark of professional computationalists and their connection to the power of capital is a sense of entitlement and individual importance (and here, Google, despite its avowed avoidance of evil, is one of the most serious offenders); that its exponents carry themselves as if they are substantially more important than regular citizens, and even that they know better the good use of computational power than do the *lumpenproletariat*. If true, if our democracy is conditioned on the development of tools which only experts can understand and manipulate, it is hard to see how republican democracy itself can persist through such a condition; if it is not true, as I suspect, then computer evangelists and experts must learn to doubt themselves much more openly, to admit that our philosophical problems will and must remain open, and that Google programmers possess no more self-knowledge than does anybody else.

At several points in this study I have taken issue with some popular critiques of computing, both because they give too much credence to computationalist thinking and because they criticize developments that from what we might call a critical cultural studies perspective would appear salutary. Yet some critiques that have received less traction in popular media point to the kinds of issues raised here. One of the most compelling lines of research that is especially relevant to my own concerns is the one currently being conducted by the Canadian cognitive psychologist Adele Diamond and her collaborators, and at a variety of experimental preschool curricula, of which the best known is called Tools of the Mind (Davidson, et. al. 2006; Diamond 2006; Diamond, et. al. 2007; Spiegel 2008a, 2008b). Within this strand of child development research the primary interest is the child's development of so-called executive functions: the ability of children to learn to regulate themselves and their drives as part of the process of growing up in and accommodating oneself to the social spheres of which adults must be a part.

In an argument that may seem counterintuitive, these researchers demonstrate that an environment in which goals are clearly indicated prohibits children from developing their ability to regulate themselves. In imaginative and unstructured play, Diamond and other researchers suggest, precisely what is at issue is the creation of rules and their violation; in such apparently irresponsible activity children develop their own sense of what rules are, why and how they should be followed, and perhaps most critically, what are the consequences for the *socius* when rules cannot be collectively followed. It seems only a small stretch to take this lesson politically: a person with a fully developed sense of self-regulation will see him- or herself as an active, powerful *member* of the democratic body, a person with a limited but critical responsibility toward the general governance of society (seeŽižek 1997)

But from the perspective we have been developing here, the computer encourages a Hobbesian conception of this political relation: one is either the person who makes and gives orders (the sovereign), or one follows orders. There is no room in this picture for exactly the kind of distributed sovereignty on which democracy itself would seem to be predicated. The point is not that computers encourage violence or do not deliver the benefits their advocates promise: it is rather that they are too good at delivering those promises, too accurate at setting out terms of engagement for the child, and in this way, replace the social activity of children creating and modifying arbitrary rules for themselves (in what is now known as "unstructured play" precisely because of the amount of structure provided in computer play environments; Diamond 2006 provides a good overview of her work on early childhood development of executive function).

Thus while providing the user with an enormous sense of personal power and mastery, in some ways, by externalizing this experience and by, in fact, providing clear and consistent rules that the user *must* follow, engagement with the computer deprives the user of exactly the internal creation not of an authoritarian master but instead of a reasonable governor with whom negotiation and compromise are possible. In Freudian terms, the superego never learns to talk with the id via the ego; the modules remain separate, and in this sense both retain too much control over the modularized ego. Diamond and her collaborators suggest provocatively that in this way the persistent use of computers may be at part the cause of the widespread (in, one notes, fully "modernized" or "developed" societies) phenomenon of what is today called Attention Deficit-Hyperactivity Disorder (ADHD). Precisely because the mechanisms for self-mastery are not developed, the child cannot teach herself to function in social groups unless under direct and complete (i.e., authoritarian) supervision. As worrying as this observation is about child development, it strikes me as that much more dismaying when applied to the political individual. Perhaps it is no accident, despite the tremendous rhetoric otherwise, that especially centralized and quasi-authoritarian forms of political rule have been the norm in recent times, despite the universal adoption of the supposedly democratizing technology of networked computing.

I AM NOT ARGUING that we need to eliminate computers from society. I am instead suggesting that our discourse about computing is almost wholly oriented toward technical capability: what can computers do? What more can they do? What operations in our world can they replace or augment? These are all vital questions—but they seem to stand in for a series of questions that are much more difficult to ask, and whose answers seem much more difficult to envision: *should* computers be used for everything of which they are capable? Does the bare fact that computers can do something mean that it is better to have that thing done on computers than in the analog world? Does the fact that computers provide us with a significant pleasure of mastery license their use for things we must master? Are there situations and actions in which cultivating mastery might be a detriment, rather than an advantage? If we could show, as I have suggested here is plausible, that the relationship between individuals (and institutions) and computers produces problematic psychological and/or ideological formations, what correctives might we develop to these formations?

The rush of evangelical thinking about computers seems at one level unavoidable; computers do amazing things, and like all human creations of this sort, they must and should produce wonder in us. This book has argued that we must also guard ourselves against seeing that wonder as definitive, or exclusive: that especially when we take that enthusiastic wonder to mean that everything is inherently moving toward a Utopian future, we need then to question with particular intensity whether that presumption is rooted in careful observation of social realities, or instead in ideological formations that propel us to overlook the material conditions of the world we hope to better.

Notes

Chapter 1 The Cultural Functions of Computation

1. For the most overt rhetorical presumptions of the newness of new media, see Hansen (2004), Manovich (2001), and the editor's comentaries in Wardrip-Fruin and Montfort (2003). Gitelman (2006) and some of the essays and commentary in Chun and Keenan (2003) and Gitelman and Pingree (2004) raise critical questions about the utility (though not as often the purpose) of this rhetoric.
2. See, e.g., Mosco (2005).
3. Deleuze and Guattari (1987), 375.
4. For the *savoir/connaissance* distinction, see Foucault (2000), especially "Truth and Juridical Forms."
5. Deleuze and Guattari (1987), 376.
6. Negroponte (1995), 229.
7. Ibid., 230.
8. Ibid., 231.
9. See OLPC (2009).
10. Agre (2002) and Sloman (2002) provide convincing typologies of current computational practice that highlight the importance of "traditional" (if massive) computation and the relative and surprising unimportance of Turing machine-style algorithmic processing to contemporary computational practice.
11. See, e.g., Campbell-Kelly and Aspray (2004); Hayles (1999).
12. Grier (2005). See also, e.g., Campbell-Kelly and Aspray (2004).
13. Gottfried Wilhelm Leibniz, letter of December 1678 to Jean Galloys. Quoted in and translated by Davis (2000), 16.
14. Marian Hobson, p.c.

15. In this sense the position I describe here is meant to be completely consistent with what is usually, but perhaps misleadingly, called antihumanism in post-structuralist theory; see, in addition to the Derrida and Foucault material cited elsewhere in this chapter, Althusser (2003, 221–305), and Badiou (2001, 4–17).

Chapter 2 Chomsky's Computationalism

1. In a widely circulated Usenet text whose authorship Chomsky has never disputed (Chomsky 1996), and which strongly resembles many of his other writings in tone and subject matter, Chomsky explains that Foucault offers "simple and familiar ideas . . . dressed up in complicated and pretentious rhetoric" and that Lacan, whom Chomsky "met several times," was "an amusing and perfectly self-conscious charlatan."

2. In all his publications, "computations" and "computational system" are the terms most closely identified with language and syntax, and if anything these references have become more explicit in recent work. For example, in Hauser, Chomsky, and Fitch (2002), an article in *Science* that serves in part to distill Chomsky's recent thought for working biologists, the authors "submit that a distinction should be made between the faculty of language in the broad sense (FLB) and in the narrow sense (FLN). FLB includes a sensory-motor system, a conceptual-intentional system, and the computational mechanisms for recursion, providing the capacity to generate an infinite range of expressions from a finite set of elements. We hypothesize that FLN only includes recursion and is the only uniquely human component of language" (Hauser, Chomsky, and Fitch 2002, 1569)—thus identifying "computational mechanisms" as the true components of human language. In *New Horizons in the Study of Language and Mind* (2000), a collection of philosophical essays, Chomsky repeatedly writes that the "I-Language consists of a computational procedure and a lexicon" (Chomsky 2000b, 120). "Three Factors in Language Design" (2005) calls language a "computational system" (6) and speaks of language requiring "efficient computation" and "cyclic computation" (6), all terms that also feature prominently as well in *The Minimalist Program* (1995).

3. Interpolated quotations from Miller are from George A. Miller, "A Very Personal History," unpublished presentation to Cognitive Science Workshop, MIT, June 1, 1979, ms. 6, 9 (cited in Edwards 1996, 414n54). A version of what Miller calls "Three Models of Grammar" was published as Chomsky (1956).

4. The term *natural languages* is widely accepted in linguistics to distinguish the set of logical and mathematical formalisms from the languages spoken by human beings. The terminology rests on problematic assumptions that are not of direct relevance to this study, and while I use the term *natural languages* throughout to refer to this distinction, it must always be understood in square quotes—nothing could be more profoundly "cultural" than "natural language".

5. Throughout Chomsky's work he goes to great pains to distinguish between two entities he today calls "I-Language" and "E-Language." "E-Language," in general, is what we refer to popularly as "language," where "I-Language" refers to the system inside the brain on which the faculty of language operates ("I

"stands for at least three terms: individual, internal, and intensional; e.g., Chomsky 2000b, 169). Chomskyans would insist that some of the statements quoted here refer to "I-Language," but this is a distinction internal to the Chomskyan system that few non-Chomskyans accept (arguably, to admit the existence of I-Language entails much of the rest of the Chomskyan system). While the distinction deserves sustained treatment, what I am interested in here is how Chomsky's theories engaged with the object we all recognize as language, and as such I avoid much direct discussion of the distinction in this text.

6. Because they reflect at length on Context-Free Grammars (CFGs), this work of Chomsky's is sometimes referred to by the shorthand "CFG essays" or "CFG research."

7. Interview with Postal in Huck and Goldsmith (1995), p. 128. Postal's dissertation was eventually published in 1979; see Postal (1962).

8. Chomsky's source here is a then-current study and partial translation of Humboldt, M. Cowan, *Humanist without Portfolio*. Detroit: Wayne State University Press, 1963, p. 42.

9. Humboldt's progressivist and racialist views are well documented throughout the history of linguistics; see, for example, Harris and Taylor (1989), Chapter 13; and Joseph (2002), Chapter 1.

10. Barsky (1997) continues to identify Chomsky's position as anarcho-syndicalist, although explicit identifications with this position are confined to Chomsky's early political writings; it is not always easy to see what political system Chomsky advocates in later work.

11. Miller, in an interview with the *Baltimore Sun* of October 23, 1982, cited in Edwards (1996), 415n74. Edwards goes on to note that Miller's student Ulric Neisser, "who consolidated the field with his *Cognitive Psychology* (New York: Appleton-Century-Crofts, 1967), which explicitly touted the computer metaphor, repudiated it almost bitterly nine years later in *Cognition and Reality*" (San Francisco: Freeman, 1976).

12. Chomsky, letter of March 31, 1995, to Robert Barsky, cited in Barsky (1997, 98).

13. Chomsky, letter of March 31, 1995, to Robert Barsky, cited in Barsky (1997, 93).

Chapter 3 Genealogies of Philosophical Functionalism

1. The critical essays are numbers 14, 18, 19, and 20, (Putnam 1973, 1960, 1964, and 1967 respectively).

2. To be fair, Chomsky explicitly cites Davis (1958) and Kleene's (1952) volume on metamathematics as his sources, but Davis (1958) is a core volume in the explication of Turing's and Church's logical ideas and their computational framework, and cites Turing (1936) and (1937) extensively; and Putnam refers to Turing's Universal Machine as the "Turing Machine," its common name in computer science and logical theory.

3. Fodor writes that this formulation is "owing to Steven Schiffer" (Fodor 1987, 136) but he does not provide a reference for it in Schiffer's published work.

4. In addition to Putnam's work on the question, several philosophers have directly considered this question. An authoritative mainstream philosophical cognitive

science text, Pylyshyn's *Computation and Cognition* (1984), ultimately raises serious problems for orthodox functionalism (see especially 257–63 of Chapter 9, "What is Cognitive Science a Science Of?"). Penrose (1989, 1994) and van Gelder (1995) offer intriguing proposals for some of the mechanisms other than computation that must be involved in cognition.

5. See Agamben (2003) and Derrida (2002) for attempts to raise the question of the category of "the animal" along lines that read closely to Wittgenstein's remarks at §475 and elsewhere in the *Investigations* (1953).

Chapter 4 Computationalist Linguistics

1. See especially Rorty (1979) and Ryle (1949).
2. Chomsky's early work at MIT was funded in part by the Research Laboratory of Electronics, one of whose topics was MT, though Chomsky himself did not work directly on the project (Harris 1993). For Chomsky's skepticism about MT, quite similar to the line of thought offered here, see, e.g., *Language and Mind* (1972): "The technological advances of the 1940s simply reinforced the general euphoria. Computers were on the horizon. . . . There were few so benighted as to question the possibility, in fact the immediacy, of a final solution to the problem of converting speech into writing by available engineering technique. And just a few years later, it was jubilantly discovered that machine translation and automatic abstracting were just around the corner" (3).
3. The editors of *Machine Translation* write in a footnote to "Translation": "When [Weaver] sent [the memorandum] to some 200 of his acquaintances in various fields, it was literally the first suggestion that most had ever seen that language translation by computer techniques might be possible" (Booth and Locke, in Weaver 1949, 15).
4. Leo Wiener, Norbert's father, professor of Slavic Languages and Literature at Harvard, claimed to speak more than 40 languages (Conway and Siegelman 2005, 13). Under his guidance, Norbert, who started Tufts in 1906 at age eleven when he was reputed to be the "youngest college man in the history of the United States" (ibid., 3), read Greek, Latin, German, and several other languages as well as English by his early teens, and later considered a career in Comparative Philology (ibid., 3–17).
5. See Google's documentation of its translation tools, at http://www.google.com/intl/en/help/faq_translation.html, as well as other pages in the Language Tools section of its site.

Chapter 5 Linguistic Computationalism

1. Also see, for the structured markup view of textuality, Bradley (2001), DeRose (1999), Renear (2001), Sperberg-McQueen (2001), and Willett (2001). Buzzetti (2002) and Hayles (2003) come closest to situating digital text in material textual history, but they do not advance the sort of thesis I am presenting about structured and semantically based markup.

2. This is apparent throughout Wittgenstein (1953), but we can also note in particular the readings of Wittgenstein in Putnam (1981a, 1981b, 1988) and the explicitly Wittgensteinian heritage of Lakoff (1987), whose view of categorization also raises very difficult questions about any sort of explicit strong-AI-style representations of lexical knowledge as suggested by the Semantic Web.

3. See Putnam (1981a, 1988, 1992).

4. See Putnam (1981a, 1981b, 1988).

5. For the characterization of such a view as ideological see, for example, Edwards (1997), Galloway (2004), and Golumbia (2003).

6. Liu (2004), especially Chapters 3 and 4, comes closest in the recent literature to discussing how databases in particular implement a culturally specific division between form and content.

7. Lakoff (1987) provides a sympathetic overview of much of the recent, Wittgenstein-inspired research into categorization that, read carefully, poses significant problems for many aspects of the structured data approach to semantics. At the same time, perhaps the most ardent rationalist in contemporary philosophy, Jerry Fodor, also sees deep problems in the category models that underlie what Lakoff calls "classical" views of categorization; this has been a hallmark of Fodor's career, from Fodor (1970) to Fodor (1998).

8. For the fully articulated vision of the Semantic Web and the extensive use of structured semantic markup in it, see, e.g., Antoniou and van Harmelen (2004), Berners-Lee, Hendler, and Lassila (2001), and Fensel, Hendler, Lieberman, and Wahlster (2003). Tim Berners-Lee, the inventor of the HTML protocol, explains his belief in the necessity of augmenting the web's semantic processing capabilities in more detail in Berners-Lee (1999).

9. For prototype theory see Lakoff (1987).

10. For discussions of language ideologies and their relationship to ideology more generally see Kress and Hodge (1979), the essays in Kroskrity (1998), and Schieffelin, Woolard, and Kroskrity (1998).

11. See Biber, Conrad, and Reppen (1998) for a general overview of computational manipulation of large text corpora.

12. See, e.g., Crystal (2004), Edwards (1997), Galloway (2004), Golumbia (2003), Warschauer (2000), and comments throughout Spivak (1999).

13. It is difficult enough simply to identify languages in terms appropriate for computers; see Constable and Simons (2000) for a metadata proposal that shows how far the computer environment is from being truly multilingual. (Still, today, most computers cannot effectively process the majority of the world's 6,000 languages).

14. See, for example, the Wikipedia entry on embedded systems: http://en.wikipedia.org/wiki/Embedded_system.

Chapter 6 Computation, Globalization, and Cultural Striation

1. "Racialist" is used here in distinction to "racist"; "racialist" refers to "a belief in the existence and significance of racial categories, but not necessarily in a hierarchy between the races, or in any political or ideological position of racial

supremacy" (Wikipedia, "Racialism," accessed 12/22/2008). As used here, racialist practices are those that reify racial categories, without a necessary commitment to racist ideology.

Chapter 7 Computationalism, Striation, and Cultural Authority

1. "Beniger (1986), especially pp. 390–436." (Liu's note, 442).

Chapter 8 Computationalism and Political Individualism

1. Putnam discusses "individualism" most famously and expansively in "The Meaning of 'Meaning'" (Putnam 1975, 215–71), but it is a persistent theme in his later writings. Also see Burge (1979, 1986).
2. *Modus ponens* is the logician's name for one of the simplest and most familiar of these math-like principles, made up of three steps: (1) If P, then Q; (2) P; (3) therefore, Q. The idea is that propositions having this form are true regardless of the contents one assigns to P and Q. Most famously: (1) all men are mortal; (2) Socrates is a man; (3) therefore Socrates is mortal.

Chapter 9 Computationalism and Political Authority

1. Hobbes (1651), 81.
2. Ibid., 110–1.
3. See Goldsmith and Wu (2006) on the notion of borderlessness; Sunstein (2001) and especially Hindman (2008) present skeptical reviews of claims for automatic radical democratic transformation via computerization.

References

Abram, David. 1996. *The Spell of the Sensuous: Perception and Language in a More-than-Human World.* New York: Pantheon.

Adam, Alison. 1998. *Artificial Knowing: Gender and the Thinking Machine.* New York: Routledge.

Adam, Frédéric, and David Sammon, eds. 2004. *The Enterprise Resource Planning Decade: Lessons Learned and Issues for the Future.* Hershey, PA: Idea Group Publishing.

Adas, Michael. 1989. *Machines as the Measure of Man: Science, Technology, and Ideologies of Western Dominance.* Ithaca, NY: Cornell University Press.

———. 2006. *Dominance by Design: Technological Imperatives and America's Civilizing Mission.* Cambridge, MA: Harvard University Press.

Agamben, Giorgio. 2003. *The Open: Man and Animal.* Stanford, CA: Stanford University Press.

Age of Empires II: The Conquerors. 2000. Computer game. Redmond, WA: Microsoft Corporation.

Age of Empires III: The War Chiefs. 2006. Computer game. Redmond, WA: Microsoft Corporation.

Agre, Philip E. 1997. *Computation and Human Experience.* Cambridge, MA: Cambridge University Press.

———. 2002. "The Practical Logic of Computer Work." In Scheutz (2002), 129–142.

Althusser, Louis. 1968. "Ideology and Ideological State Apparatuses: Notes Toward an Investigation." In Althusser (1971), 127–186.

———. 1971. *Lenin and Philosophy and Other Essays.* New York: Monthly Review Press.

————. 2003. *The Humanist Controversy and Other Writings.* New York: Verso.

————. 2006. *Philosophy of the Encounter: Later Writings, 1978–1987.* New York: Verso.

Amadae, S. M. 2003. *Rationalizing Capitalist Democracy: The Cold War Origins of Rational Choice Liberalism.* Chicago: University of Chicago Press.

Anderson, Perry. 1974. *Lineages of the Absolutist State.* London: New Left Books.

Antoniou, Grigoris, and Frank van Harmelen. 2004. *A Semantic Web Primer.* Cambridge, MA: The MIT Press.

Badiou, Alain. 2001. *Ethics: An Essay on the Understanding of Evil.* New York: Verso.

Baran, Paul A., and Paul M. Sweezy. 1966. *Monopoly Capital: An Essay on the American Economic and Social Order.* New York: Monthly Review Press.

Barsky, Robert F. 1997. *Noam Chomsky: A Life of Dissent.* Cambridge, MA: The MIT Press.

Bates, Madeleine, and Ralph M. Weischedel, eds. 1993. *Challenges in Natural Language Processing.* New York: Cambridge University Press.

Bauerlein, Mark. 2008. *The Dumbest Generation: How the Digital Age Stupefies Young Americans and Jeopardizes Our Future (Or, Don't Trust Anyone Under 30).* New York: Penguin.

Bechtel, William, and Adele Abrahamsen. 2002. *Connectionism and the Mind: Parallel Processing, Dynamics, and Evolution in Networks.* Second edition. Malden, MA: Blackwell.

Beniger, James R. 1986. *The Control Revolution: Technological and Economic Origins of the Information Society.* Cambridge, MA: Harvard University Press.

Benkler, Yochai. 2006. *The Wealth of Networks: How Social Production Transforms Markets and Freedom.* New Haven, CT: Yale University Press.

Bennington, Geoffrey, and Jacques Derrida. 1993. *Jacques Derrida.* Chicago: University of Chicago Press.

Berlinski, David. 2000. *The Advent of the Algorithm: The 300-Year Journey from an Idea to the Computer.* San Diego: Harcourt.

Berners-Lee, Tim. 1999. *Weaving the Web: The Original Design and Ultimate Destiny of the World Wide Web by Its Inventor.* New York: HarperCollins Publishers.

Berners-Lee, Tim, J. Hendler, and O. Lassila. 2001. "The Semantic Web." *Scientific American* 284 (May), 34–43.

Berwick, Robert C. 1985. *The Acquisition of Syntactic Knowledge.* Cambridge, MA: The MIT Press.

Biber, Douglas, Susan Conrad, and Randi Reppen. 1998. *Corpus Linguistics: Investigating Language Structure and Use.* New York: Cambridge University Press.

Birkerts, Sven. 1994. *The Gutenberg Elegies: The Fate of Reading in an Electronic Age.* New York: Ballantine.

Black, Edwin. 2002. *IBM and the Holocaust: The Strategic Alliance Between Nazi Germany and America's Most Powerful Corporation.* New York: Three Rivers Press.

Block, Ned. 1990. "The Computer Model of the Mind." In Daniel N. Osherson and Edward E. Smith, eds., *Thinking: An Invitation to Cognitive Science, Volume 3.* Cambridge, MA: The MIT Press, 247–289.

Bogard, William. 1996. *The Simulation of Surveillance: Hypercontrol in Telematic Societies.* New York: Cambridge University Press.

Booth, A. Donald, and William N. Locke. 1955. "Historical Introduction." In Locke and Booth (1955), 1–14.

Bowers, C. A. 2000. *Let Them Eat Data: How Computers Affect Education, Cultural Diversity, and the Prospects of Ecological Sustainability.* Athens, GA: University of Georgia Press.

Bradley, J. 2001. "Text Tools." In Schreibman, Siemens, and Unsworth (2001), 505–522.

Braverman, Harry. 1974. *Labor and Monopoly Capital: The Degradation of Work in the Twentieth Century.* New York: Monthly Review Press.

Brunn, Stanley D., ed. 2006. *Wal-Mart World: The World's Biggest Corporation in the Global Economy.* New York: Routledge.

Burge, Tyler. 1979. "Individualism and the Mental." *Midwest Studies in Philosophy* 4, 73–121.

———. 1986. "Individualism and Psychology." *Philosophical Review* 43, 3–45.

Burnham, David. 1983. *The Rise of the Computer State.* New York: Vintage.

Bush, Vannevar. 1945. "As We May Think." In Wardrip-Fruin and Montfort (2003), 37–47.

Butler, Judith. 1997. *The Psychic Life of Power: Theories in Subjection.* Stanford, CA: Stanford University Press.

Buzzetti, Dino. 2002. "Digital Representation and the Text Model." *New Literary History* 33:1, 61–88.

Campbell, Jeremy. 1982. *Grammatical Man: Information, Entropy, Language, and Life.* New York: Simon and Schuster.

Campbell-Kelly, Martin, and William Aspray. 2004. *Computer: A History of the Information Machine.* Second edition. Boulder, CO: Westview Press.

Carnap, Rudolf. 1937. *The Logical Syntax of Language.* London: Routledge and Kegan Paul.

Carr, Nicholas G. 2003. "IT Doesn't Matter." *Harvard Business Review* (May), 41–49.

———. 2004. *Does IT Matter? Information Technology and the Corrosion of Competitive Advantage.* Cambridge, MA: Harvard Business School Press.

Castells, Manuel. 2003. *The Information Age: Economy, Society, and Culture.* Three Volumes. Malden, MA: Blackwell Publishers.

"Chomsky Is Citation Champ." 1992. *MIT Tech Talk,* http://web.mit.edu.

Chomsky, Noam. 1955. "The Logical Structure of Linguistic Theory." Manuscript, University of Pennsylvania.

———. 1956. "Three Models for the Description of Language." *IRE Transactions on Information Theory* IT-2, Number 3 (September), 113–124.

———. 1957. *Syntactic Structures.* The Hague: Mouton.

———. 1959a. "On Certain Formal Properties of Grammars." *Information and Control* 2, 137–167.

———. 1959b. "Review of Skinner's *Verbal Behavior*." *Language* 35, 26–57.

———. 1965. *Aspects of the Theory of Syntax*. Cambridge, MA: The MIT Press.

———. 1966. *Cartesian Linguistics: A Chapter in the History of Rationalist Thought*. New York: Harper & Row.

———. 1972. *Language and Mind*. New York: Cambridge University Press.

———. 1973. "Introduction." In Chomsky (1975), 1–53.

———. 1975. *The Logical Structure of Linguistic Theory*. New York: Plenum. Revised & edited version of Chomsky 1955 with new introduction.

———. 1995. *The Minimalist Program*. Cambridge, MA: The MIT Press.

———. 1996. "Chomsky on Postmodernism." Usenet text. http://www.cscs.umich.edu/~crshalizi/.

———. 2000a. *The Architecture of Language*. New Delhi: Oxford University Press.

———. 2000b. *New Horizons in the Study of Language and Mind*. New York: Cambridge University Press.

———. 2004. "Beyond Explanatory Adequacy." In Adriana Belletti, ed., *The Cartography of Syntactic Structures. Volume 3: Structures and Beyond*. New York: Cambridge University Press, 104–131.

———. 2005. "Three Factors in Language Design." *Linguistic Inquiry* 36 (Winter), 1–22.

Chomsky, Noam, and George Miller. 1958. "Finite State Languages." *Information and Control* 1, 91–112.

Chomsky, Noam, and M.P. Schützenberger. 1963. "The Algebraic Theory of Context-Free Languages." In P. Braffort and D. Hirschberg, eds., *Computer Programming and Formal Systems*. Amsterdam: North-Holland, 118–161.

Chun, Wendy H.K. 2006. *Control and Freedom: Power and Paranoia in the Age of Fiber Optics*. Cambridge, MA: The MIT Press.

Chun, Wendy H.K., and Thomas Keenan, eds. 2003. *New Media, Old Media: Interrogating the Digital Revolution*. New York: Routledge.

Civilization II, aka *Sid Meier's Civilization II*. 1996. Computer game. Hunt Valley, MD: MicroProse Software, Inc.

Civilization III, aka *Sid Meier's Civilization III*. 2001. Computer game. Hunt Valley, MD: Firaxis Games.

Claritas. 2007. "Claritas PRIZM NE: 66 Marketing Segments." Claritas corporate website. Online at http://www.claritas.com/.

Constable, Peter, and Gary Simons. 2000. "Language Identification and IT: Addressing Problems of Linguistic Diversity on a Global Scale." *SIL Electronic Working Papers* (SILEWP). Dallas, TX: SIL International. http://www.sil.org/.

Conway, Flo, and Jim Siegelman. 2005. *Dark Hero of the Information Age: In Search of Norbert Wiener, The Father of Cybernetics*. New York: Basic Books.

Copeland, B. Jack. 1996. "What Is Computation?" *Synthese* 108, 335–359.

———. 2002. "Narrow versus Wide Mechanism." In Scheutz (2002), 59–86.

Coulmas, Florian. 1989. *The Writing Systems of the World*. Oxford: Blackwell.

———. 1996. *The Blackwell Encyclopedia of Writing Systems*. Oxford: Blackwell.

Coombs, James H., Allen Renear, Steven J. DeRose. 1987 "Markup Systems and The Future of Scholarly Text Processing." *Communications of the ACM* 30:11, 933–947.

CPM Marketing Group. 2001. "OSF Healthcare System Earns Substantial ROI with CPM Customer Relationship Management Solution." Press Release (November 7, 2001). Online at http://biz.yahoo.com/bw/011107/72048_1.html.

Crosby, Alfred W. 1997. *The Measure of Reality: Quantification and Western Society, 1250–1600.* New York: Cambridge University Press.

Crystal, David. 2001. *Language and the Internet.* New York: Cambridge University Press.

———. 2004. *The Language Revolution.* New York: Polity Press.

Dahlberg, Lincoln, and Eugenia Siapera, eds. 2007. *Radical Democracy and the Internet: Interrogating Theory and Practice.* New York: Palgrave.

Dale, Robert, Hermann Moisl, and Harold Somers, eds. 2000. *Handbook of Natural Language Processing.* New York: Marcel Dekker.

Darnell, Rick. 1997. "A Brief History of SGML." In *HTML Unleashed 4.* Indianapolis, IN: Sams Publishing. §3.2. http://www.webreference.com/.

Davenport, David. 2000. "Computationalism: The Very Idea." *Conceptus-Studien* 14, 121–137.

Davidson, Matthew C., Dima Amso, Loren Cruess Anderson, and Adele Diamond. 2006. "Development of Cognitive Control and Executive Functions from 4 to 13 years: Evidence from Manipulations of Memory, Inhibition, and Task Switching." *Neuropsychologia* 44, 2037-2078.

Davis, Martin. 1958. *Computability and Unsolvability.* New York: McGraw-Hill.

———. 2000. *Engines of Logic: Mathematicians and the Origin of the Computer.* New York: Norton.

Davis, Martin, and Elaine J. Weyuker. 1983. *Computability, Complexity, and Languages: Fundamentals of Theoretical Computer Science.* New York: Academic Press.

De Landa, Manuel. 1991. *War in the Age of Intelligent Machines.* New York: Zone Books.

———. 2002. *Intensive Science and Virtual Philosophy.* New York: Continuum.

Deleuze, Gilles. 1980. "Course on Leibniz." http://www.webdeleuze.com/.

———. 1992. "Postscript on the Societies of Control." *October* 59 (Winter), 3–7.

Deleuze, Gilles, and Félix Guattari. 1983. *Anti-Oedipus: Capitalism and Schizophrenia.* Minneapolis: University of Minnesota Press.

Deleuze, Gilles, and Félix Guattari. 1987. *A Thousand Plateaus: Capitalism and Schizophrenia.* Minneapolis: University of Minnesota Press.

Dennett, Daniel C. 1991. "Granny's Campaign for Safe Science." In Loewer and Rey (1991), 87–94.

DeRose, Stephen J. 1999. "XML and the TEI." *Computers and the Humanities* 33:1–2 (April), 11–30.

DeRose, Stephen J., D. Durand, E. Mylonas, and Allen H. Renear. 1990. "What is Text, Really?" *Journal of Computing in Higher Education* 1:2, 3–26.

Derrida, Jacques. 1967. "Structure, Sign, and Play in the Discourse of the Human Sciences." In *Writing and Difference.* Chicago: University of Chicago Press, 1978, 278–293.

———. 1976. *Of Grammatology.* Revised edition. Baltimore, MD: Johns Hopkins University Press, 1998.

———. 1979. "Scribble (Writing-Power)." In Derrida (1998), 50–73.

———. 1988. *Limited Inc.* Evanston, IL: Northwestern University Press.

———. 1990. "Force of Law: The 'Mystical Foundation of Authority.' " In David Gray Carlson, Drucilla Cornell, and Michel Rosenfeld, eds., *Deconstruction and the Possibility of Justice.* New York: Routledge, 1992, 3–67.

———. 1992. "A 'Madness' Must Watch Over Thinking." In *Points . . . : Interviews, 1974–1994.* Stanford, CA: Stanford University Press, 1995, 339–364.

———. 1993. "Nietzsche and the Machine." In *Negotiations: Interventions and Interviews 1971–2001.* Stanford, CA: Stanford University Press, 2002, 215–256.

———. 1996a. *Monolingualism of the Other; or, The Prosthesis of Origin.* Stanford, CA: Stanford University Press.

———. 2002. "This Animal That Therefore I Am (More to Follow)." *Critical Inquiry* 28:2 (Winter), 369–418.

———. 2005. *Rogues: Two Essays on Reason.* Stanford, CA: Stanford University Press.

Diamond, Adele. 2006. "The Early Development of Executive Functions." In Ellen Bialystok and Fergus I. M. Craik, eds., *Lifespan Cognition: Mechanisms of Change.* New York: Oxford University Press, 70–95.

Diamond, Adele, W. Stephen Barnett, Jessica Thomas, and Sarah Munro. 2007. "Preschool Program Improves Cognitive Control." *Science* 318, 1387-1388.

Dixon, R. M. W. 1997. *The Rise and Fall of Languages.* New York: Cambridge University Press.

Dreyfus, Hubert L. 1992. *What Computers Still Can't Do: A Critique of Artificial Reason.* Third edition. Cambridge, MA: The MIT Press.

Edwards, Paul N. 1996. *The Closed World: Computers and the Politics of Discourse in Cold War America.* Cambridge, MA: The MIT Press.

Eichenwald, Kurt. 2005. *Conspiracy of Fools: A True Story.* New York: Broadway Books.

Ellul, Jacques. 1964. *The Technological Society.* New York: Vintage.

———. 1980. *The Technological System.* New York: Continuum.

———. 1990. *The Technological Bluff.* Grand Rapids, MI: William B. Eerdmans Publishing.

Empire Earth. 2001. Computer game. Los Angeles, CA: Sierra Entertainment.

Empire Earth II. 2005. Computer game. Paris, France: Vivendi Universal.

Fair, Isaac and Co. n.d. "Fair, Isaac MarketSmart Decision System™ for Retail." Press release. http://www.fairisaac.com.

Fensel, Dieter, J. Hendler, H. Lieberman, and W. Wahlster, eds. 2003. *Spinning the Semantic Web: Bringing the World Wide Web to Its Full Potential.* Cambridge, MA: The MIT Press.

Filman, Robert E., Tzilla Elrad, Siobhán Clarke, and Mehmet Aksit. 2004. *Aspect-Oriented Software Development.* Reading, MA: Addison-Wesley.

Fodor, Jerry A. 1964. "On Knowing What We Would Say." In Lyas (1971), 297–308.

———. 1970. "Three Reasons for Not Deriving 'Kill' from 'Cause to Die.' " *Linguistic Inquiry* 1, 429–438.

———. 1975. *The Language of Thought.* New York: Thomas Crowell.

————. 1981. *RePresentations: Philosophical Essays on the Foundations of Cognitive Science.* Cambridge, MA: The MIT Press.

————. 1983. *The Modularity of Mind: An Essay on Faculty Psychology.* Cambridge, MA: The MIT Press.

————. 1987. *Psychosemantics: The Problem of Meaning in the Philosophy of Mind.* Cambridge, MA: The MIT Press.

————. 1990. *A Theory of Content and Other Essays.* Cambridge, MA: The MIT Press.

————. 1994. *The Elm and the Expert: Mentalese and Its Semantics.* Cambridge, MA: The MIT Press.

————. 1998a. *Concepts: Where Cognitive Science Went Wrong.* New York: Oxford University Press.

————. 1998b. *In Critical Condition: Polemical Essays on Cognitive Science and the Philosophy of Mind.* Cambridge, MA: The MIT Press.

————. 2000. *The Mind Doesn't Work That Way: The Scope and Limits of Computational Psychology.* Cambridge, MA: The MIT Press.

————. 2003. *Hume Variations.* New York: Oxford University Press.

Fodor, Jerry A., and Jerrold J. Katz. 1962. "What's Wrong with the Philosophy of Language?" In Lyas (1971), 269–283.

Fodor, Jerry A., and Jerrold J. Katz. 1963. "The Availability of What We Say." In Lyas (1971), 190–203.

Fodor, Jerry A., and Jerrold J. Katz, eds. 1964. *The Structure of Language: Readings in the Philosophy of Language.* Englewood Cliffs, NJ: Prentice-Hall.

Fodor, Jerry A., and Ernest Lepore. 1992. *Holism: A Shopper's Guide.* Cambridge, MA: Blackwell.

Fodor, Jerry A., and Ernest Lepore. 2002. *The Compositionality Papers.* New York: Oxford.

Foucault, Michel. 1969. "What Is An Author?" In Foucault, *Language, Counter-Memory, Practice: Selected Essays and Interviews.* Ithaca, NY: Cornell University Press, 1977, 113–138.

————. 1973. *The Order of Things: An Archaeology of the Human Sciences.* New York: Vintage Books.

————. 1975. *Discipline and Punish: The Birth of the Prison.* New York: Vintage Books,.

————. 2000. *Power. Essential Works of Foucault Volume 3.* New York: The New Press.

Freud, Sigmund. 1905. *Three Essays on the Theory of Sexuality.* Standard Edition of the Complete Works of Sigmund Freud, Vol. 7. London: Hogarth Press, 135–243.

Friedman, Thomas. 2005. *The World Is Flat: A Brief History of the Twenty-First Century.* Third edition. New York: Picador, 2007.

Galloway, Alexander R. 2004. *Protocol: How Control Exists after Decentralization.* Cambridge, MA: The MIT Press.

————. 2006. *Gaming: Essays on Algorithmic Culture.* Minneapolis: University of Minnesota Press.

Galloway, Alexander R., and Eugene Thacker. 2007. *The Exploit: A Theory of Networks*. Minneapolis, MN: University of Minnesota Press.

Gates, Bill. 1995. *The Road Ahead*. New York: Viking.

Gauthier, Jay. 2001. "Business Architects for the Front Office: CRM and Its Impact on the Healthcare Industry." Berkeley Enterprise Partners, Inc., Sales presentation (February 2, 2001). http://www.mahealthdata.org/.

Gelb, I. J. 1952. *A Study of Writing*. Second edition. Chicago: University of Chicago Press, 1963.

Gitelman, Lisa. 2006. *Always Already New: Media, History, and the Data of Culture*. Cambridge, MA: The MIT Press

Gitelman, Lisa, and Geoffrey B. Pingree, eds. 2004. *New Media, 1740–1915*. Cambridge, MA: The MIT Press.

Goldsmith, Jack, and Tim Wu. 2006. *Who Controls the Internet? Illusions of a Borderless World*. New York: Oxford University Press.

Goldsmith, John. 2004. "From Algorithms to Generative Grammar and Back Again." Paper delivered at Chicago Linguistics Society. Ms. University of Chicago.

Golumbia, David. 1996a. "Black and White World: Race, Ideology, and Utopia in *Triton* and *Star Trek*." *Cultural Critique* 32 (Winter), 75–96.

———. 1996b. "Hypercapital." *Postmodern Culture* 7:1 (September).

———. 1999. "Quine, Derrida, and the Question of Philosophy." *The Philosophical Forum* 30 (September), 163–186.

———. 2001. "The Computational Object: A Poststructuralist Approach." Paper delivered at ACH/ALLC, New York University, New York, NY.

———. 2003. "Metadiversity: On the Unavailability of Alternatives to Information." In Mark Bousquet and Katherine Wills, eds., *The Politics of Information*. New York: Alt-X.

———. 2004. "Computation, Gender, and Human Thinking." *Differences: A Journal of Feminist Cultural Studies* 14 (Summer), 27–48.

Gresh, Louis H., and Robert Weinberg. 1999. *The Computers of Star Trek*. New York: Basic Books.

Grier, David Alan. 2005. *When Computers Were Human*. Princeton, NJ: Princeton University Press.

Grimes, Barbara, ed. 2000. *Ethnologue*. 14th Edition. CD-ROM. Dallas, TX: SIL International.

Hansen, Mark B. N. 2006. *Bodies in Code: Interfaces with Digital Media*. New York: Routledge.

Hardcastle, Valerie Gray. 1995. "Computationalism." *Synthese* 105:3 (December), 303–317.

Hardt, Michael, and Antonio Negri. 2000. *Empire*. Cambridge, MA: Harvard University Press.

Hardt, Michael, and Antonio Negri. 2004. *Multitude: War and Democracy in the Age of Empire*. Cambridge, MA: Harvard University Press.

Harris, Randy Allen. 1993. *The Linguistics Wars*. New York: Oxford University Press.

Harris, Roy. 1987. *The Language Machine*. Ithaca, NY: Cornell University Press.

Harris, Zellig. 2002. "The Background of Transformational and Metalanguage Analysis." In Bruce E. Nevin, ed., *The Legacy of Zellig Harris: Language and*

Information into the 21st Century. Volume One: Philosophy of Science, Syntax, and Semantics. Philadelphia: John Benjamins, 1–15.

Harrison, William, and Harold Ossher. 1993. "Subject-Oriented Programming: A Critique of Pure Objects." *Proceedings of 1993 Conference on Object-Oriented Programming Systems, Languages, and Applications.* http://www.research.ibm.com/.

Haugeland, John. 1985. *Artificial Intelligence: The Very Idea.* Cambridge, MA: The MIT Press.

Hauser, Marc D., Noam Chomsky, and W. Tecumseh Fitch. 2002. "The Faculty of Language: What Is It, Who Has It, and How Did It Evolve?" *Science* 298 (November 22), 1569–1579.

Hausser, Roland. 2001. *Foundations of Computational Linguistics: Human-Computer Communication in Natural Language.* Second edition. New York: Springer-Verlag.

Hayles, N. Katherine. 1999. *How We Became Posthuman: Virtual Bodies in Cybernetics, Literature, and Informatics.* Chicago: University of Chicago Press.

———. 2003. "Translating Media: Why We Should Rethink Textuality." *Yale Journal of Criticism* 16:2 (Fall), 263–290.

———. 2005. *My Mother Was a Computer: Digital Subjects and Literary Texts.* Chicago: University of Chicago Press.

Headrick, Daniel R. 1981. *The Tools of Empire: Technology and European Imperialism in the Nineteenth Century.* New York: Oxford University Press.

———. 1988. *The Tentacles of Progress: Technology Transfer in the Age of Imperialism, 1850–1940.* New York: Oxford University Press.

Heidegger, Martin. 1954. "The Question Concerning Technology." In *Basic Writings.* Revised and expanded edition. San Francisco: HarperCollins Publishers, 1993, 311–341.

Hindman, Matthew. 2008. *The Myth of Digital Democracy.* Princeton, NJ: Princeton University Press.

Hobbes, Thomas. 1651. *Leviathan, or, The Matter, Forme, & Power of a Common-Wealth Ecclesiasticall and Civill.* Ed. C. B. Macpherson. New York: Penguin, 1985.

Hobson, Marian. 1998. *Jacques Derrida: Opening Lines.* New York: Routledge.

Huck, Geoffrey J., and John A. Goldsmith. 1995. *Ideology and Linguistic Theory: Noam Chomsky and the Deep Structure Debates.* New York: Routledge.

Hull, David. 1986. "On Human Nature." *PSA: Proceedings of the Biennial Meeting of the Philosophy of Science Association,* Vol. Two: Symposia and Invited Papers, 3–13.

Hutchins, W. J. 1986. *Machine Translation: Past, Present, Future.* Chichester and New York: Ellis Horwood Limited/John Wiley & Sons.

Hymes, Dell, and John Fought. 1981. *American Structuralism.* The Hague: Mouton.

Illich, Ivan 1980. "Vernacular Values." *CoEvolution Quarterly.* http://www.preservenet.com/.

Innis, Harold. 1950. *Empire and Communications.* Second edition, revised by Mary Q. Innis. Toronto: University of Toronto Press, 1972.

———. 1951. *The Bias of Communication*. Revised edition. Toronto: University of Toronto Press, 1964.

Jameson, Fredric. 1981. *The Political Unconscious: Narrative as a Socially Symbolic Act*. Ithaca, NY: Cornell University Press.

———. 1991. *Postmodernism, or, The Cultural Logic of Late Capitalism*. Durham, NC: Duke University Press.

Jenkins, Henry, and David Thorburn, eds. 2003. *Democracy and New Media*. Cambridge, MA: The MIT Press.

Jeter, Lynne W. 2003. *Disconnected: Deceit and Betrayal at Worldcom*. New York: Wiley.

Joseph, John E. 2002. *From Whitney to Chomsky: Essays in the History of American Linguistics*. Philadelphia: John Benjamins.

Katz, Jerrold J. 1990. *The Metaphysics of Meaning*. Cambridge, MA: The MIT Press.

———. 1996. "The Unfinished Chomskyan Revolution." *Mind and Language* 11, 270–294.

———. 1998. *Realistic Rationalism*. Cambridge, MA: The MIT Press.

Katz, Jerrold J., and Jerry A. Fodor. 1963. "The Structure of a Semantic Theory." In Fodor and Katz (1964), 479–518.

Katz, Jerrold J., and Paul Postal. 1991. "Realism vs. Conceptualism in Linguistics." *Linguistics and Philosophy* 14, 515–554.

Keen, Andrew. 2007. *The Cult of the Amateur: How Today's Internet Is Killing Our Culture*. New York: Doubleday.

Kleene, Stephen Cole. 1952. *Introduction to Metamathematics*. New York: Van Nostrand.

Kolko, Beth E., Lisa Nakamura, and Gilbert B. Rodman, eds. 2000. *Race in Cyberspace*. New York: Routledge.

Kreml, William P. 1984. *Relativism and the Natural Left*. New York: Columbia University Press.

Kress, Gunther, and Robert Hodge. 1979. *Language as Ideology*. London: Routledge and Kegan Paul.

Kurzweil, Ray. 1990. *The Age of Intelligent Machines*. Cambridge, MA: The MIT Press.

———. 1999. *The Age of Spiritual Machines: When Computers Exceed Human Intelligence*. New York: Viking.

———. 2006. *The Singularity Is Near: When Humans Transcend Biology*. New York: Penguin.

Lakoff, George. 1987. *Women, Fire, and Dangerous Things: What Categories Reveal about the Mind*. Chicago and London: University of Chicago Press.

Lakoff, George, and Mark Johnson. 1999. *Philosophy in the Flesh: The Embodied Mind and Its Challenge to Western Thought*. New York: Basic Books.

Landow, George. 1992. *Hypertext: The Convergence of Contemporary Critical Theory and Technology*. Baltimore, MD: Johns Hopkins University Press.

Lash, Scott. 2002. *Critique of Information*. London: Sage Publications.

Lawler, John M. 1999. "Metaphors We Compute By." In D. Hickey, ed., *Figures of Thought: For College Writers*. Mayfield Publishing. http://www-personal.umich.edu/~jlawler/.

Leibniz, Gottfried Wilhelm. 1684. *Meditations on Knowledge, Truth, and Ideas.* Trans. Jonathan Bennett. Modified by Bennett from his Cambridge University Press edition of Leibniz's works. http://www.earlymoderntexts.com/.

Lenat, Douglas B., and R. V. Guha. 1990. *Building Large Knowledge-Based Systems: Representation and Inference in the Cyc Project.* Reading, MA: Addison-Wesley.

Lessig, Lawrence. 2002. *The Future of Ideas: The Fate of the Commons in a Connected World.* New York: Vintage.

———. 2005. *Free Culture: The Nature and Future of Creativity.* New York: Penguin.

Lévy, Pierre. 2001. *Cyberculture.* Minneapolis: University of Minnesota Press.

Lichtenstein, Nelson, ed. 2006. *Wal-Mart: The Face of Twenty-First-Century Capitalism.* New York: The New Press.

Litman, Jessica. 2001. *Digital Copyright.* Amherst, NY: Prometheus Books.

Liu, Alan. 2004. *The Laws of Cool: Knowledge Work and the Culture of Information.* Chicago: University of Chicago Press.

Locke, William N., and A. Donald Booth, eds. 1955. *Machine Translation of Languages: Fourteen Essays.* Cambridge, MA: The MIT Press.

Loewer, Barry, and Georges Rey, eds. 1991. *Meaning in Mind: Fodor and His Critics.* Cambridge, MA: Blackwell.

Lorde, Audre. 1984. *Sister Outside: Essays and Speeches.* Berkeley, CA: Crossing Press.

Lunenfeld, Peter. 2000. *Snap to Grid: A User's Guide to Digital Arts, Media, and Cultures.* Cambridge, MA: The MIT Press.

———, ed. 1999. *The Digital Dialectic: New Essays on New Media.* Cambridge, MA: The MIT Press.

Lyas, Colin, ed. 1971. *Philosophy and Linguistics.* London: Macmillan.

Macpherson, C. B. 1962. *The Political Theory of Possessive Individualism: Hobbes to Locke.* New York: Oxford University Press.

Manning, Christopher D., and Hinrich Schütze. 1999. *Foundations of Statistical Natural Language Processing.* Cambridge, MA: The MIT Press.

Manovich, Lev. 2001. *The Language of New Media.* Cambridge, MA: The MIT Press.

Marvin, Carolyn. 1988. *When Old Technologies Were New: Thinking About Electric Communication in the Late Nineteenth Century.* New York: Oxford University Press.

Marx, Leo. 1964. *The Machine in the Garden: Technology and the Pastoral Ideal in America.* New York: Oxford University Press.

Massumi, Brian. 2002. *Parables for the Virtual: Movement, Affect, Sensation.* Durham, NC: Duke University Press.

Mattelart, Armand. 2000. *Networking the World (1794–2000).* Minneapolis: University of Minnesota Press.

———. 2003. *The Information Society: An Introduction.* London: Sage Publications.

May, Christopher T. 2002. *The Information Society: A Skeptical View.* New York: Polity Press.

McChesney, Robert. 2007. *Communication Revolution: Critical Junctures and the Future of Media.* New York: New Press.

McCumber, John. 2001. *Time in the Ditch: American Philosophy and the Mc-Carthy Era*. Evanston, IL: Northwestern University Press.

McGann, Jerome. 1983. *Critique of Modern Textual Criticism*. Chicago: University of Chicago Press.

———. 1991. *The Textual Condition*. Princeton, NJ: Princeton University Press.

McKenzie, Donald F. 1999. *Bibliography and the Sociology of Texts*. New York: Cambridge University Press.

Microsoft Project. 1987–. Software application. Redmond, WA: Microsoft Corporation.

Miller, George A., Eugene Galanter, and Karl H. Pribham. 1960. *Plans and the Structure of Behavior*. New York: Holt.

Mills, C. Wright. 1956. *The Power Elite*. New York: Oxford University Press.

Minsky, Marvin. 1967. *Computation: Finite and Infinite Machines*. Englewood Cliffs, NJ: Prentice-Hall.

Mosco, Vincent. 2005. *The Digital Sublime: Myth, Power, and Cyberspace*. Cambridge, MA: The MIT Press.

Mumford, Lewis. 1934. *Technics and Civilization*. New York: Harcourt, Brace & World, Inc.

———. 1964. *The Pentagon of Power*. New York: Harcourt, Brace, Jovanovich.

Nakamura, Lisa. 2002. *Cybertypes: Race, Ethnicity, and Identity on the Internet*. New York: Routledge.

———. 2007. *Digitizing Race: Visual Cultures of the Internet*. Minneapolis, MN: University of Minnesota Press.

Negroponte, Nicholas. 1995. *Being Digital*. New York: Alfred A. Knopf.

Nelson, Ted H. 1997. "Embedded Markup Considered Harmful." In Dan Connolly, ed., *XML: Principles, Tools, and Techniques*. Sebastopol, CA: O'Reilly, 129–134.

Nettle, Daniel. 1999. *Linguistic Diversity*. Oxford: Oxford University Press.

Nettle, Daniel, and Suzanne Romaine. 2000. *Vanishing Voices: The Extinction of the World's Languages*. New York and London: Oxford University Press.

Newell, Allen. 1990. *Unified Theories of Cognition*. Cambridge, MA: Harvard University Press.

Newell, Allen, and Herbert A. Simon. 1972. *Human Problem Solving*. Englewood Cliffs, NJ: Prentice-Hall.

Newmeyer, Frederick J. 1996. *Generative Linguistics: A Historical Perspective*. New York: Routledge.

———. 1998. *Language Form and Language Function*. Cambridge, MA: The MIT Press.

Nichols, Johanna. 1992. *Linguistic Diversity in Space and Time*. Chicago: University of Chicago Press.

Noble, David F. 1977. *America by Design: Science, Technology, and the Rise of Corporate Capitalism*. New York: Knopf.

———. 1997. *The Religion of Technology: The Divinity of Man and the Spirit of Invention*. New York: Penguin Books.

Nye, David E. 2003. *America as Second Creation: Technology and Narratives of New Beginnings*. Cambridge, MA: The MIT Press.

OLPC. 2008. "One Laptop Per Child: Vision: Mission." http://www.laptop.org.

O'Gorman, Bill. 2004. "The Road to ERP: Has Industry Learned or Revolved Back to the Start?" In Adam and Sammon (2004), 22–46.

Ong, Walter S. J. 1977. *Interfaces of the Word: Studies in the Evolution of Consciousness and Culture*. Ithaca, NY: Cornell University Press.

———. 1982. *Orality and Literacy: The Technologizing of the Word*. New York and London: Routledge.

Penrose, Roger. 1989. *The Emperor's New Mind: Concerning Computers, Minds, and the Laws of Physics*. New York: Oxford University Press.

———. 1994. *Shadows of the Mind: A Search for the Missing Science of Consciousness*. New York: Oxford University Press.

Phillipson, Robert. 1992. *Linguistic Imperialism*. Oxford: Oxford University Press.

Pichler, Alois. 1995. "Advantages of a Machine-Readable Version of Wittgenstein's *Nachlass*." In Johannessen and Nordenstam, eds., *Culture and Value: Philosophy and the Cultural Sciences*. The Austrian Ludwig Wittgenstein Society, Vienna.

Pierrehumbert, Janet. 1993. "Prosody, Intonation, and Speech Technology." In Bates and Weischedel (1993), 257–282.

Pinker, Steven. 1997. *How the Mind Works*. New York: Norton.

Postal, Paul M. 1979. *Some Syntactic Rules in Mohawk*. Written 1962; first published version, New York: Garland Publishing.

Poster, Mark. 1990. *The Mode of Information: Poststructuralism and Social Context*. Chicago: University of Chicago Press.

———. 2001. *What's the Matter with the Internet?* Minneapolis: University of Minnesota Press.

———. 2006. *Information Please: Culture and Politics in the Age of Digital Machines*. Durham, NC: Duke University Press.

Putnam, Hilary. 1960. "Minds and Machines." In Putnam 1975, 362–385.

———. 1964. "Robots: Machines or Artificially Created Life?" In Putnam (1975), 386–407.

———. 1967. "The Mental Life of Some Machines." In Putnam (1975), 408–428.

———. 1973. "Philosophy and Our Mental Life." In Putnam (1975), 291–303.

———. 1975. *Mind, Language and Reality: Philosophical Papers, Volume Two*. New York: Cambridge University Press.

———. 1977. "Models and Reality." In Putnam (1983), 1–25.

———. 1979. *Mathematics, Matter, and Method: Philosophical Papers, Volume One*. Second Edition. New York: Cambridge University Press.

———. 1981a. *Reason, Truth and History*. New York: Cambridge University Press.

———. 1981b. "Why There Isn't a Ready-Made World." In Putnam (1983), 205–228.

———. 1981c. "Why Reason Can't Be Naturalized." In Putnam (1983), 229–247.

———. 1982. "A Defense of Internal Realism." In Putnam (1990), 30–42

———. 1983. *Realism and Reason: Philosophical Papers, Volume Three*. New York: Cambridge University Press.

———. 1988. *Representation and Reality*. Cambridge, MA: The MIT Press.

———. 1990. *Realism with a Human Face*. Cambridge, MA: Harvard University Press.

———. 1992. *Renewing Philosophy*. Cambridge, MA: Harvard University Press.

Pylyshyn, Zenon W. 1984. *Computation and Cognition: Toward a Foundation for Cognitive Science*. Cambridge, MA: The MIT Press.

Quine, W. V. O. 1960. *Word and Object*. Cambridge, MA: The MIT Press.

Reisch, George A. 2005. *How the Cold War Transformed Philosophy of Science: To the Icy Slopes of Logic*. New York: Cambridge University Press.

Renear, Allen H. 1995. "Theory and Metatheory in the Development of Text Encoding." Working draft, Brown University. http://www.rpi.edu/~brings/renear .target.

———. 2001. "Text Encoding," In Schreibman, Siemens, and Unsworth (2001), 218–239.

Renear Allen H., E. Mylonas, and David Durand. 1996. "Refining Our Notion of What Text Really Is: The Problem of Overlapping Hierarchies." *Research in Humanities Computing*. http://www.stg.brown.edu/.

Rheingold, Howard. 2000. *Tools for Thought: The History and Future of Mind-Expanding Technology*. Revised edition. Cambridge, MA: The MIT Press.

Robins, Kevin, and Frank Webster. 1999. *Times of the Technoculture: From the Information Society to the Virtual Life*. New York: Routledge.

Rorty, Richard. 1979. *Philosophy and the Mirror of Nature*. Princeton, NJ: Princeton University Press.

———, ed. 1967. *The Linguistic Turn: Recent Essays in Philosophical Method*. Reprint edition. Chicago: University of Chicago Press, 1988.

Roszak, Theodore. 1986. *The Cult of Information: A Neo-Luddite Treatise on High-Tech, Artificial Intelligence, and the True Art of Thinking*. Berkeley: University of California Press.

Ryle, Gilbert. 1949. *The Concept of Mind*. Chicago: University of Chicago Press, 1984.

Sammon, David, and Frédéric Adam. 2004. "Setting the Scene: Defining and Understanding ERP Systems." In Adam and Sammon (2004), 1–21.

Sapir, Edward. 1921. *Language: An Introduction to the Study of Speech*. London: Granada.

Saul, John Ralston. 1992. *Voltaire's Bastards: The Dictatorship of Reason in the West*. New York: Vintage Books.

Schank, Roger C., and Kenneth Colby, eds. 1973. *Computer Models of Thought and Language*. San Francisco: Freeman.

Schiller, Dan. 2000. *Digital Capitalism: Networking the Global Market System*. Cambridge, MA: The MIT Press.

Schreibman, Susan, Ray G. Siemens, and John Unsworth, eds. 2001. *A Companion to Digital Humanities*. Malden, MA: Blackwell Publishing.

Scheutz, Matthias, ed. 2002. *Computationalism: New Directions*. Cambridge, MA: The MIT Press.

Schumpeter, Joseph. 1942. *The Process of Creative Destruction*. London: Unwin.

Scott, James C. 1999. *Seeing Like a State: How Certain Schemes to Improve the Human Condition Have Failed*. New Haven, CT: Yale University Press.

Searle, John. 1977. "Reiterating the Differences: A Reply to Jacques Derrida." *Glyph* 1, 198–208.

———. 1983. *Intentionality: An Essay in the Philosophy of Mind*. New York: Cambridge University Press.

———. 1984. *Minds, Brains and Science*. Cambridge, MA: Harvard University Press.

———. 1992. *The Rediscovery of the Mind*. Cambridge, MA: The MIT Press.

Shannon, Claude. 1951. "Prediction and Entropy of Printed English." *Bell Systems Technical Journal* 30, 50–64.

Shannon, Claude, and Warren Weaver. 1949. *The Mathematical Theory of Communication*. Urbana, IL: University of Illinois Press.

Sharp, Duane E. 2003. *Customer Relationship Management Systems Handbook*. Boca Raton, FL: Auerbach/CRC Press.

Shields, Rob. 2003. *The Virtual*. New York: Routledge.

Shirky, Clay. 2008. *Here Comes Everybody: The Power of Organizing Without Organizations*. New York: Penguin.

Simon, Leslie David, Javier Corrales, and Donald R. Wolfensberger. 2002. *Democracy and the Internet: Allies or Adversaries?* Washington and Baltimore: Woodrow Wilson Center/Johns Hopkins University Press.

Skutnabb-Kangas, Tove. 2000. *Linguistic Genocide in Education—Or Worldwide Diversity and Human Rights?* Mahwah, NJ, and London: Lawrence Erlbaum.

Sloman, Aaron. 2002. "The Irrelevance of Turing Machines to Artificial Intelligence." In Scheutz (2002), 87–128.

Smith, Brian Cantwell. 1996. *On the Origin of Objects*. Cambridge, MA: The MIT Press.

———. 2002. "The Foundations of Computing." In Scheutz (2002), 23–58.

Smith, George. 1991. *Computers and Human Language*. New York: Oxford University Press.

Sperberg-McQueen, Christopher M. 2001. "Classification and Its Structures." In Schreibman, Siemens, and Unsworth (2001), 161–176.

Spiegel, Alix. 2008a. "Old-Fashioned Play Builds Serious Skills." National Public Radio Morning Edition (February 21). http://www.npr.org.

Spiegel, Alix. 2008b. "Creative Time Makes for Kids in Control." National Public Radio Morning Edition (February 28). http://www.npr.org.

Spivak, Gayatri Chakravorty. 1999. *A Critique of Postcolonial Reason: Toward a History of the Vanishing Present*. Cambridge, MA: Harvard University Press.

———. 2005. "Translating into English." In Sandra Berman and Michael Wood, eds., *Nation, Language, and the Ethics of Translation*. Princeton, NJ: Princeton University Press, 93–110.

Sproat, Richard, ed. 1998. *Multilingual Text-to-Speech Synthesis: The Bell Labs Approach*. Dordrecht: Kluwer Academic Publishers.

Stallman, Richard. 2002. *Free Software, Free Society: Selected Essays of Richard M. Stallman*. Joshua Gay, ed. Boston: GNU Press.

Staten, Henry. 1984. *Wittgenstein and Derrida*. Lincoln: University of Nebraska Press.

Stein, Gertrude. 1990. *Selected Writings of Gertrude Stein*. New York: Vintage.

Strauss, Leo. 1953. *Natural Right and History.* Chicago: University of Chicago Press.

Suchman, Lucy. 1987. *Plans and Situated Actions: The Problem of Human-Machine Communication.* New York: Cambridge University Press.

Sullivan, Laurie. 2004. "Wal-Mart's Way: Heavyweight Retailer Looks Inward to Stay Innovative in Business Technology." *Information Week* (September 27). http://www.informationweek.com.

Sunstein, Cass R. 2001. *Republic.com.* Princeton, NJ: Princeton University Press.

Surowiecki, James. 2005. *The Wisdom of Crowds.* New York: Anchor Books.

Swartz, Mimi, with Sherron Watkins. 2003. *Power Failure: The Inside Story of the Collapse of Enron.* New York: Doubleday.

Sweezy, Paul M. 1972. *Modern Capitalism and Other Essays.* New York: Monthly Review Press.

Tanselle, G. Thomas. 1992. *A Rationale of Textual Criticism.* Philadelphia, PA: University of Pennsylvania Press.

Taylor, R. Gregory. 1998. *Models of Computation and Formal Languages.* New York: Oxford University Press.

Trippi, Joe. 2004. *The Revolution Will Not Be Televised: Democracy, the Internet, and the Overthrow of Everything.* New York: Regan Books.

Turing, Alan. 1936. "On Computable Numbers, with an Application to the *Entscheidungsproblem.*" *Proceedings of the London Mathematical Society,* Series 2, Volume 42 (1936–37), 230–265.

———. 1937. "Computability and λ-Definability." *The Journal of Symbolic Logic* 2, 153–163.

———. 1950. "Computing Machinery and Intelligence." *Mind: A Quarterly Review of Psychology and Philosophy* 59, Number 236 (October), 433–460.

Turkle, Sherry. 1984. *The Second Self: Computers and the Human Spirit.* New York: Simon & Schuster.

———. 1995. *Life on the Screen: Identity in the Age of the Internet.* New York: Simon & Schuster.

Turner, Fred. 2006. *From Counterculture to Cyberculture: Stewart Brand, the Whole Earth Network, and the Rise of Digital Utopianism.* Chicago: University of Chicago Press.

Ullman, Ellen. 1997. *Close to the Machine: Technophilia and Its Discontents.* San Francisco: City Lights.

Vaidhyanathan, Siva. 2003. *Copyrights and Copywrongs: The Rise of Intellectual Property and How It Threatens Creativity.* New York: New York University Press.

van Gelder, Tim. 1995. "What Might Cognition Be, If Not Computation?" *Journal of Philosophy* 92 (July), 345–381.

Virilio, Paul. 1983. *Pure War.* With Sylvère Lotringer. New York: Semiotext(e).

———. 1989. *War and Cinema: The Logistics of Perception.* New York: Verso.

———. 1997. *Open Sky.* New York: Verso.

———. 2000. *The Information Bomb.* New York: Verso.

von Baeyer, Hans Christian. 2005. *Information: The New Language of Science.* Cambridge, MA: Harvard University Press.

von Neumann, John. 1958. *The Computer and the Brain*. New Haven, CT: Yale University Press.

——. 1966. *Theory of Self-Reproducing Automata*. ed. Arthur Banks. Champaign, IL: University of Illinois Press.

von Neumann, John, and Oskar Morgenstern. 1944. *Theory of Games and Economic Behavior*. Reprint edition. Princeton, NJ: Princeton University Press, 2007.

Wal-Mart. 2007. "The Wal-Mart Story." http://www.walmartfacts.com/.

Wallace, James, and Jim Erickson. 1992. *Hard Drive: Bill Gates and the Making of the Microsoft Empire*. New York: HarperBusiness.

Wardrip-Fruin, Noah, and Nick Montfort, eds. 2003. *The New Media Reader*. Cambridge, MA: The MIT Press.

Wark, McKenzie. 2004. *A Hacker Manifesto*. Cambridge, MA: Harvard University Press.

——. 2007. *Gamer Theory*. Cambridge, MA: Harvard University Press.

Warschauer, Mark. 2000. "Language, Identity, and the Internet." In Kolko, Nakamura, and Rodman (2000), 151–170.

——. 2002. "Reconceptualizing the Digital Divide." *First Monday* 7 (July). http://www.firstmonday.org/.

——. 2003. *Technology and Social Inclusion: Rethinking the Digital Divide*. Cambridge, MA: The MIT Press.

Weaver, Warren. 1949. "Translation." In Locke and Booth (1955), 15–23.

——. 1955. "Foreword: The New Tower." In Locke and Booth (1955), v–vi.

Weinberger, David. 2003. *Small Pieces Loosely Joined: A Unified Theory of the Web*. New York: Basic Books.

——. 2007. *Everything Is Miscellaneous: The Power of the New Digital Disorder*. New York: Times Books.

Weizenbaum, Joseph. 1976. *Computer Power and Human Reason: From Judgment to Calculation*. San Francisco: Freeman.

Whyte, William H. 1957. *The Organization Man*. New York: Doubleday.

Wiener, Norbert. 1954. *The Human Use of Human Beings: Cybernetics and Society*. Garden City, NY: Doubleday & Company.

——. 1964. *God and Golem, Inc. A Comment on Certain Points where Cybernetics Impinges on Religion*. Cambridge, MA: The MIT Press.

Willett, P. 2001. "Electronic Texts: Audiences and Purposes." In Schreibman, Siemens, and Unsworth (2001), 240–253.

Williams, Raymond. 1980. *Culture and Materialism*. New York: Verso.

Wilson, Robert A. 1994. "Wide Computationalism." *Mind: A Quarterly Review of Psychology and Philosophy* 103, Number 411 (July), 351–372.

——. 1995. *Cartesian Psychology and Physical Minds: Individualism and the Sciences of the Mind*. New York: Cambridge University Press.

Winner, Langdon. 1977. *Autonomous Technology: Technics-out-of-Control as a Theme in Political Thought*. Cambridge, MA: The MIT Press.

——. 1988. *The Whale and the Reactor: A Search for Limits in an Age of High Technology*. Chicago: University of Chicago Press.

Winograd, Terry. 1972. *Understanding Natural Language*. New York: Academic Press.

———. 1973. "A Procedural Model of Language Understanding." In Schank (1973) 152–186.

———. nd1. "How SHRDLU Got Its Name." Author's website. http://hci.stanford .edu/~winograd/shrdlu/.

———. nd2. "SHRDLU." Author's website. http://hci.stanford.edu/~winograd/ shrdlu/.

Winograd, Terry, and Fernando Flores. 1987. *Understanding Computers and Cognition: A New Foundation for Design.* Norwood, NJ: Ablex Publishing.

Wittgenstein, Ludwig. 1922. *Tractatus Logico-Philosophicus.* Trans. D. F. Pears and B. F. McGuinness. First paperback edition. New York: Routledge, 1974.

———. 1953. *Philosophical Investigations.* Third edition. Cambridge, MA: Blackwell, 2002.

———. 1972. *On Certainty.* New York: Harper & Row.

———. 1984. *Culture and Value.* Chicago: University of Chicago Press.

Wolfram, Stephen. 1994. *Cellular Automata and Complexity: Collected Papers.* Boulder, CO: Westview Press.

———. 2002. *A New Kind of Science.* Champaign, IL: Wolfram Media.

Wright, Ronald. 2005. *A Short History of Progress.* New York: Carroll & Graf Publishers.

Ziff, Paul. 1961. *Semantic Analysis.* Ithaca, NY: Cornell University Press.

Zittrain, Jonathan. 2008. *The Future of the Internet—and How to Stop It.* New Haven, CT: Yale University Press.

Žižek, Slavoj. 1997. "Cyberspace, Or, The Unbearable Closure of Being." In *The Plague of Fantasies.* New York: Verso, 127–167.

Zuboff, Shoshana. 1988. *In the Age of the Smart Machine: The Future of Work and Power.* New York: Basic Books.

Zuse, Konrad. 1993. *The Computer—My Life.* New York: Springer-Verlag.

Acknowledgments

THE FRIENDSHIP and support of Suzanne Daly, Shaun Fletcher, Sonali Perera, Elliott Trice, Chandan Reddy, Jen Leibhart, Lisa Henderson, Peter Mahnke, and Jodi Melamed were indispensible for writing this book; so was the inspiration offered by many people in the English Department at the University of Pennsylvania, especially James F. English, Marjorie Levinson, and Margreta de Grazia.

At the University of Virginia, Jennifer Wicke, Susan Fraiman, Michael Levenson, Lise Dobrin, Ellen Contini-Morava, Jahan Ramazani, Christopher Krentz, Herbert Tucker, Dan Lefkowitz, Deborah McDowell, Eve Danziger, Bruce Holsinger, Anna Brickhouse, Peter Brooks, Grace Hale, Rita Felski, Eleanor Kaufman, and Nitin Govil all read parts of this manuscript during its preparation or talked with me about the ideas in it. Outside of UVa, Lisa Gitelman, Paul Smith, Matt Kirschenbaum, David Herman, Kevin Russell, Marie-Odile Junker, Roger Lancaster, Meredith McGill, Talbot Taylor, and Ira Livingston provided helpful comments on this project or research related to it. Audiences at the 2006 MLA Annual Convention, the 2001 ACH/ALLC Conference, MIT, the University of Virginia, and George Mason University provided helpful feedback on some of the material presented here.

Generous grants from the University of Virginia College of Arts and Sciences, the Department of English, and a fellowship from the National Endowment for the Humanities provided invaluable support for the research and composition of this book.

Like so many others, I owe Jennifer Wicke a special note of thanks. This is by no means the only project of this sort for which her guidance and judgment have proven decisive. In my case her guidance and judgment have extended far beyond my book, just as decisively.

At Harvard University Press, Lindsay Waters and Phoebe Kosman have been encouraging, gracious, demanding, critical, and supportive, all at just the moments when they were needed most.

George Justice, Devoney Looser, Nitin Govil, Denise McKenna, 莫茜 (Mo Qian), Suzanne Daly, Sonali Perera, Lise Dobrin, Ira Bashkow, Eleanor Kaufman, Lisa Alspector, and Jim English are more than friends. My family—Linda A. Golumbia, Nancy Golumbia, Susan Eachus, Jacob Golumbia, and Scout, and especially my parents, Arthur and Linda R. Golumbia—have supported and encouraged me in more ways than I can count.

I remain responsible for any errors in the text.

Index

www.ingramcontent.com/pod-product-compliance
Ingram Content Group UK Ltd.
Pitfield, Milton Keynes, MK11 3LW, UK
UKHW041428250325
456663UK00007B/18/J